For Collectors Only®

The Mosin-Nagant Rifle

by

Terence W. Lapin

6th Edition

North Cape Publications®, Inc.

Acknowledgments

I am privileged to be able to thank those without whose assistance the production of this book would have passed from the merely difficult to the nearly impossible. My thanks to those who made it possible to wend my way through the labyrinths and arcana of the National Archives, the Defense Intelligence Agency, the Smithsonian Institution and the Library of Congress. It would have been impossible without the assistance and expertise of so many members of their staffs: my sincerest thanks to all of them.

In my search I also benefitted from the kindness and assistance of Lt. Cdr. Markus Aarnio (Embassy of Finland, Washington, D.C.), Lt. Col. William A. Allanson USMC (ret), Mr. Rich Baker (U.S. Army Military History Institute), Mr. Ralph Denton, Mr. John Griffiths (USMC Air-Ground Museum), Mr. Harry Hunter (National Museum of American History), Mr. Steve Kehaya (Century International Arms), Ms. Susan Mayer (National Rifle Association of America), Ms. Louise McGovern (Army Research Laboratory, Aberdeen Proving Grounds), Mr. Tim Sanz (Foreign Military Studies Office, Ft. Leavenworth), Mr. Karl-Heinz Wrobel, and Messrs. Michael Metzgar, Ken Flaydrich and Woody Travis (Armory of Orange, Orange, California).

Lastly—but most of all—very special thanks to my wife, Laura, whose unflagging encouragement in this project made all things possible.

Terence W. Lapin

ISBN 978-1-882391-21-9

North Cape Publications, P.O. Box 1027, Tustin, California 92781
Voice: 800 745-9714 **Fax:** 714 832-5302 **E-mail**: northcape@ix.netcom.com.
Website: http://www.northcapepubs.com

Printed in USA by Bang Printing, Valencia, CA 91355

Table of Contents

Cover Photograph. L-r, M1891/30 Sniper Rifle with PU Scope and Mount and Model 1891 Infantry Rifle. North Cape Publications Collection

This photograph, taken in 1904, shows an Imperial Russian soldier, preparing to leave for the front in the Far East. He is holding a Model 1891 Infantry Rifle. The clip contains the M1891 round-nosed cartridge.

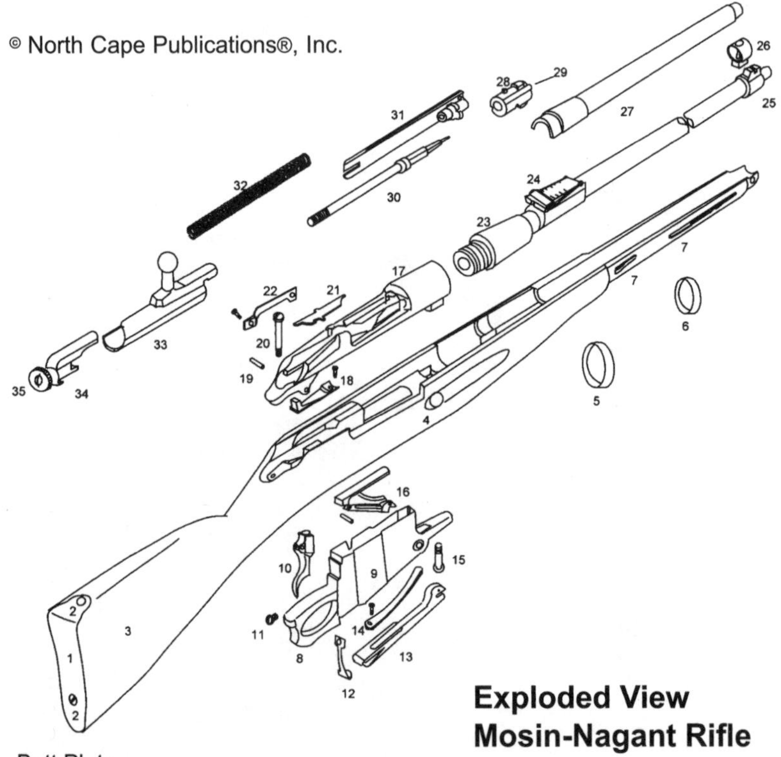

Exploded View
Mosin-Nagant Rifle

1. Butt Plate
2. Butt Plate Screws
3. Stock
4. Reinforcing Bolt
5. Lower Barrel Band
6. Upper Barrel Band
7. Barrel Band Spring
8. Trigger Guard
9. Magazine
10. Trigger
11. Floorplate Latch Screw
12. Floorplate Latch
13. Magazine Floorplate
14. Lower Magazine Spring and Screw
15. Front Guard Screw
16. Magazine Follower Assembly
17. Receiver
18. Trigger Spring/ Bolt Stop and Screw
19. Trigger Pin
20. Rear Guard (Tang) Screw
21. Ejector
22. Ejector Spring/ Interrupter & Screw
23. Barrel
24. Rear Sight Assembly
25. Front Sight Base
26. Front Sight
27. Handguard
28. Bolt Head
29. Extractor
30. Firing Pin
31. Bolt Connector/ Guide Bar
32. Bolt Spring
33. Bolt
34. Cocking Piece
35. Cocking Head

Introduction

The Mosin-Nagant rifle is not an attractive firearm. It has none of the elegance of, say, the 1903 Springfield, nor is it particularly arresting in appearance. This venerable rifle is, however, robust, dependable, reasonably accurate, and has a long and often fascinating history. Although it was last manufactured almost forty years ago it is still in use as a reserve or militia weapon in a number of countries. Unlike the Mauser with its myriad variants the Mosin-Nagant has a sufficiently limited number of models to challenge, but not bankrupt, the collector and to keep the student of arms and their history interested but not overwhelmed.

Note: In Russian the name "Mosin" is МОСИН and pronounced MO-seen; in American publications the name is often misspelled "Moisin" and accordingly mispronounced. "Nagant", a Walloon (Belgian French) name, is pronounced rather like Nah-GON, the second syllable being nasalized.

The going-out-of-business sale which accompanied the collapse of the Soviet Union and the Communist regimes of Eastern Europe sent large numbers of Mosin-Nagant rifles and carbines into the surplus market, substantially reducing their prices and adding to the earlier Finnish and Chinese imports and the American-made rifles of World War I vintage. Consequently, shootable and collectable examples of many of the weapons and ammunition described in this book can now be obtained inexpensively.

Although a certain amount of basic information on the Mosin-Nagant series appears in general firearms books there is no comprehensive text in English available on these weapons. Much of the information commonly found is garbled, minimal or — surprisingly often — simply wrong. Some of the best material on the rifles has not been translated into English, and I have endeavored to extract and present new and useful material from sources not found in the local library or bookstore.

The information encountered in researching this book was almost always fragmented, frequently inaccurate, and often contradictory. The words 'allegedly', 'reportedly' and so on appear in this text more frequently than I would like, but I do not wish to report as fact details which may be true, but which cannot be established as fact.

Where such conflicts arose I resolved the matter by accepting the consensus supported by the weight of the evidence; or by reliance on my own experience; or by presenting the conflicting assertions (with or without comment) and allowing the reader to draw his own conclusions.

I make no apology for the number of Russian and Finnish terms and notes throughout the book. The Mosin-Nagant is, essentially, a weapon of Russia and

Finland; much of its history took place in those countries, and most of the people and institutions having to do with development, production, and use of the rifle spoke and wrote in Russian or Finnish. Some brief sections at the end of the book are devoted to matters of language and contain English translations for all foreign words used and not otherwise explained in the text.

T. W. Lapin, 1998

Introduction to the Second Edition

Since I researched and wrote the first edition of this book in the early and mid-1990s a considerable amount of information about the Mosin-Nagant has been disgorged from foreign sources, especially Central and Eastern Europe (the Chinese and North Koreans remain resolutely silent). Using this new data I corrected and amended some of the text of the first edition, expanded upon some of the materials already present, and added some new information and features. I hope these changes are of use and interest to the reader.

To all those readers who have given me encouragement and compliments, as well as those who have pointed out errata, please accept my appreciation and thanks.

T.W. Lapin, 2000

Introduction to the Third Edition

In the five years since the first edition of this book was published the Mosin-Nagant scene in the United States has changed beyond recognition. Thousands of these rifles and carbines have been imported from eastern Europe; prices have dropped dramatically.

One of a number of gratifying results of this trend is the fact that Mosins are now so common — especially in the form of arsenal-refinished rifles and carbines with no collector value — that one can shoot them extensively without the nagging dread that one is abusing a potential museum piece.

In preparing this edition of *The Mosin-Nagant Rifle* I must express my indebtedness to A.N. Kulinskii for his pioneering work in the study of the odder varieties of Mosin bayonets; I would like to thank Mr. Hervé Melet for his thoughtfulness and generosity in furnishing me interesting and useful material on the French-made Mosin-Nagants of Châtellerault.

T. W. Lapin, 2003

Introduction to the Fourth Edition

It is now just short of a decade since the first edition of this book was published, and the changes in the world of information, as well as the world in general, have been astounding. What began as a casual inquiry, ambling around local libraries to satisfy my own idle curiosity about the Mosin-Nagant rifles, grew into an undertaking I pursued on the ground as far afield as Eastern Europe. These days I could just as well have sat at home, playing with a computer, and acquired a certain amount of information that went into this book; but had I done so I would not have had nearly as much fun at it, nor would I have gained remotely as much understanding of the subject. Much as I value the Internet, I still believe there is no substitute for hands-on experience: prowling through airy museums, dusty storage rooms, and some rather peculiar places that clearly have never felt the tread of the fire marshal's boots.

It is very gratifying to know that I have added, in some way, to the available knowledge of these fascinating old weapons, and I hope the reader gets as much fun out of learning about them as I have.

T. W. Lapin, 2007

Introduction to the Fifth Edition

In the twelve years since the first edition of this book was published interest in the Mosin-Nagant has grown far beyond what anyone reasonably would have thought in 1998, when they were still the ugly old guns no one particularly wanted and cost very little in the dustier kind of pawnshops. Although these days some models — especially Finnish ones such as the m/39 — have become quite pricey, a respectable collection of M1891/30 rifles and M1938 and M1944 carbines still can be acquired for less than $80.00 each, a result of the seemingly never-ending supply that flows out of Eastern Europe, often shortly after "This is the last shipment!" ads from major and minor retailers have run their course.

Despite the huge influx of these old warhorses there are doubtless some surprises still lurking in the military-surplus shadows, and I hope to see, in the not too distant future, an opportunity to pick up some Mosin-Nagants with, say, North Korean markings. We'll see.

T. W. Lapin, 2010

Introduction to the Sixth Edition

The Mosin-Nagant scene has continued to evolve in the three years since the fifth edition of this book appeared. The evidently limitless harvest of M1891/31s from Eastern Europe now includes a growing number of "sniper" rifles with bent bolt handles and scopes of—some would say—questionable vintage. Chinese Type 53 carbines are entering the market again, mostly in very used condition (they should be inspected by a gunsmith before firing) but of historical interest nonetheless.

I am still waiting for the North Koreans to discover the benefit of exporting something other than missiles and counterfeit goods. Mosins would be an excellent start.

T.W. Lapin, 2013

Conventions

1) "Right side" or "left side" refers to the side of the firearm to the shooter's right or left when shouldered properly. 2) All directions are given from the shooter's point of view—i.e., looking toward the muzzle. 3) It was not always possible to equate parts changes to serial number ranges as in previous books in the "For Collectors Only®" series as serial numbering conventions used by the manufacturing nations vary too widely. 4) The design of certain Mosin-Nagant parts were modified during the course of manufacture. In the text, these parts and their changes are identified as "Type 1," "Type 2" and so on. The use of "type" was not part of any official nomenclature and is used here for convenience only. 5) Quotation marks are often used in the text to indicate factory-applied markings. The quotation marks were not part of the factory-applied marking unless noted otherwise. 6) The reader may find information repeated several times throughout the text. This has been done deliberately to save having to turn back and forth to find specific information. 7) If you are uncertain of the meaning of a Russian or Finnish term used in the text, refer to the glossary in Appendix H.

Measurements

Measurements in this book are given in both metric and English units unless otherwise noted. One centimeter (cm) = 10 millimeters (mm) and 1,000 mm = 1 meter (m). To convert millimeters to inches, multiply by 0.03937; meters to feet, multiply by 3.28. A kilogram (kg) is 1,000 grams (g); 1 kg. = 2.2 lbs; 1 lb. = 453.59 g, and 28.3495 g = 1 oz. The weights of bullets and propellants are given both in grams (g) and grains (gr (troy)); 480 gr = 1 oz.

An *arshin* (*arshini*, pl.) is an old Imperial Russian measurement equal to 2.33 feet or 28 inches or 0.777 yards.

A Word of Caution

Firearms are dangerous when handled carelessly. Inanimate objects do not themselves cause injuries but human error, carelessness, ignorance, or malice does. Be careful. Assume that all weapons are loaded until *you* check to see that they are not. Never take anyone's word that a weapon is unloaded.

The Mosin-Nagant Rifle

Chapter 1
Mosin-Nagant Parts Analysis

The Mosin-Nagant in its various forms was manufactured in Russia, China, Poland, Hungary, France, Finland, Czechoslovakia, Romania, the United States and possibly North Korea. Reworks of this famous rifle were also undertaken in Austria, Bulgaria, Czechoslovakia, Finland, Germany, and Poland and parts were made in Belgium, Germany and Switzerland. Production of the Mosin-Nagant began in 1892 and continued into the 1960s, and they were still in service all over the world in the 1980s. The Mosin-Nagant story is complex and fascinating, which means it is also sometimes very difficult to determine the origin and model of a particular Mosin-Nagant. The author hopes this text will ease that task.

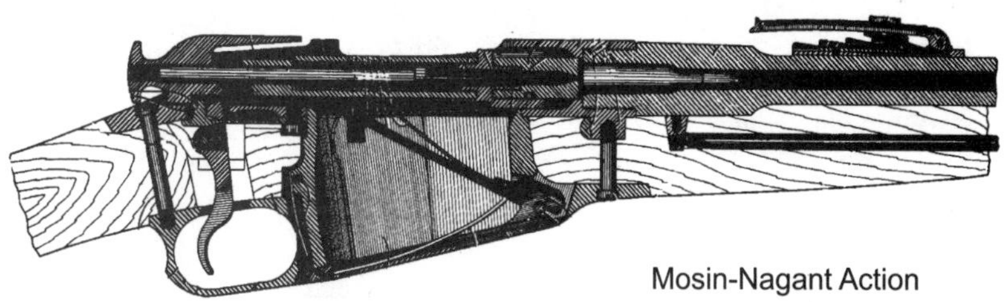

Mosin-Nagant Action

There are eighty-one parts to the M1891 Infantry Rifle, of which sixty-one are not duplicates. The figure above shows the Mosin-Nagant action and principal parts. The numbers correlate to those parts specified in the official U. S. Army manual of August 1918 for the "Russian Three-line Rifle, Caliber 7.62 mm (.3 Inch)":

Band screws (2)
Band screw button (2)
Barrel
Bolt
Bolt head
Butt plate
Butt plate screws (2)
Hand guard rivets (6)
Lower band
Lower band stop
Main spring
Nose cap
Nose cap screw
Rear sight base

Cleaning rod
Cleaning rod retainer
Cocking piece
Connecting bar
Ejector-interrupter
Ejector-interrupter screw
Extractor
Floor plate
Floor plate catch
Floor plate catch screw
Floor plate hinge pin
Follower
Follower carrier
Follower carrier hinge pin
Follower carrier spring
Follower carrier spring screw
Follower hinge pin
Follower spring
Front sight
Guard screw, front
Guard screw, rear
Hand guard
Hand guard liner, front
Hand guard liner, rear
Rear sight base screw
Rear sight base spring screw
Rear sight joint pin
Rear sight leaf
Rear sight slide
Rear sight slide catch (2)
Rear sight slide catch spring (2)
Rear sight slide cap spring cap (2)
Receiver
Recoil bolt
Recoil bolt nut
Sear
Sear screw
Sling eye, lower (2)
Sling eye, upper (2)
Sling eye screw (8)
Stock
Striker
Trigger
Trigger guard
Trigger pin
Upper band
Upper band stop

Most Mosin-Nagant parts — excluding stocks and handguards — are, theoretically, interchangeable among all models, though it is always advisable to use the part appropriate to its original firearm, e.g., M1891 Infantry rifle parts with M1891 Infantry rifles, etc., for reasons of both safety and authenticity. Because of differences in headspace a rifle whose bolt is not original to it should ***not*** be fired without having first been checked by a competent gunsmith. Following is a list of fully interchangeable parts:

1) The bolt and bolt assembly (although rifles mounted with sniper scopes will not function properly with any bolt but the type with an extended, turned-down bolt handle).

2) Butt plate and butt plate screws.
3) Trigger assembly.
4) Trigger guard and magazine assembly.
5) Trigger guard screws.
6) Interrupter/ejector (1- and 2-piece types).

In the Soviet era the Communists were wont to deface the two-headed imperial eagle of the tsars. The marking *Imperatorskii Petra Velikago* ("Imperial [sic] Peter the Great's") on Tula arsenal products often suffered this fate. Moreover, many Russian-made parts recycled into Finnish-reworked Mosin-Nagants had all the Russian markings deliberately ground off. In some instances a missing mark is simply the result of normal wear. If a particular part should have a manufacturer or arsenal mark, but does not, it is usually because of one of the foregoing reasons.

Dozens of arsenal and other identification marks can be found on Mosin-Nagants, and the reader is directed to Appendix C: Identification and Attribution for their explanation.

There are ten basic models of the Mosin-Nagant rifle and carbine and many subtypes. Therefore, it is not surprising that there are only three specifications common to all models: 1) Operating System, bolt action, 2) Magazine Capacity, 5 rounds and 3) Rifling: 4-groove, right-hand, concentric.

As a basis for comparison Table 1-1 provides the specifications for the M1891 Infantry Rifle, from the U. S. Army manual of 1918 for the "Russian Three-Line Rifle," as adopted by the United States at that time.

To the extent that specifications are applicable to certain basic types of Mosin-Nagants, Table 1-2, Specifications — Russian Models and Table 1-3, Specifications — Finnish Models are good early steps in determining which model is which. Next, consult the illustrations in Appendix C: Identification and Attribution, as the markings on the receiver ring will aid greatly in identifying a given model.

Table 1-1 Specifications for the M1891 Infantry Rifle	
Barrel	
Diameter of the bore	0.300 in
Exterior diameter at the muzzle	0.585 in
Exterior diameter at the breech	1.180 in
Length of chamber and bore	31.50 in
Diameter at rear of chamber	0.491 in
Diameter at front end of chamber body	0.460 in
Diameter at rear of chamber neck	0.339 in
Diameter at front of chamber neck	0.312 in
Length of chamber body	1.500 in
Length of chamber neck	0.490 in
Length of chamber shoulder	0.180 in
Total length of chamber	2.170 in
Rifling	
Number of grooves	4
Twist, uniform 1 turn in	9.5 in
Width of grooves	0.150 in
Width of lands	0.0776 in
Depth of grooves	0.0006 in
Stock	
Length with butt plate	41.38 in
Crook, i.e., axis of bore to heel of butt	1.9 in (approx)
Distance, trigger to butt plate	13 in (approx)

Table 1-1, cont.	
Rifle Overall	
Weight of rifle, complete	9.5 lbs
Weight of rifle, complete with bayonet	10.5 lbs
Stress of mainspring (about)	20 lbs
Trigger pull (at middle of finger piece)	8 lbs

BUTT PLATES

All models of the Mosin-Nagant have a blued, stamped steel butt plate which is slightly curved to fit the shoulder, see Figure 1-1. It is 105 mm (4 3/16 in) tall, and 40 mm (1 5/8 in) at its widest; it is 3 mm (1/8 in) thick. A flange extends 35 mm (1 3/8 in) over and onto the top of the butt. There is only one size butt plate; it fits all Mosin-Nagants of whatever pattern or origin. The butt plate is secured by two wood screws ±30 mm (1.18 in) long; the heads are 8 mm (0.314 in) in diameter.

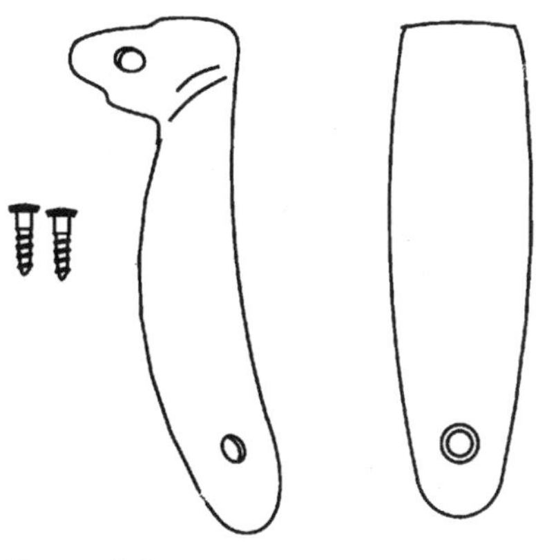
Figure 1-1

Russian Mosin-Nagants from the tsarist era have the arsenal logo stamped on the butt plate tang. On some, but not all, the serial number will be found just below the arsenal logo. Soviet rifle butt plates, like their tsarist forebears, are usually marked with the arsenal logo as well as the serial number, although these are not commonly found on the M1938 and M1944 carbines. American, Hungarian, Romanian and Polish Mosin-Nagants butt plates also show a serial number. Chinese Type 53 carbines may or may not have a serial number on the butt plate.

Table 1-2, Mosin-Nagant Specifications, Russian Models

Model	**Rifle M1891**	**Cossack Rifle**	**Dragoon Rifle**	**Rifle M91/30**	**Carbine M1907**	**Carbine M1938**	**Carbine M1944**
Weight	9.62 lbs 4.36 kg	8.75 lbs 3.97 kg	8.75 lbs 3.97 kg	8.7 lbs 3.95 kg	7.5 lbs 3.4 kg	7.25 lbs 3.28 kg	8.9 lbs 4.0 kg
Length	51.37 in 1.30 m	48.75 in 1.238 m	48.75 in 1.238 m	49.5 in 1.257 m	40 in 1.016 m	40 in 1.016 m	40.4 in 1.026 m
Barrel Length	31.6 in 803 mm	28.8 in 732 mm	28.8 in 732 mm	28.7 in 729 mm	20 in 510 mm	20 in 510 mm	20.47 in 520 mm
Front Sight	Unhooded Blade	Unhooded Blade	Unhooded Blade	Hooded Post	Hooded Post	Hooded Post	Hooded Post
Rear Sight	Ramp & Leaf	Tangent	Ramp & Leaf	Tangent	Tangent	Tangent	Tangent

Table 1-3, Mosin-Nagant, Finnish Models					
Model	m/27 Rifle	m/27 Cavalry Carbine	m/28 Rifle	m/28-30 Rifle	m/39 Rifle
Weight	9.04 lbs 4.10 kg	8.76 lbs 3.97 kg	9.2 lbs 4.17 kg	9.6 lbs 4.35 kg	10 lbs 4.54 kg
Length	46.6 in 1.184 m	43.7 in 1.110 m	43.7 in 1.110 m	43.7 in 1.110 m	46.6 in 1.184 m
Barrel Length	27 in 685 mm	24 in 610 mm	27 in 685 mm	27 in 685 mm	27 in 685 mm
Front Sight	Ear Protected Blade	Ear Protected Blade	Ear Protected Blade	Ear Protected Blade	Ear Protected Blade
Rear Sight	Ramp & Leaf	Ramp & Leaf	Tangent	Tangent	Tangent

Butt Plate Screws

Two wood screws secure the butt plate to the stock, one just above the toe and the other through the tang. The screws are unmarked, blued, and indistinguishable from model to model. Each screw is ±30 mm (1.18 in) long, and the head is 8 mm (0.3 in) in diameter. Refer to Figure 1-1.

Stocks

With the exception of the M1891 Infantry rifle, Dragoon rifle, and, possibly, Cossack rifle, which were made without an upper handguard from the beginning of production until about 1910, all Mosin-Nagants have wooden furniture consisting of a buttstock and a handguard. See Figure 1-2 for a generic assembly. Handguards are discussed below.

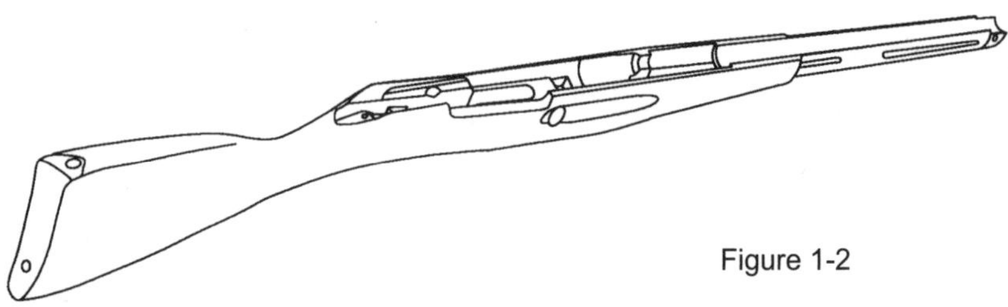

Figure 1-2

From the earliest production to the last, all Mosin-Nagants, regardless of country or model, have a finger groove approximately 120 mm (4.72 in) long routed into both sides of the stock from the receiver to past the center of the rear sight. The left groove is almost invariably about 1/4 inch longer than the right groove to accommodate the right-handed shooter.

Stock Bolts

On all stocks made after circa 1910 a metal bolt was inserted through the stock at the rear of the finger groove to help absorb recoil and strengthen the stock. Many M1891/30 rifles and M1938 and M1944 carbines refurbished in Soviet arsenals after World War II have an additional bolt inserted just behind the action, see Figure 1-3.

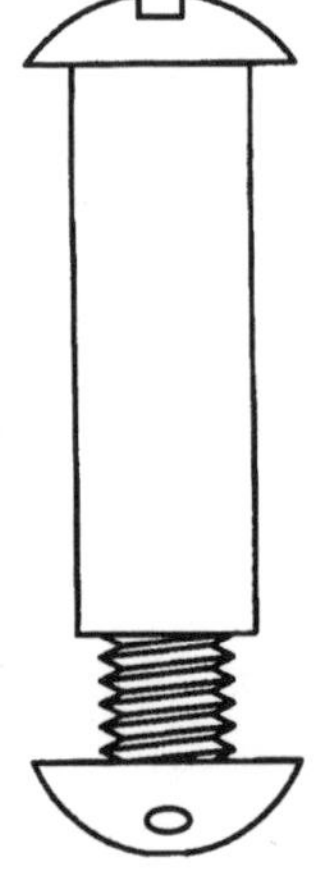

Figure 1-3

The bolt head is on the left; it is plain, smooth and convex, and is 15 mm (0.6 in) in diameter. The nut opposite has two small holes by which it is attached with a spanner wrench.

Caution: The stock bolt was *not* intended to be removed and attempting to do so may damage the stock.

A threaded metal nut, or stop, is sunk flush into the stock bed forward of the receiver cut; this accepts the screw-end of the cleaning rod of all Mosin-Nagants to secure it against recoil. Many stocks are found with a hole through the underside of the stock to aid in removing the rod nut.

Following is a descriptive list of stocks which are interchangeable among the specified models without adjustment, even though the assembly will not be authentic.

STOCK INTERCHANGEABILITY

a) The M1891 Infantry rifle stock and handguard will fit the M1891 Dragoon, the Cossack rifle, the M1891/30 and its foreign copies, and the following Finnish patterns: m/91 (except those with stepped barrels) and m/24 (except those with stepped barrels). If the Infantry rifle stock and handguard are used on the Dragoon, Cossack and M1891/30 models the stock's length prevents attachment of a bayonet; if used on a sniper rifle a scope cannot be properly mounted unless the necessary cuts are made to the left side of the stock rail.

b) The M1891 Dragoon rifle stock and handguard will fit the Cossack rifle, the M1891 Infantry rifle, and the M1891/30 rifle; if used on a sniper rifle a scope cannot be properly mounted unless the necessary cuts are made to the left side of the stock.

c) The M1907 carbine stock will fit the M1938 carbine.

d) The M1891/30 stock and handguard will fit the M1891 Infantry rifle, Dragoon rifle, and Cossack rifle; if used on a sniper rifle a scope cannot be properly mounted unless the necessary cuts are made to the left side of the stock.

e) The M1938 carbine stock will fit the M1907 carbine; the handguard will also fit the M1944 and its foreign copies, but the stock will not.

f) The M1944 carbine stock and handguard will fit the M1907 carbine and the M1938 carbine. This stock will appear — and is — inappropriate on other models because of the folding-bayonet groove along the right side, but it will fit.

RUSSIAN STOCKS

Russian Mosin-Nagant stocks of all types are made of birch and are protected by a military-type oil finish. Carbine stocks on weapons refurbished in Soviet arsenals beginning in the latter 1940s often are of laminated birch. Stocks made during and after the Second World War were commonly treated with a heavy coating of clear varnish as additional protection from the elements.

All Russian models' stocks terminate in a blued metal nosecap which is secured by a single screw, see Figure 1-4. The screw head is on the right side of the stock. The arsenal or manufacturer's logo appears on some nosecaps, but this is not common.

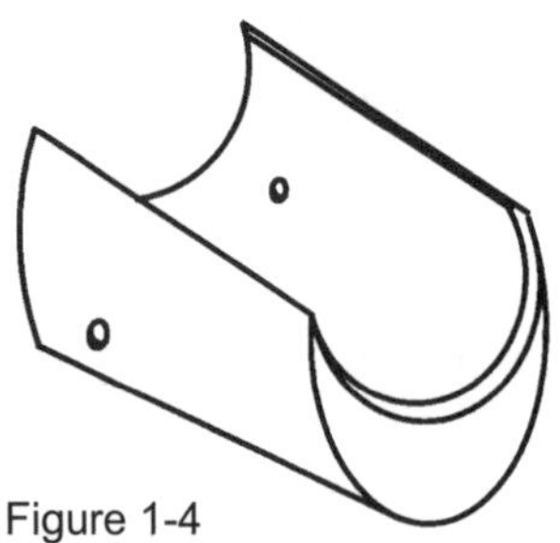
Figure 1-4

There are also stocks which have a wedge-shaped insert spliced into the underside; this may have been used to repair damaged stocks or, possibly, to salvage inferior grade stock blanks, as the Japanese did with their rifles.

Table 1-4 provides dimensions for all Russian Mosin-Nagant stocks.

Table 1-4 Russian-Style Stocks	
Model	**Stock Length in Inches***
M1891 Infantry Rifle	47.5
Dragoon Rifle	45
Cossack Rifle	45
M1907 Carbine	38.19
M1891/30 Rifle	45
M1938 Carbine	36.25
M1944 Carbine	36.25
*Measure from middle of butt plate to end of nose cap	

M1891 Infantry Rifle Stock

The original M1891 Infantry rifle stock was made both with and without a handguard. It was 1,206.5 mm (47.5 inches) long, including nosecap. This type was produced to circa 1910, when significant changes were made to accommodate the new M1908 *spitzer* bullet. Stocks for the first several years' output of the M1891 had a steel finger rest behind the trigger guard. The finger rest was eliminated circa 1894, in order to reduce costs and simplify production. Original-configuration stocks without the cross-bolt (introduced in 1910), and especially those with the finger rest, are extremely rare as many were lost, captured or destroyed during the Russo-Japanese War (1904–05), and most surviving rifles were retrofitted with the new style stock. See Figure 1-5.

Early M1891 stocks had a very short cleaning rod — about 15 inches long. When these rods were replaced by the later version towards the end of the 1890s the cleaning rod channel on the underside of the stock was lengthened to accept the new rod; this alteration can be seen on some stocks. When this work was done, the hole in the stock bed containing the rod retaining nut

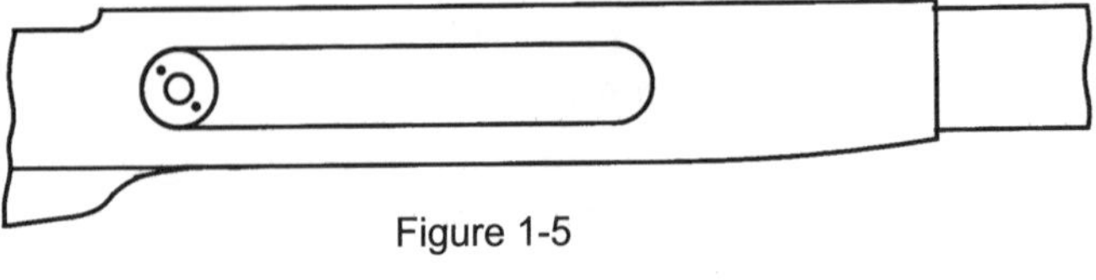
Figure 1-5

was filled in with a wooden plug and the nut moved towards the receiver. It is possible that this was necessary only for stocks from the Châtellerault contract.

Sling slots were introduced circa 1910 to replace the sling swivels. Two slots were installed: one in the butt midway between the butt plate and the trigger guard, and the second in the fore end, midway between the barrel bands. The slots are lined with metal washers, which are faced with blued metal plates or escutcheons ("sling eyes", in American military terminology) secured to both sides of the stock by two small screws for each of the four plates. See Figure 1-6. Pre-Soviet, Russian-made plates are often marked with the arsenal's logo, but this becomes less common in the Soviet era. The sling slot escutcheons are 38 mm (1.5 in) long by 10 mm (0.39 in) wide.

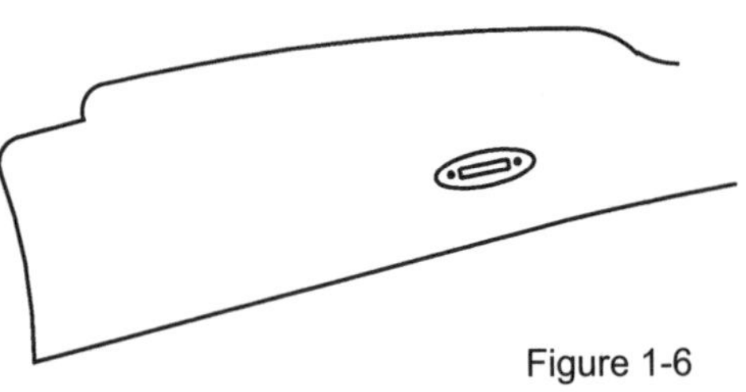
Figure 1-6

M1891 Dragoon Stock

This model did not have the finger rest of the early type Infantry rifle stock but did have a handguard. The stock is 1,143.0 mm (45.0 in) long, including nosecap. Except in length the stock is otherwise identical to that of the post-1909 Infantry rifle (rifles made or retrofitted after circa 1909).

Metal-lined sling slots with their escutcheons, rather than swivels, were always standard.

Unlike the Infantry rifle the Dragoon has barrel band retaining springs, which are blued flat steel strips resting in two grooves routed into the right side of the stock's fore end. The front spring is 60 mm (2.36 in) long and the rear one 40 mm (1.57 in) long; both are 5 mm (0.197 in) wide.

Some stocks of Dragoon rifles made in the 1920s are found stamped with the letters CCCP (i.e., SSSR in the Cyrillic alphabet, for *Soyuz Sovietskikh Sotsialisticheskikh Respublik*: Union of Soviet Socialist Republics).

Cossack Rifle Stock

This stock is identical to the Dragoon rifle stock. The author has seen one suggestion that this model was originally produced fully stocked, like the M1907 carbine; given the configuration of other Russian long arms, that seems unlikely.

M1907 Carbine Stock

This stock is similar to other models in its configuration and materials. It is approximately 970 mm (38.19 in) long overall, including the 18 mm (0.70 in) long nosecap, and extends to within 50 mm (1.97 in) of the muzzle, see Figure 1-7. It has the usual sling slots and butt plate, all of which are arsenal-marked.

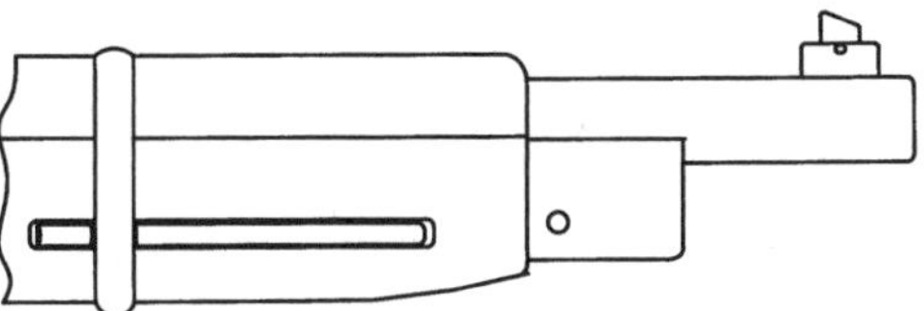

Figure 1-7

M1891/30 Rifle Stock

This is similar to the stock made for the Dragoon rifle. M1891/30 stocks made at the Tula Arsenal were often stamped on the right side of the butt with a Soviet five-pointed star, 20 mm (0.787 in) in width. The Izhevsk arsenal logo is a circle containing the hammer and sickle in a wreath of laurel leaves and the letters "CCCP". These markings are more common on pre-1941 stocks than in wartime production.

M1891/30 Sniper Rifle Stock

The same stock was used on this model as on the standard M1891/30,

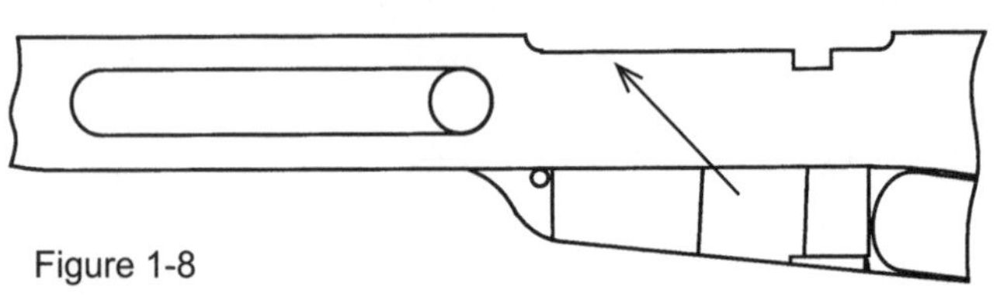
Figure 1-8

but it is inletted on the left-side rail (arrow) to allow a telescopic sight to be mounted. Figure 1-8.

M1938 Carbine Stock

The M1938 stock is made of solid birch, oil-finished, and is usually found coated with varnish, see Figure 1-9. Carbines refurbished in Soviet arsenals during and after the late 1940s were often given replacement laminated birch stocks. Some stocks were fitted with an additional stock bolt through the wrist just behind the trigger guard during refurbishing, but this is relatively uncommon.

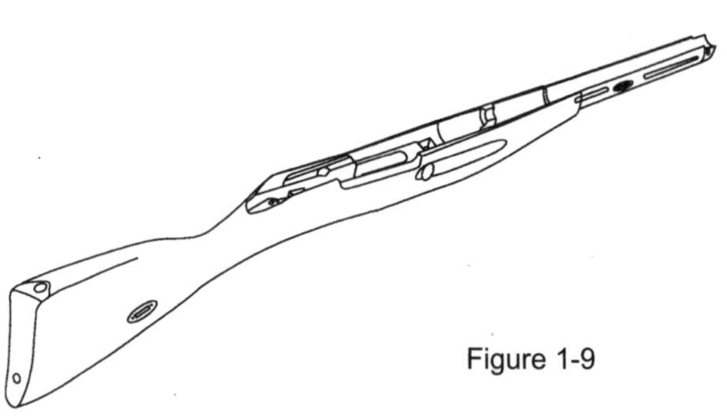
Figure 1-9

Carbine stocks will be noted with a wedge-shaped insert spliced into the underside; this technique may have been used to repair damaged stocks or, possibly, to salvage inferior grade stock blanks, as the Japanese did on some of their own rifles.

Carbine stocks have the metal nosecap common to all Russian-style Mosin-Nagants. The stocks have two barrel band springs of flat, blued steel; they rest in grooves on the right side of the fore arm. Both barrel bands are 5 mm (0.19 in) wide; the front band is 60 mm (2.36 in) long and the rear one 50 mm (1.97 in) long.

There are two sling slots, each approximately 25 mm (0.98 in) long and 5 mm (0.19 in) wide. The slots are lined with metal washers, although these are very often omitted from one — usually the rear — or both slots in wartime production stocks. These washers differ from those used in the slots of the rifles in that they often are no more than half-liners, covering only the bottom of the slots and crimped to cover the outer edge. Slot escutcheons are rare, and almost nonexistent in wartime production.

Some stocks bear an inspector's or other acceptance mark on the butt in the form of a Cyrillic letter in a circle about 5 mm (0.19 in) in diameter, or a diamond of comparable size.

Some M1938 carbine stocks have a single Cyrillic letter stamped into the finger groove on the right side, which is probably an inspector's or stock fitter's mark.

M1944 Carbine Stock

This stock is almost identical to the M1938 stock, with the addition of a groove for the folding bayonet in the right side of the stock, see Figure 1-10. The groove (arrow) extends from the front of the receiver ring to the back edge of the rear barrel band, about 122.5 mm (4.82 in) in length.

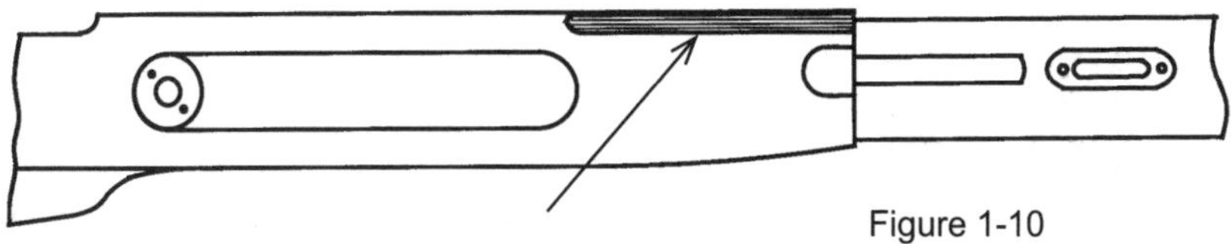

Figure 1-10

To be authentic, an M1944 stock must have the bayonet groove.

Many late-production M1944 stocks have the sling slot escutcheons set into the stock and are not secured by screws. This was a post-World War II innovation.

M1944 stocks, unlike those of the M1938, have a bullet-shaped dimple in both sides of the stock. The base of the dimple is tangent to the rear edge of the rear barrel band and the point faces rearwards. Inspectors' stock marks on the M1944 are the same as those found on the M1938 carbine.

Some M1944 carbine stocks have a single Cyrillic letter stamped into the finger groove on the right side, which is probably an inspector's or stock fitter's mark.

FINNISH STOCKS

Many Finnish Mosin-Nagants have stocks which, like the metal parts, can be products of any country which produced Mosin-Nagants prior to World War II. Like the Russian varieties, Finnish-made stocks are of solid Arctic birch; they are oil-finished and sometimes lacquered or varnished. Some stocks made in or after the late 1930s — especially those for the m/39 — are somewhat darker because they were stained with potassium permanganate dye.

Finnish-made stocks are characterized by their high-quality workmanship: e.g., the stock bolt will almost always be neatly installed and centered at the rear end of the finger groove, unlike the typically off-centered Russian product.

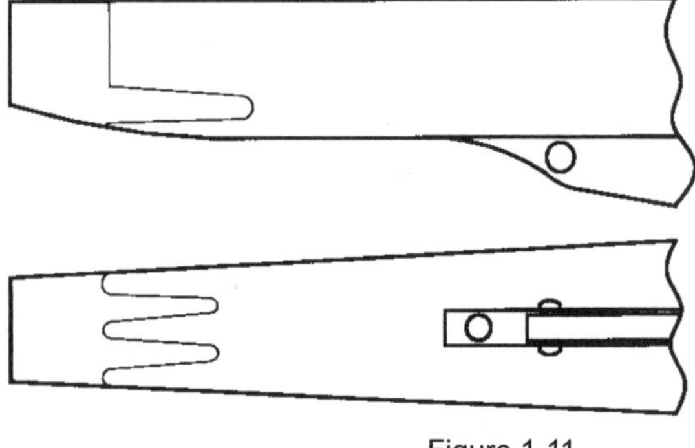

Figure 1-11

One element unique to Finnish-made or reworked stocks is fabrication of the stock in two pieces, finger-mortised together on the underside below the rear sight, see Figure 1-11. The purpose of this feature is to prevent the wood from warping in the extreme cold of Arctic winters. These two-piece stocks consist either of new wood or of recycled foreign Mosin-Nagant stock pieces, or both. While not all Finnish stocks are of the two-piece variety, all two-piece stocks are Finnish.

Finger-mortised stocks made before the end of World War II have rounded or pointed mortises. Post-War replacement stocks have squared mortises.

Unlike the Russians, who abandoned sling swivels around 1909, the Finns preferred them to sling slots. On many, but not all, ex-Russian stocks used by the Finns the sling slots will have been filled in and mounted with sling swivels. On many other such stocks the sling slots will still be intact but will have swivels mounted through them.

To remedy the problem of barrel bands coming loose and shifting forward, the Finns placed a small screw in front of and touching each barrel band (usually on the right side) on many of their Mosin-Nagants. These screws are about 0.375 to 0.5 inch long, with a slotted head about 0.125 inch in diameter; they can be found in-the-white, blued, or finished with a blackish coating sometimes used on other metal parts. One does not often find the screws still in the stock, but the tiny screw holes remain as evidence.

Arsenal-made, repaired or reworked Finnish stocks will usually have an identifying mark on the right side of the butt consisting of a circle superimposed on two crossed cannons; in the circle is a capital letter: "L," "S," or "Z." Some early models have a symbol which appears to be a wheel, rather than a letter. SAKO-made stocks usually have the SAKO logo (a capital "S" crowned with three evergreen sprigs, in a cogwheel) stamped on the right side of the butt; some rifles also have the stock's date stamped under the cogwheel. Many Finnish stocks have a capital "V" stamped on the underside of the stock, either behind or in front of the trigger guard/magazine assembly.

When Finnish rifles were rechambered to fit the new Finnish D166 round, as most were, the stocks were stamped with a capital D, usually — but not always — on the right side of the butt. See Chapter 7, Ammunition.
On some stocks a brass disc was inset into the right side of the butt, show-

ing the unit number and type of unit to which the weapon was issued. These were ordered removed in 1941, probably for security reasons. The space left by the removed disc was filled in with a matching wood plug and the stock refinished. Not all discs were removed; some can still be found intact on various rifles.

M1891 Infantry Rifle-type Stocks

Finnish-made stocks for all models which take the M1891 Infantry rifle-length action/barrel combination (m/91, m/24, and "P" series) have a noticeably thicker wrist than M1891 stocks made by other countries: ± 6.125 inches in circumference rather than the usual ± 5.25 in; the stocks are often also somewhat heavier. (See Chapter 3 for information on shortened m/24 stocks.)

Many of the m/24s, and the m/91s made by Tikkakoski in 1925–27, have "stepped" barrels rather than the tapered barrels of earlier M1891 Infantry rifles (Figure 1-12). The m/24s, even those with unstepped barrels, have larger, heavier barrels than their predecessors. The stock bed between the rear and front barrel bands was widened to an untapered 20 mm (0.79 in) on preexisting stocks (normal taper in the same area is 18 mm to 15 mm (0.71 in to 0.59 in). If the stock was originally Russian-manufactured, it was altered to fit the new barrel; if it was Finnish, it may have been altered or may be new-production, but the two cannot be distinguished.

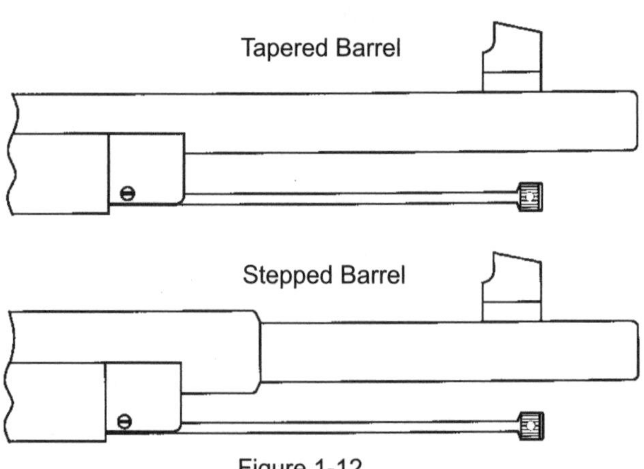

Figure 1-12

m/27 Rifle Stock

Although new stocks were made for this variety, many of the stocks used for it were existing Infantry and Dragoon M1891s with the fore ends shortened to fit the 27-inch barrel. These stocks are characterized by the sling swivel added to the underside of the butt; sometimes the existing sling slot was filled in, sometimes left intact. The butt swivel is of bent wire attached to a 2 in long x 1/2 in wide plate secured to the stock by two wood screws. The swivel can rotate through 360°.

The m/27 was the first Mosin-Nagant model to have a new nosecap. Two types were developed. **Type 1** was hinged on the right side, secured on the left by a machine screw parallel to the stock and had a bayonet lug on the underside, see Figure 1-13.

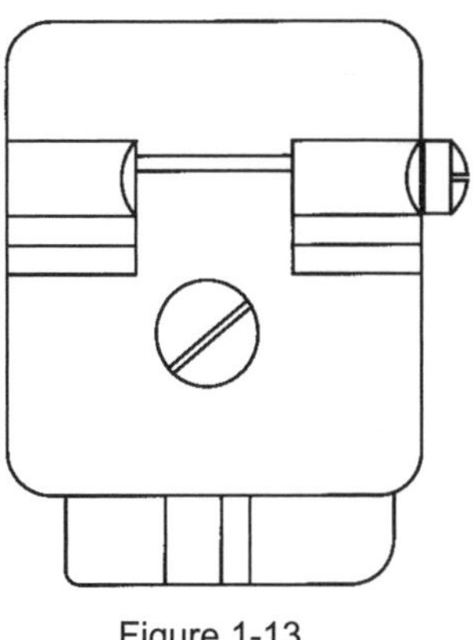

Figure 1-13

Because the nosecap tended to rotate when the bayonet was used, cracking the stock, the **Type 2** m/27 nosecap was developed. It had two parallel metal braces, one on each side, added in 1935 to new rifles and retrofitted to old through 1937. The braces are 75 mm (2.95 in) long by 10 mm (0.39 in) wide. They are set atop the nosecap, extend rearward and are seated in grooves in the stock. The braces are attached to the stock by a transverse bolt, with the head on the right. Each brace is spot-welded to the nosecap on some examples, but this is uncommon.

Note: A **Type 3** m/27 hinged nosecap was developed for use on the m/39 rifle, described below. The nosecap screw is perpendicular to the stock, rather than parallel.

m/27 Cavalry Carbine Stock

The m/27 stock was shortened by about 3 in to accommodate the shorter carbine barrel. It is also characterized by the m/27-type sling swivel mounted on the underside of the butt in addition to a Mauser-style recess on the right side of the butt. The stock is inletted on the right side above the magazine (arrow) to accommodate the turned-down bolt handle, see Figure 1-14.

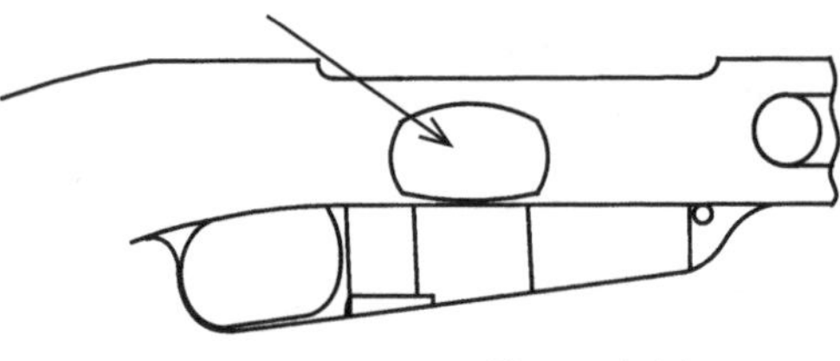
Figure 1-14

Note: The m/27 Cavalry Carbine is extremely rare: fewer than 300 of the 2,500 produced are reported to survive.

m/28 Civil Guard Rifle Stock

As with the m/27, preexisting stocks were altered to fit this model. The m/28 Civil Guard Rifle stock has the usual Russian-style sling slots and a new nosecap was devised for the m/28 to eliminate the problems with the earlier model. The new nosecap was made in two types, both of which have a bayonet lug on the underside.

The **Type 1** m/28 nosecap was made in two pieces, is open in front and, unlike its predecessor, has no hinge; it was attached to the stock by one machine screw running completely through the stock from right to left. See also the section on nosecaps, below.

The **Type 2** nosecap was made in a single piece and also was fastened to the stock by a single machine screw through the stock from right to left. The front of the second pattern is solid, with a hole through which the cleaning rod passes.

m/28-30 Civil Guard Rifle Stock

The stock is the same as that of the m/27 and employs only the m/27 Type 2 nosecap. Some stocks have a brass bolt, approximately 6.5 mm (.25 in) in diameter, placed through the fore end about 1 inch behind the nosecap: this was to reinforce the stock in the event the improved nosecap did not alleviate the breakage problem caused by bayonet use. This addition is comparatively uncommon.

m/91-30 Stock

The Finnish-made version of this Russian model is typically found with original Russian M1891/30 stocks; however, some exist with stocks evidently made from preexisting M1891 Infantry and Dragoon rifle stocks. The reworked stocks are identifiable by the characteristic Finnish two-piece construction, the finger-mortising clearly discernible on the underside. Entirely new two-piece stocks were made as well.

m/39 Stock

The only Mosin-Nagant model which has a distinctively different buttstock is the Finnish m/39 rifle. This weapon has a pistol-grip wrist as opposed to the straight, 'English' style of all other varieties; the butt comb is slightly higher than that of other models, which reduces the impact of recoil. All m/39 stocks consist of two pieces mortised together under the rear sight.

Note: The first 7,000 m/39s stocks reportedly were made with the earlier-style stock, i.e., without the pistol grip, in 1940 and 1941.

The wood at the front end of the stock was strengthened, enabling the m/39 to be made with the Type 3 nosecap (a variation of the Type 1 m/27 hinged nosecap). On the m/39, the nosecap screw is on the right side and is *perpendicular* to the stock, rather than parallel as on the earlier m/27. A groove routed into the left side of the stock holds the single barrel band retaining spring, which is 68 mm (2.68 in) long and 4 mm (0.157 in) wide.

The sling mounting system consists of two swivels mounted on the front barrel band: one each on the left side and bottom, and two on the butt — a swivel on the underside and a sling bar set in a depression in the left side. Unlike the swivel of the m/27 that of the m/39 cannot rotate, but swings fore and aft.

AMERICAN STOCKS

American-made stocks for the M1891 Infantry rifle were produced by

Remington-UMC and New England Westinghouse for the Russian government during World War I. They are made of American black walnut and have an appearance and finish very similar to the U.S. military rifles of the period, i.e., they are a dark — almost purple — brown and have a military-type oil finish. The workmanship is excellent.

Some stocks may have a Russian acceptance mark on the side of the butt in the form of a Cyrillic letter п in a circle. Some American M1891s manufactured by New England Westinghouse — perhaps all those actually received by the Russians before January 1918 — have the Russian words "АНГЛІЙСКИ ЗАКАЗЪ" meaning "English Contract" in the pre-Revolution alphabet and spelling, within a circle about 0.875 inch in diameter stamped on the left side of the butt.

Occasionally a two-headed Russian imperial eagle in a circle on the right buttstock with the letters п and к (P and K in Cyrillic for *Probaya Komissiya* or Proof Commission) on either side of the eagle will also be observed.

Note: Great Britain owned the New England Westinghouse machinery on which the Mosin-Nagant rifles were manufactured; it was also the guarantor of payment for the weapons (in effect, the British government was a 'co-signer' for the tsar). The old saw that the "English contract" mark was meant to fool the Central Powers as to the origin of the rifles is imbecilic.

Some of these American-made stocks may also be found with an imperial two-headed Romanov eagle flanked by the Cyrillic letters п and к in a circle also about 0.875 inch in diameter, on the right side of the butt. At the bottom is a date from the 1890s to circa 1917, and at the top is an arsenal logo (a T-like hammer for Tula, an arrow for Sestroryetsk, or a bow-and-arrow for Izhevsk). This is a Russian proof commission acceptance mark and not a factory proof mark.

CHINESE STOCKS

The only Mosin-Nagant produced by the People's Republic of China is the M1944, designated the "Type 53". Chinese stocks are made of a local wood, usually catalpa also called tulip wood, which is similar in appearance to the beech often used for rifle stocks by some European countries. The Chinese stocks have a military-style oil finish, and are not varnished.

Unlike the Europeans the Chinese stamped their stocks with a profusion of inspection and acceptance marks: stars, triangles, etc., on the interior and exterior, which makes them relatively easy to identify.

The buttstock is sometimes, but not always, serial-numbered, in which instance the number must match that of the receiver to be considered original to the piece.

HUNGARIAN STOCKS

Hungarian-made stocks for the M1891/30 rifle and M1944 carbine (in Hungarian usage 48.M and 44.M, respectively) are of solid birch and are characterized by excellent workmanship. The finish is a standard military oil type, with a low sheen.

The stocks commonly bear a "B" (for the Budapest arsenal) in a circle on the right side of the buttstock, and the numbers 02 — the East Bloc code for Hungary — stamped in the same area.

POLISH STOCKS

wz. 91/98/25 Rifle

The stock for the Polish-developed wz. 91/98/25 is a hybrid of Russian and German features. The stock is that of the M1891 Infantry rifle on which the front has been altered to accept a Mauser-style H-form nosecap and bayonet lug. See Figure 1-16.

The handguard is the standard M1891, but shortened to accommodate the new nosecap. Only the rear barrel band is used and a sling swivel is mounted on the left side. A second swivel is affixed to the left side of the

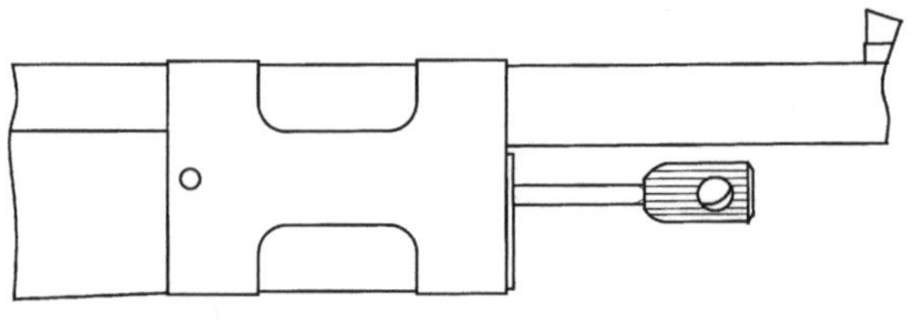

Figure 1-16

butt several inches behind the sling slot; the slot is retained in its original form.

M1944 Carbine

The Polish M1944 stock is identical to that used on the Russian M1944, described above. A common buttstock marking is a diamond containing the letters "OW", as is the occasional small (3mm–5mm) diamond found elsewhere on the stock.

ROMANIAN STOCKS

The Romanian M1944 carbine stock is identical to those made in Russia and Hungary and can be distinguished only by local markings such as a "C" in a diamond, a "2" in a circle and a triangle containing numerals and a letter.

HANDGUARDS

RUSSIAN HANDGUARDS

M1891 Infantry Rifle Handguard

The original model did not have a handguard until circa 1910. Thereafter a wooden handguard was added, finished to match the stock. It covered the barrel from about 2 in forward of the front of the rear sight to about 2.125 in to the rear of the nosecap. The handguard was 440 mm (17.3 in) long and was reversible, i.e., either end could face either end of the rifle, see Figure 1-16.

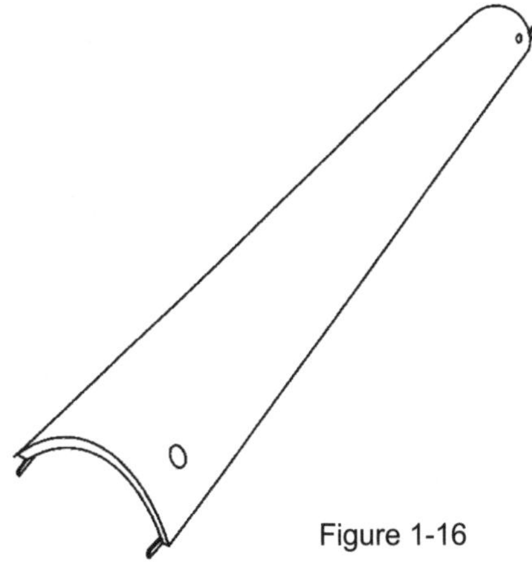

Figure 1-16

At each end of the handguard, held by three rivets to the underside, is a 25 mm (0.98 in) long metal liner. The rivet heads are visible on the top of the handguard. Extending from each liner are two metal tabs 5 mm (0.196 in) long and 3 mm (0.12 in) wide which slide under the front and rear barrel bands to secure the handguard to the stock.

This handguard is authentic to all M1891 Infantry rifles made after c. 1910, and to all Finnish rifles with the full-length Infantry rifle stock.

Note: Handguards for American-made M1891 Infantry rifles, like the stocks, are of American black walnut. Because handguards are thin and relatively fragile, American-stocked rifles are often found with Russian or Finnish birch replacement handguards, which of course are not the original.

Dragoon Rifle Handguard

This model was made without a handguard until circa 1910. The Dragoon handguard is 465 mm (18.30 in) long and is different than that used on the Infantry rifle. It has a distinct front and rear, the rear being a 30 mm (1.18 in) long arched area slightly wider and higher than the rest of the handguard.

The ends are lined with a metal strip secured by a screw and a rivet (two rivets on some examples) at each end of the handguard, the heads of which are visible on top of the handguard. The rear top of the handguard is slightly scalloped to fit against the front end of the rear sight base. Unlike the Infantry model, the handguard is held on the stock by the front and rear barrel bands, so there are no tabs protruding from the metal caps. See Figure 1-17.

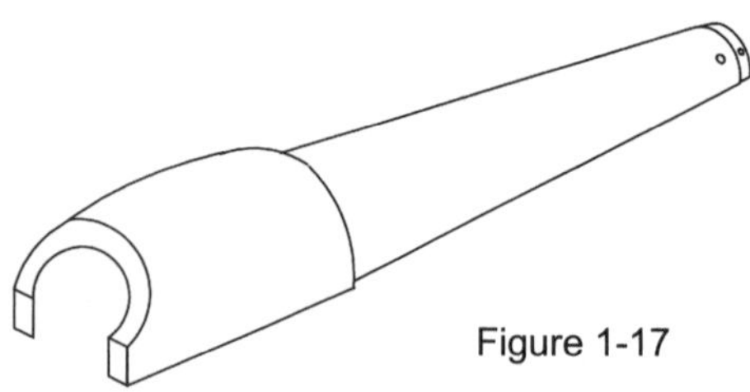
Figure 1-17

This handguard is authentic to the Dragoon and Cossack rifles; it will fit, but is not authentic to, the M1891/30.

Cossack Rifle Handguard

This handguard is identical to that used on the Dragoon rifle. The original design is reported to have had a rather long handguard, making the rifle fully stocked, like the M1907 carbine, to within about 2 in of the muzzle crown, and thereby precluding attachment of a bayonet. I have found no documentation to substantiate this report.

M1907 Carbine Handguard

This handguard is 375 mm (14.76 in) long and extends from the receiver ring to within 50 mm (1.97 in) of the muzzle, see Figure 1-18. The rear sight is mounted on the barrel 1 inch forward of the receiver and protrudes through a somewhat rectangular hole 65 mm (2.56 in) long. Metal liners front and rear are secured by brads.

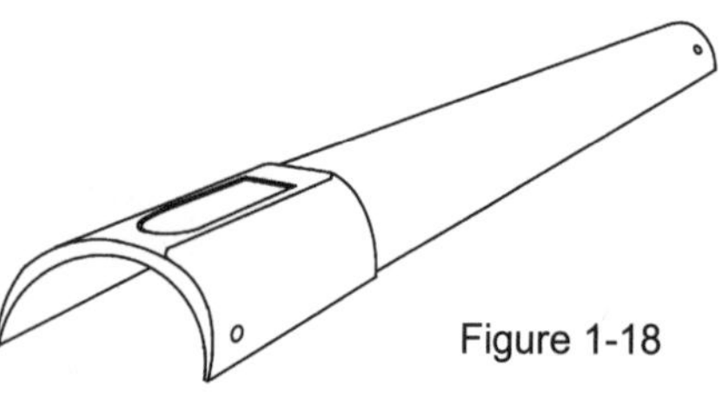
Figure 1-18

M1891/30 Rifle Handguard

This handguard is 455 mm (17.91 in) long, and both ends are finished and lined with a 15 mm (0.59 in) long metal cap secured by two rivets each. The rivet heads are visible on top of the handguard. The handguard is held on the stock by the front and rear barrel bands, so there are no tabs protruding from the metal caps. See Figure 1-19. This handguard will also fit the Dragoon model and is often found on those rifles reworked by the Finns.

Figure 1-19

M1938 Carbine Handguard

This handguard is 260 mm (10.23 in) long, and is finished at each end by a metal cap/liner 10 mm (0.39 in) wide. The rear 50 mm (1.968 in), between the barrel band and the rear sight base, is somewhat higher than the forward portion, see Figure 1-20.

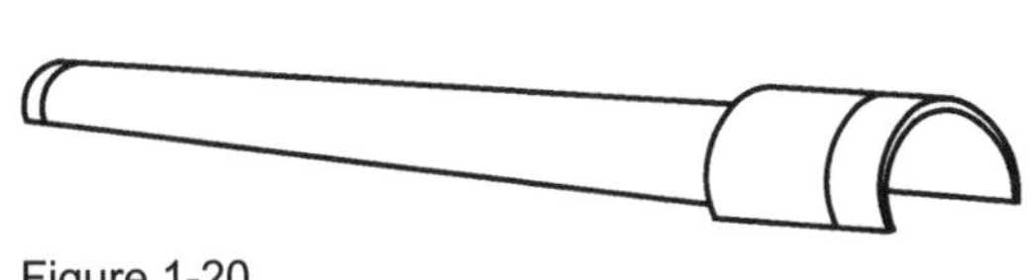

Figure 1-20

M1944 Carbine Handguard

Identical to the M1938 carbine. The handguards of all foreign copies of the M1944 (Chinese, Hungarian, etc.) are made of the same wood as their respective stocks, and are of the same pattern as the Soviet originals.

FINNISH HANDGUARDS

Finnish m/27 Rifle Handguards

The front 28 mm (1.10 in) of the handguard is covered by a nosecap 20 mm (0.787 in) wide. Thereafter the handguard increases slightly in height, and the width increases to 25 mm (0.98 in) at the front of the barrel band. At the rear of the barrel band the handguard again increases slightly in height, and broadens to 30 mm (1.18 in). The rear of the handguard is shaped into a forward-facing beveled arc 15 mm (0.590 in) deep to accommodate the front of the rear sight base. See Figure 1-21.

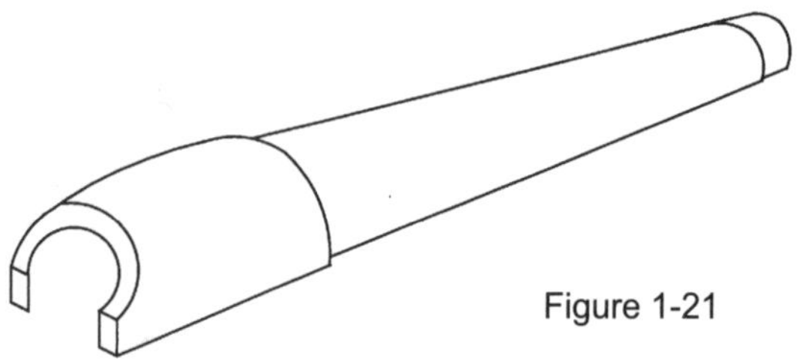

Figure 1-21

Finnish m/28 Rifle Handguard

Identical to that of the m/27 (see above).

Finnish m/28-30 Rifle Handguard

The handguard is unique to this model. It is 430 mm (16.92 in) long; the area under the nosecap is 20 mm (0.787 in) wide, increasing to 25 mm (0.98 in) from the rear of the nosecap to the barrel band, and ending in a slighly higher raised portion 33 mm (1.299 in) wide which extends to the rear sight base. See Figure 1-22.

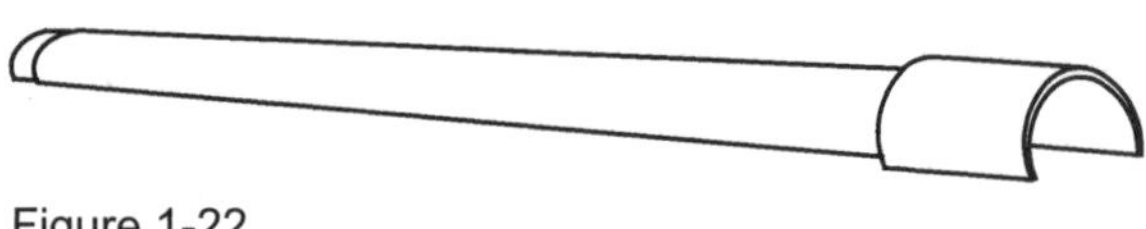

Figure 1-22

Finnish m/39 Rifle Handguard

This handguard is unique to the m/39. It is 410 mm (16.14 in) long. The front half is 30 mm (1.18 in) wide from the nosecap to the barrel band; the rear half is 35 mm (1.377 in) wide. The front 30 mm (1.18 in) is covered and secured by the nosecap. See Figure 1-23.

There is a barrel band 170 mm (6.69 in) behind the nosecap, at which point the handguard increases slightly in height and width for 190 mm (7.48 in) rearwards to a point where it is beveled forward. The rear end of the handguard then decreases in height and is covered by a blued steel rim 8 mm (0.314 in) wide, which is integral with the rear sight base.

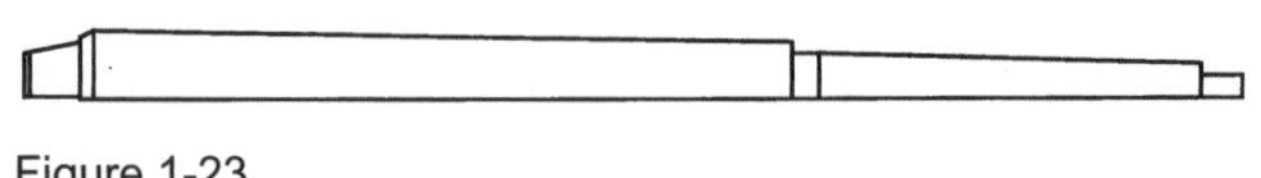

Figure 1-23

BARREL BANDS

RUSSIAN BARREL BANDS

M1891 Infantry Rifle Barrel Bands

The original or **Type 1** M1891 Infantry rifle had two barrel bands which were secured by machine screws through protrusions on the underside of the bands. As with succeeding models, the screws are capped with small "buttons" on the end opposite to the head. See Figure 1-24.

The Type 1 front barrel band on the original Infantry rifle also held the forward sling swivel until the introduction of sling slots circa 1910. On many of these barrel bands the screws are *loosened* by clockwise rotation and tightened counterclockwise — the opposite of normal Western practice.

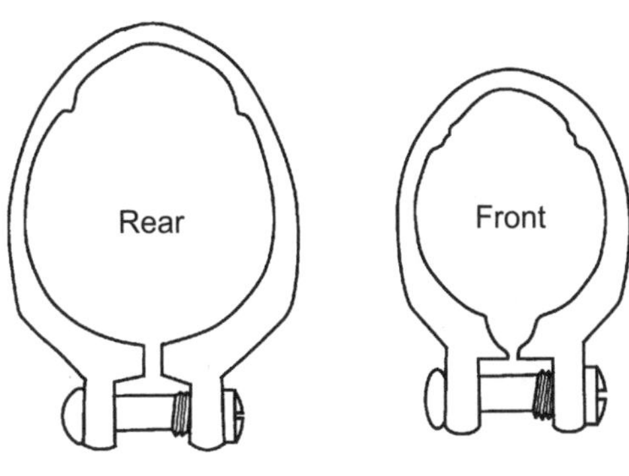

Figure 1-24

These front barrel bands are 100 mm (3.94 in) and the rear barrel bands are 135 mm (5.31 in) in diameter — both measurements exclude the screw-holding tabs, which extend 10 mm (0.393 in) from the outer rim of the bands. Both barrel bands are 8 mm (0.314 in) wide. The front barrel band's base above the screw-tabs is grooved to allow insertion of the cleaning rod.

These barrel bands are made of steel, usually blued but sometimes finished with a black coating; they are commonly marked with the arsenal logo. These Type 1 barrel bands were discontinued around 1910; they are original to M1891 Infantry rifles made before circa 1910, and to Finnish rifles which take the M1891 Infantry rifle stock. They will fit, but are not authentic to, all other Russian Mosin-Nagant M1891 Infantry rifle types and their foreign copies.

The **Type 2** M1891 Rifle barrel band, introduced circa 1910, was an improvement over the Type 1, being made of a heavier blued steel. The front band is 120 mm (4.72 in) in diameter, the rear band diameter is 140 mm (5.51 in); both bands are 10 mm (0.393 in) wide. See Figure 1-25.

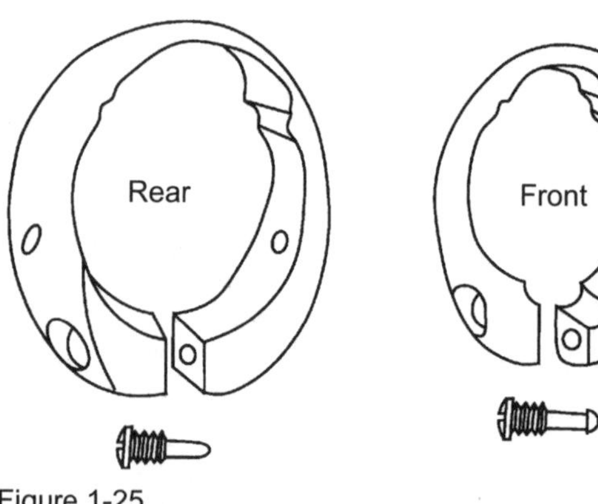

Figure 1-25

These bands are secured on the underside by a countersunk screw with a "button" to prevent its being completely unscrewed; they lack the protruding screw-tabs of the Type 1. Like the Type 1, the screws on many of these Type 2 barrel bands operate oddly: left is tight and right is loose. The front barrel band is grooved at the base to allow insertion of the cleaning rod. These barrel bands are often found marked with the arsenal or maker's logo.

The Type 2 barrel bands will fit all Mosin-Nagants with the M1891 Infantry rifle stock, and are authentic to M1891 Infantry rifles made after circa 1909, and to the Finnish m/91 and m/24 rifles. Some bands will be found with a small hole drilled completely through them: this is to accommodate a pin which was used by the Finns to secure the bands, though it is uncommon to find a rifle with the pins still in place.

Dragoon Rifle Barrel Bands
The Dragoon rifle stock and handguard are secured by two blued metal barrel bands, the front slightly smaller than the rear, with circumferences of 115 mm (4.53 in) and 125 mm (4.92 in) respectively; both are 7 mm (0.275 in) wide. See Figure 1-26.

These bands are solid and have a convex outer side; they are marked with the logo of whichever of the three Russian arsenals produced them. They are held in place by blued steel flat springs, one per band, set in grooves on the right side of the stock. The front spring is 60 mm (2.36 in) long and the rear is 50 mm (1.97 in) long; each is 5 mm (0.197 in) wide. The springs are often, but not always, arsenal-marked.

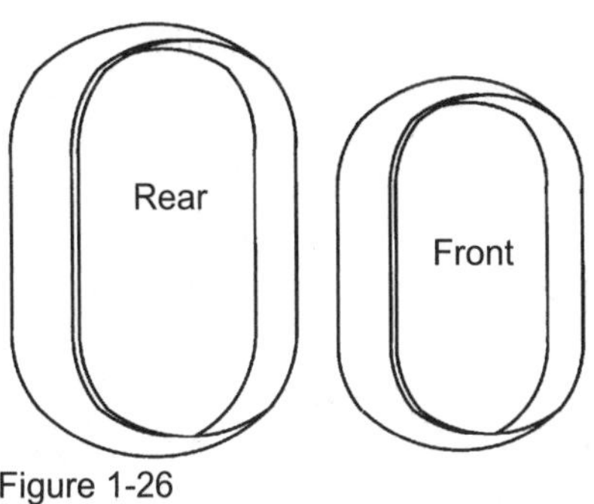

Figure 1-26

Cossack Rifle Barrel Bands
Identical to those used on the Dragoon rifle, above.

M1907 Carbine Barrel Bands
Two barrel bands were used on the M1907 carbine, both 7 mm (0.275 in) wide and made of blued steel. The front band is 115 mm (4.53 in), and the rear band is 125 mm (4.92 in) in circumference. Both are held in place by blued steel flat springs, one per band, set into grooves on the right side of the stock. The front spring is 60 mm (2.36 in) long, and the rear spring is 40 mm (1.57 in) long; both are 5 mm (0.197 in) wide. The bands are marked with the manufacturing arsenal's logo.

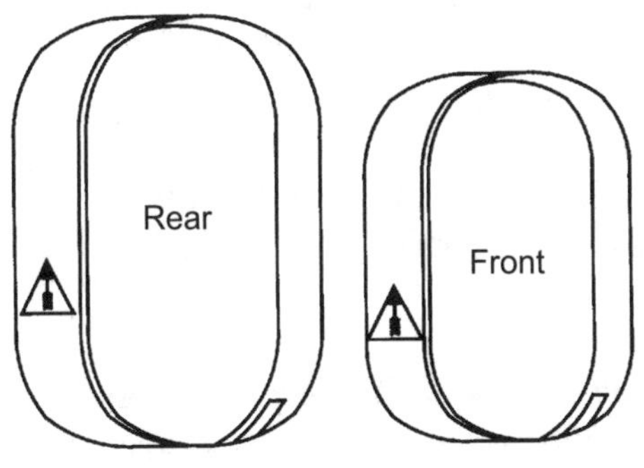

Figure 1-27

M1891/30 Rifle Barrel Bands
Although the barrel bands of the M1891/30 (Figure 1-27) are the same size as those of the M1907 carbine and the Dragoon and Cossack rifles (115 mm circumference for the front, 125 mm for the rear), they are easily distinguishable from the earlier type by

three features: a) the exterior is flat rather than convex; b) the underside is openable tongue-and-groove construction, whereas the earlier type is a solid band; and c) they have post-1930 Soviet arsenal markings.

M1938 Carbine Barrel Bands

Two blued metal barrel bands, secured by retaining springs in grooves along the stock, were used on the M1938 carbine. The circumference of the front band is 115 mm (4.53 in), that of the rear 125 mm (4.92 in). The bands have openable tongue-and-groove undersides and the usual Soviet-era arsenal logos.

M1944 Carbine Barrel Bands

Identical to the M1938. Barrel bands of the various M1944 copies made by China, Hungary, etc., are also identical to those of the M1938, but, naturally, do not have Soviet markings.

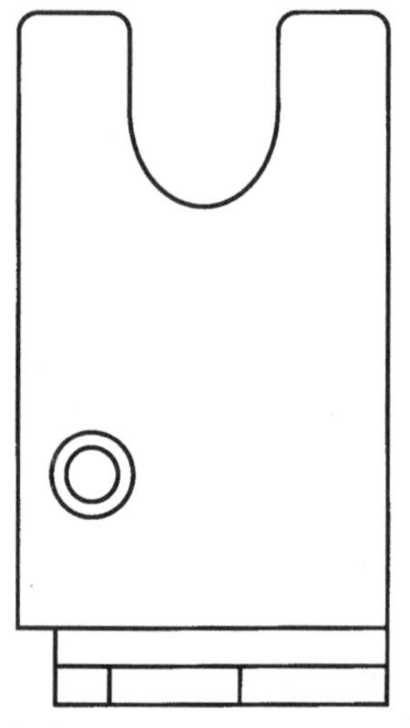
Figure 1-28

FINNISH BARREL BANDS

Finnish m/27 Rifle Barrel Bands

This rifle has a single blued steel barrel band 135 mm (5.32 in) in circumference and 12 mm (0.472 in) wide. It is secured to the stock by a single screw on the right side. See Figure 1-28. The front barrel band is actually the nosecap, described below.

Finnish m/28 Rifle Barrel Bands

These barrel bands are identical to those used on the m/27.

Finnish m/28-30 Rifle Barrel Bands

This rifle uses as a single blued steel barrel band identical in dimensions to that of the m/28 but whereas the band of the m/28 is rather flat, that of the m/28-30 is slightly convex.

Finnish m/39 Rifle Barrel Bands

The m/39's rear barrel band is made of blued steel and is 130 mm (5.118 in) in diameter and 10 mm (0.393 in) wide. It has two features unique to this model: a) the band is hinged on the left side and tightened by a screw on the right, and b) it has two sling swivels mounted to it: one on the left side and one on the underside. The band is held in place by a retaining spring set into a groove on the left side of the stock. The spring is blued steel, 68 mm (2.68 in) long and 4 mm (0.157 in) wide. It is unmarked. See Figure 1-29.

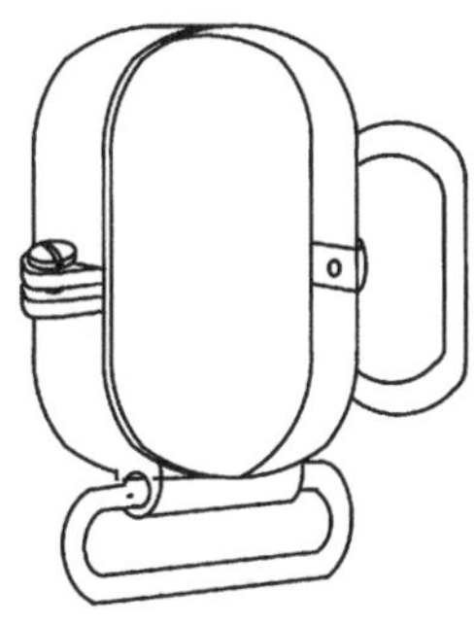

Figure 1-29

The front barrel band is also the nosecap. It is made of milled steel in two pieces, hinged on the left side and secured by a machine screw through the connecting lugs on the right side. The bottom half is 30 mm (1.18 in) at its widest, scalloped to 25 mm (0.98 in) at the top of the front; the top half is a uniform 25 mm wide. The entire assembly is attached to the stock by a machine screw running completely through the stock from right to left. There is a bayonet lug on the underside of the nosecap. See Figure 1-30.

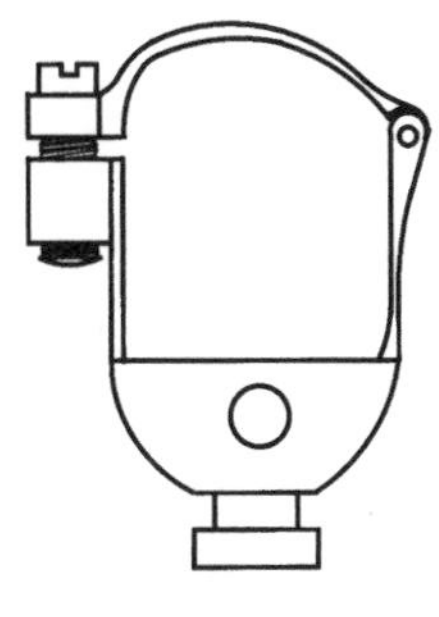

Figure 1-30

NOSECAPS

RUSSIAN NOSECAPS

M1891 Infantry Rifle Nosecap

This simple blued metal cap is 22 mm (0.86 in) long and 20 mm (0.787 in) wide. It is secured to the end of the stock by a single screw through the stock. It is authentic to all models which use the Infantry rifle stock, the Dragoon rifle, and the Cossack rifle. See Figure 1-31.

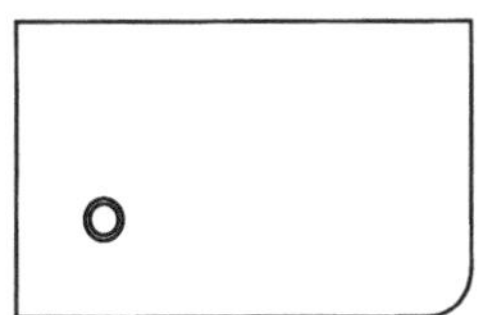

Figure 1-31

M1907 Carbine Nosecap

This nosecap is blued steel, identical to that of other models except in size: it is 18 mm (0.708 in) long and 20 mm (0.787 in) wide at its widest point.

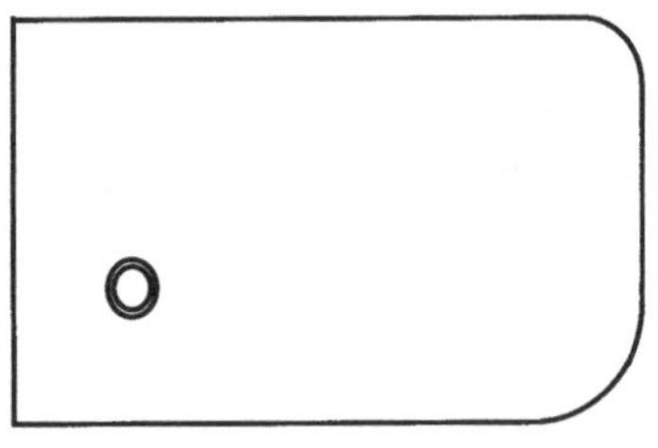

Figure 1-32

M1891/30 Rifle Nosecap

This nosecap is virtually identical to that of the M1891 Infantry rifle nosecap, but has more rounded front surfaces. Figure 1-32.

M1938 Carbine Nosecap

Identical to that of the M1891/30 rifle, but is even more rounded at the front. It is authentic to the M1944 carbine as well.

M1944 Carbine

Uses the same nosecap as the M1938.

FINNISH NOSECAPS

Finnish m/27 Rifle Nosecap

The m/27 was the first model to have a new type of nosecap. Two types were used. The **Type 1** was hinged on the right side and secured on the left by a machine screw parallel to the stock; some m/27s have the hinge on the *left* and the screw on the right. See Figure 1-33.

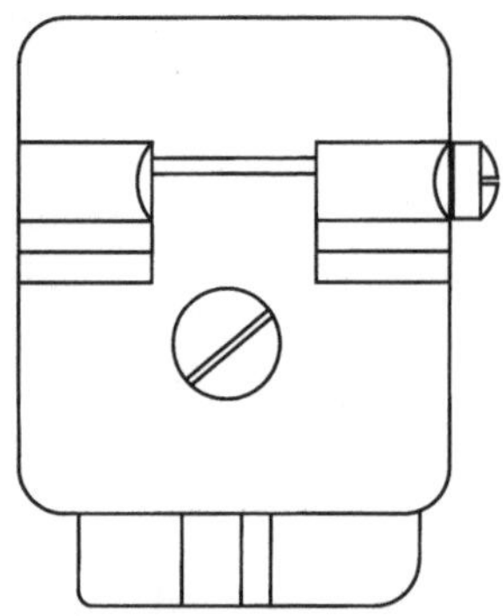

Figure 1-33

The nosecap is 28 mm (1.10 in) wide and 45 mm (1.77 in) tall, including the bayonet lug. The bayonet lug on the underside of the nosecap is 25 mm (0.98 in) long and 8 mm (0.314 in) wide. Because the nosecap tended to rotate when the bayonet was used, cracking the stock, the **Type 2** had two parallel metal braces, one on each side, added starting in 1935. The braces are 75 mm (2.95 in) long by 10 mm (0.39 in) wide. They are set atop the nosecap and extend rearwards, seated in grooves in the stock. The braces are attached to the stock by a transverse bolt whose head is on the right side of the stock approximately 1.25 in from the rear of the brace. In some examples of the Type 2, both braces are spot-welded to the rear of the nosecap, but this was uncommon. See Figure 1-34.

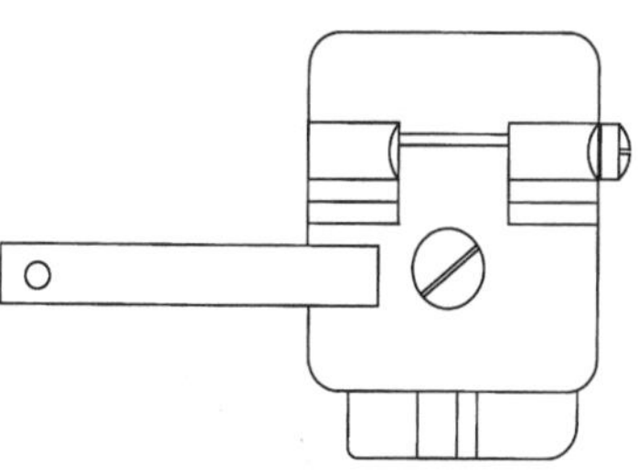
Figure 1-34

Finnish m/28 Rifle

Experience with nosecap problems led the Finns to develop a simplified nosecap having a lug which accepted all Finnish-developed knife-type bayonets: the m/27, m/28, m28/30, m/35, and m/39 Sk.Y. See Chapter 5, Bayonets.

There are two types of this nosecap: **Type 1** was made in two pieces, **Type 2** in one and was used on the m/28's successor, the m/28-30 as well. The two-piece Type 1 nosecap consisted of the band and the flat face through which the cleaning rod passed. See Figures 1-35 and 1-36 respectively.

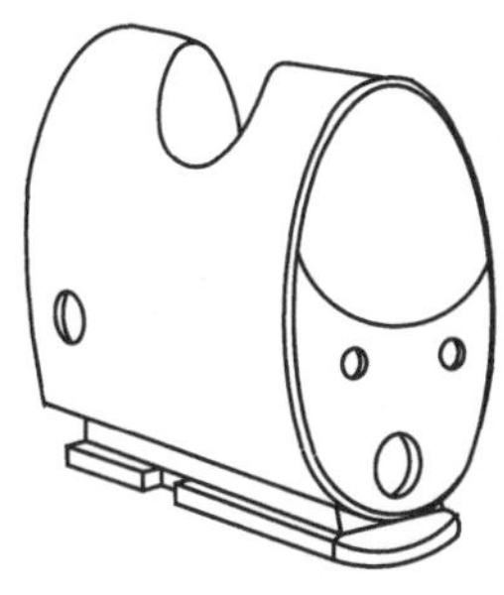
Figure 1-35

Finnish m/28-30 Rifle Nosecap

Used the one-piece nosecap described above and shown in Figure 1-36.

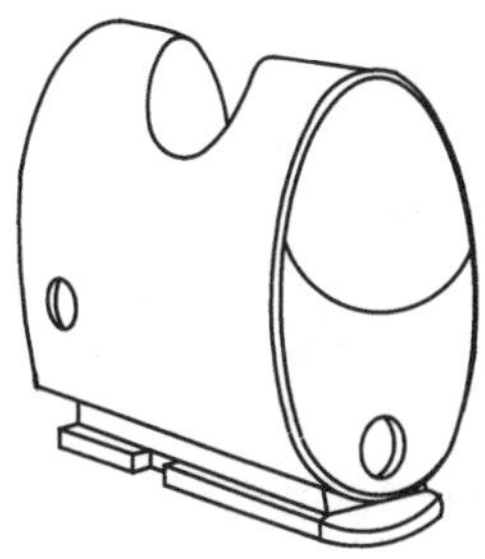
Figure 1-36

Finnish m/39 Rifle Nosecap

The front barrel band forms the nosecap. It is made of milled steel in two pieces, hinged on the left side and secured by a machine screw through the connecting lugs on the right. See Figure 1-37.

The bottom half is 30 mm (1.18 in) at its widest, scalloped to 25 mm

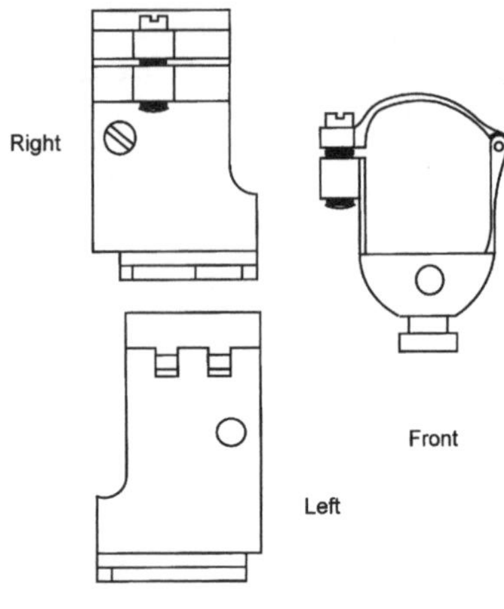

Figure 1-37

(.98 in) at the top of the front; the top half is a uniform 25 mm wide. The entire assembly is attached to the stock by a screw at the rear of the nosecap running completely through the stock from right to left. There is a bayonet lug on the underside of the nosecap.

SLING SWIVELS

RUSSIAN SLING SWIVELS

The original swivels were of simple bent metal wire, rectangular, and approximately 25 mm (.98 in) by 30 mm (1.18 in); their internal angles are rounded as are the external ones. They were blued. The author has observed one Cossack rifle fitted with rectangular, straw-colored swivels through the slots.

M1891 Infantry Rifle

The original M1891 Infantry rifle featured two sling swivels: one attached to the front of the magazine housing and the other mounted on the front barrel band. See Figures 1-38 and 1-39.

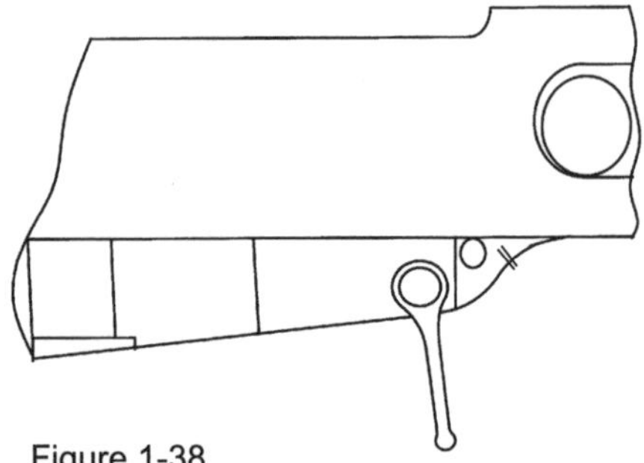

Figure 1-38

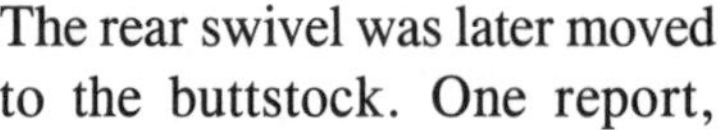

The rear swivel was later moved to the buttstock. One report, which the author has been unable to verify, suggests that this was done only to rifles issued to Guards regiments. The swivels were discontinued altogether around 1909, and existing rifles retrofitted with sling slots where the front swivel had been mounted, and on the side of the buttstock. See Figure 1-40.

FINNISH SWIVELS

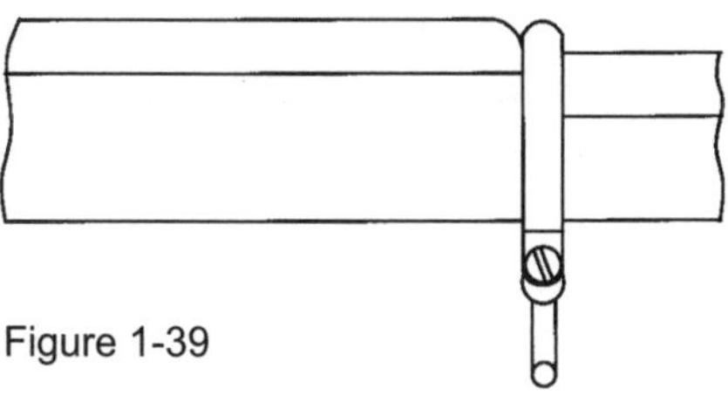

Figure 1-39

The swivels on Finnish reworks are metal, blued or finished with a blackish coating; the latter is the more common. The front swivel is 38 mm (1.5 in) wide at the top, tapering to 25 mm (.98 in), and is 25 mm (.98 in) in height; it is secured by a screw 45 mm (1.75 in) long. The rear swivel is 45 mm (1.8 in) wide at the top and tapers to 30 mm (1.18 in), and is 38 mm (1.5 in) in height; it is secured by a screw 50 mm (2.0 in) long. See Figure 1-41.

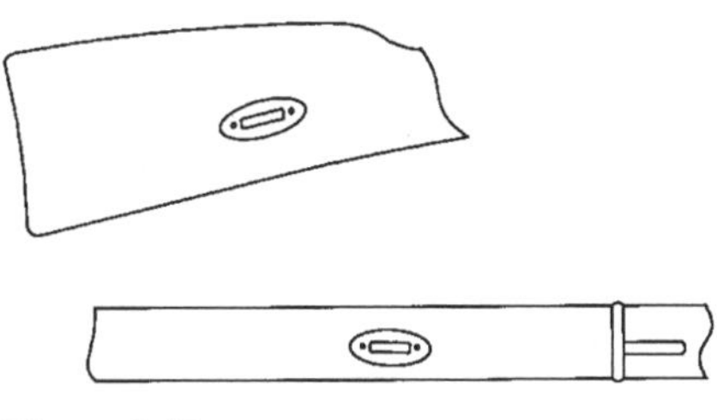

Figure 1-40

m/27 Rifle Swivel

This rifle has a swivel mounted on a blued metal plate on the underside of the butt, see Figure 1-42. The plate is approximately 2.0 in long and is secured with two screws.

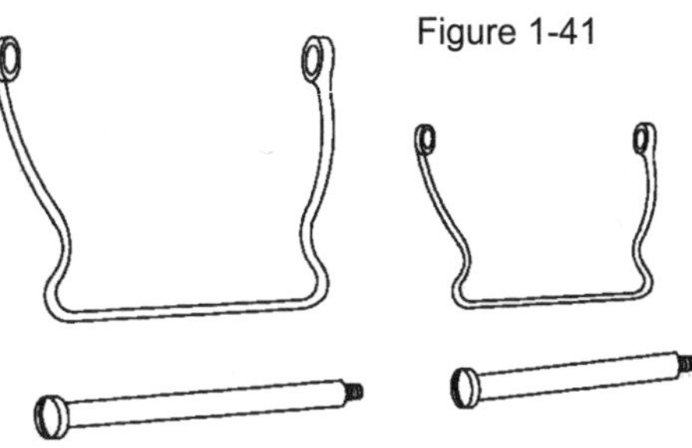

Figure 1-41

The swivel rotates through 360°. Forward attachment of the sling is through a sling slot in the forend, although it is not unusual to see a swivel mounted through the slot as well.

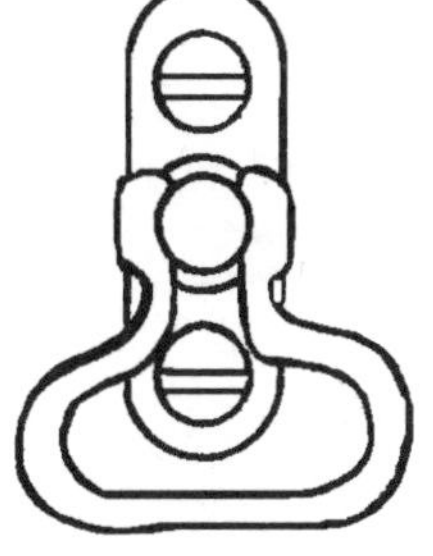

Figure 1-42

m/27 Carbine Swivel

On this exceedingly rare firearm — fewer than 300 are reported to exist — the swivel arrangement is the same as for the m/27 rifle. It differs, however, in that there is also a Mauser-type sling recess on the right side of the butt. See Figure 1-43.

m/39 Rifle Swivel

This rifle has a unique swivel arrangement. The butt configuration is similar to that of the m/27 carbine, differing only in two respects: the sling bar is on the *left* side of the butt, and the swivel on the underside of the stock does not rotate.

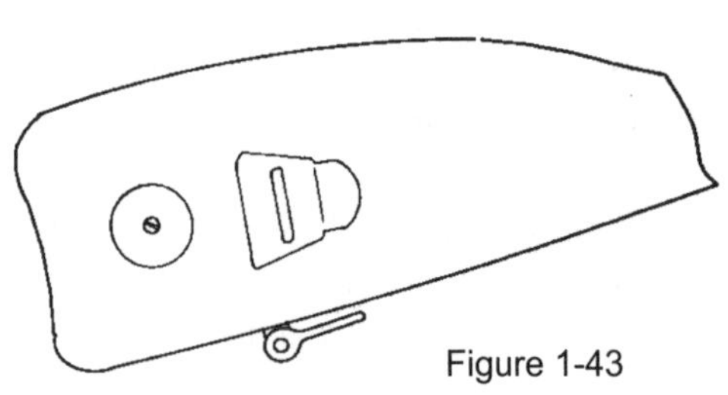

Figure 1-43

There are two front swivels, both attached to the barrel band. Each swivel is made of 3 mm (0.118 in) thick bent wire, 30 mm (1.18 in) by 12 mm (0.472 in). See Figure 1-44.

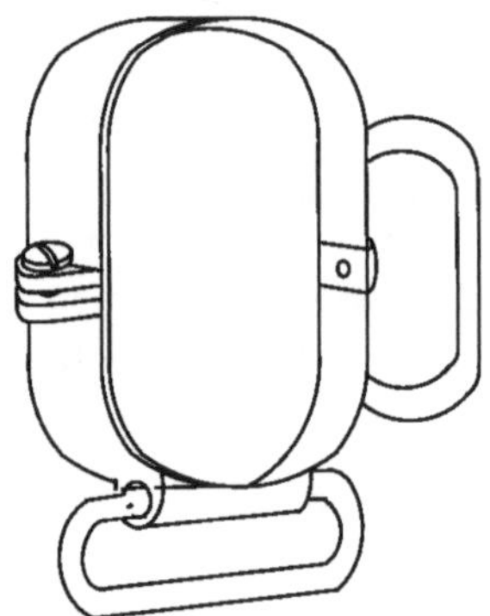

Figure 1-44

The butt swivel is identical to the two front swivels. It is mounted on a metal plate 40 mm (1.57 in) by 10 mm (0.39 in), which is set into a recess mortised into the underside of the butt. See Figure 1-45. The plate is secured by two screws.

It does not rotate, but is otherwise quite similar to the butt swivel of the m/27.

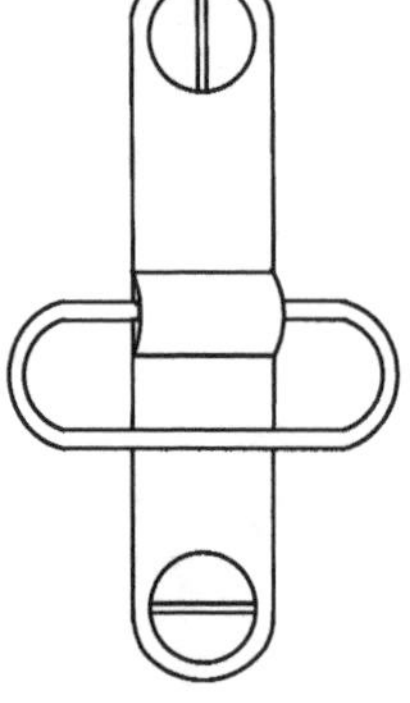

Figure 1-45

In addition to the three swivels, the m/39 has a sling bar on the left side of the butt. The bar is set into a recess 50 mm (1.968 in) long by 25 mm (0.98 in) wide, which begins 45 mm (1.77 in) from the butt plate. The metal bar is 50 mm (1.968 in) long and is secured by two screws, one through each 12 mm (0.472 in) broad end of the bar. The bar itself is set in a 50 mm mortise perpendicular to the main recess. See Figure 1-46.

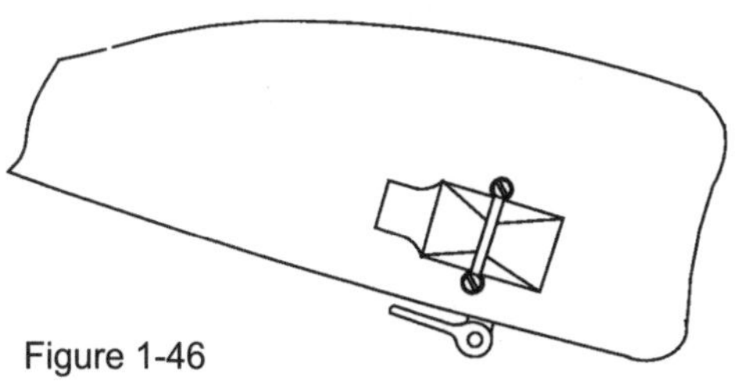
Figure 1-46

TRIGGER GUARD AND MAGAZINE HOUSING

Two types of M1891 trigger guard housings were manufactured. They are identical except for the fact that the **Type 1** has a sling swivel attached to the front of the magazine housing on Infantry rifles from the start of production to circa 1909, see Figure 1-47.

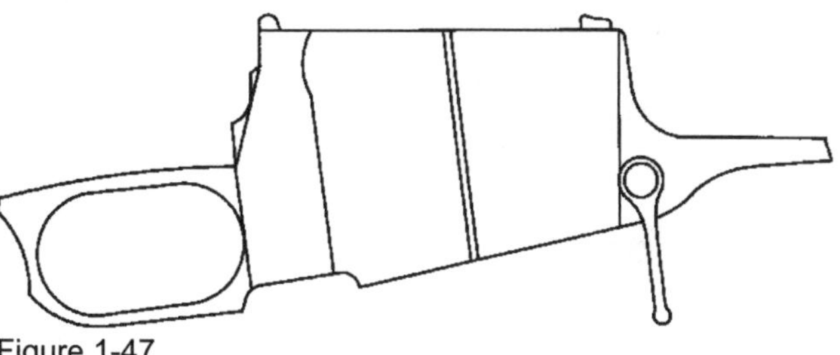
Figure 1-47

The **Type 2** trigger guard housing was identical to the Type 1 except for the lack of the swivel. It was used on all Mosin-Nagants from circa 1909 until the end of production in all countries, see Figure 1-48.

The trigger guard is secured to the action and stock by two machine screws: one from the top, through the rear tang; and one from the bottom, through the front tang.

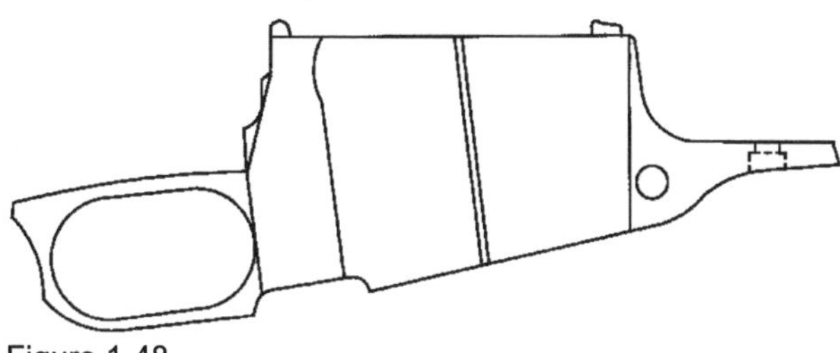
Figure 1-48

The rear screw is 48 mm (1.89 in) long; the front screw is 30 mm (1.18 in) long. The screw heads are of identical size: 9 mm (0.35 in) in diameter and 3 mm (0.12 in) thick.

The trigger guard itself is made of blued steel; it is 210 mm (8.27 in) long and, except for the magazine well, is 11 mm (0.433 in) wide. A slot 10 mm x 6 mm (0.39 in x 0.236 in) is bored through the rear tang, through which the trigger passes. The rear screw hole is 10 mm behind the trigger slot. 15 mm (0.590 in) in front of the trigger slot is a hole through which the floorplate release catch passes. This catch is blued spring steel 45 mm (1.77 in) long and is secured to the back of the magazine housing by a single screw; its purposes are to hold the floorplate shut and to allow it to be opened in order to unload the magazine.

The floorplate is 115 mm (4.527 in) long and 18 mm (0.708 in) at its widest point. There is a circular indentation 15 mm (0.590 in) in diameter at the rear of the floorplate, through which is bored a 7 mm x 8 mm (0.275 in x 0.314 in) hole to allow engagement of the floorplate latch.

The floorplate is attached to the trigger guard by a hook engaging a rivet, which rests in a beveled hole 10 mm x 20 mm (0.39 in x 0.787 in) bored through the trigger guard in front of the magazine housing 10 mm behind the front screw hole. The magazine-follower consists of two pieces of blued steel: the follower and follower carrier; they are hinged together at the rear. See Figure 1-49.

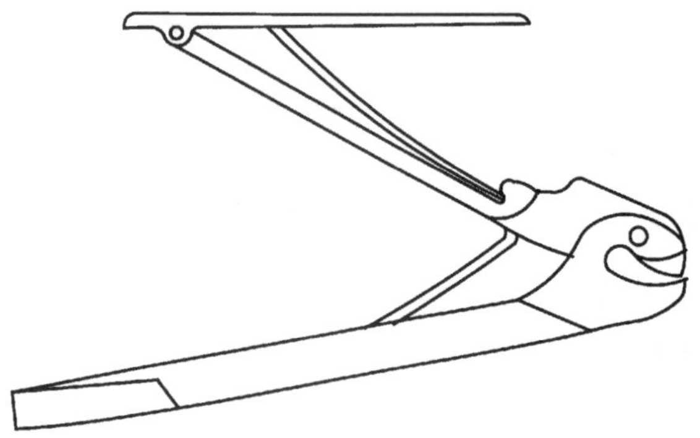

Figure 1-49.

The upper piece (the follower) is beveled downward at front and rear; the underside has a channel in which rides the top of the smaller magazine-follower spring. The follower is 65 mm (2.56 in) long and 7 mm (0.275 in) wide, and is normally stamped on the underside with inspectors' and arsenal markings. The follower carrier is 90 mm (3.54 in) long and tapers from front to back; it is 5 mm (0.196 in) for most of its length. It has inspectors' and arsenal marks on the side.

The front of the follower carrier is hinged to the front of the floorplate, and both are hooked onto the same hinge pin which holds the floorplate/follower assembly to the trigger guard. The entire assembly is removed from the trigger guard hinge pin by pinching the top of the follower together with the bottom of the floorplate, swinging them forward as far as they will go, and pulling straight down. There is no magazine cutoff on Mosin-Nagants as the follower does not lock the bolt open on an empty magazine.

The follower carrier spring is attached to the interior of the floorplate by a single screw. The spring is blued spring steel, 80 mm (3.149 in) long and tapers from 5 mm to 7 mm (0.196 in to 0.275 in) front-to-back. It is slightly indented on the top of its front to accept the bottom of the lower section of the follower carrier. The spring is unmarked.

The smaller follower spring is 50 mm x 5 mm (1.968 in x 0.196 in) and is made of spring steel finished in-the-white. The lower end is held in a parallel groove at the front of the follower carrier; the upper end rests in a channel machined into the underside of the follower. The spring is unmarked.

Russian trigger guards are always marked with the maker or arsenal logo on the exterior of the front tang, in front of the screw head. The floorplates are serial-numbered to the weapon.

Chinese Trigger Guards

Chinese trigger guards are marked on the interior of the front tang, forward of the screw hole. The floorplates are serial-numbered to the weapon.

Hungarian Trigger Guards

Hungarian trigger guards have the country code number 02 on the exterior front tang, forward from the screw hole. The floorplates are serial-number to the weapon.

Polish Trigger Guards

Polish trigger guards do not have factory or date markings, but do have various inspectors' markings. The floorplates are serial-numbered to the weapon.

Romanian Trigger Guards

Romanian trigger guards are marked on the exterior front tang with an arrowhead in a triangle. The floorplates are serial-numbered to the weapon.

TRIGGER ASSEMBLY

There are three types of triggers: the original found on all varieties, and two improved types developed by the Finns, found only on Finnish-reworked and domestically produced rifles.

The trigger is fastened by a pin to two lugs on the receiver. Near the top of the trigger is a slot for the sear. See Figure 1-50. When the trigger is pressed it swings forward and down, causing the upper end of its slot to press the sear downwards and force its nose out of engagement with the cocking-piece lug, firing the weapon.

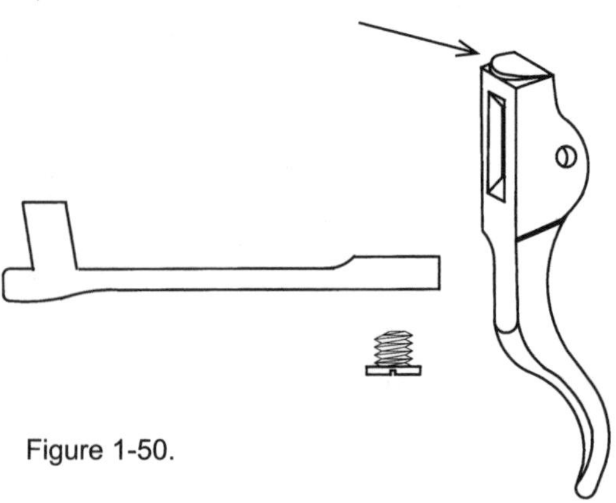

Figure 1-50.

The bolt stop (Arrows in Figures 1-50, -51 and -52) is found on the head of all triggers of whatever type. When the trigger is pressed it retracts the stop, thereby enabling the bolt to be withdrawn from the weapon.

TRIGGERS

Type 1 Russian Trigger

The **Type 1** was used on all Russian-manufactured models. It is 70 mm (2.755 in) long, made of blued steel and arsenal-marked. The trigger is secured to the receiver by a steel pin 17 mm (0.669 in) long.

Note: The arsenal's or maker's mark on the trigger is the only way to determine whether it is of Russian, American or French manufacture.

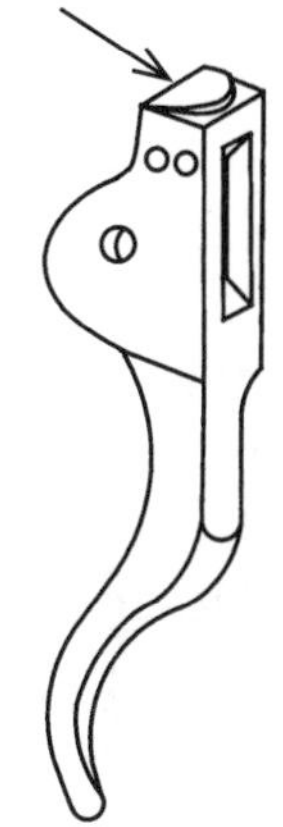

Figure 1-51

Type 2 Finnish Trigger

The **Type 2** Finnish trigger is essentially the Russian version, but with a raised and extended lug at the attachment point and a somewhat differently angled bolt stop. See Figure 1-51.

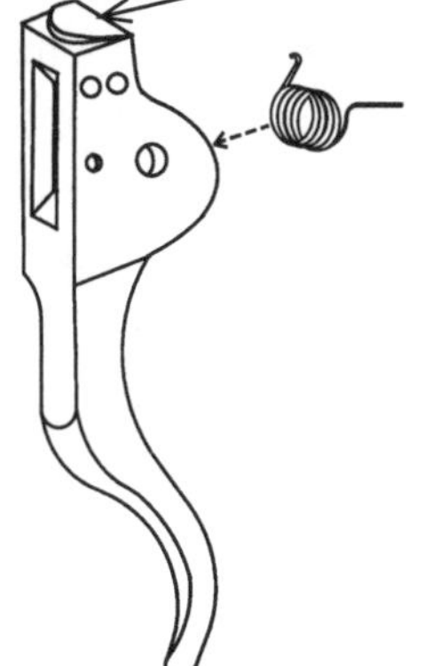

Figure 1-52

Type 3 Finnish Trigger

The **Type 3** Finnish trigger is almost identical to the Type 2, but has an additional hole forward of the mounting-pin hole and a slightly different bolt-stop. More significantly, a coiled spring has been added to smooth the trigger pull. See Figure 1-52.

SEAR

The sear is essentially a leaf spring, finished in-the-white. It is 52 mm (2.05 in) long and 12 mm (0.472 in) wide at its widest point. A hole 7 mm (0.275 in) in diameter is bored through it to receive the retaining screw, which is 10 mm (0.39 in) long and has a head 10 mm (0.39 in) in diameter and 3 mm (0.118 in) thick. The retaining screw passes through a hole at the forward end of the sear and is secured to a lug on the underside of the receiver. The sear nose protrudes through a slot into the channel in which the cocking piece lug slides. The sear spring is not arsenal-marked. Refer to Figure 1-50.

INTERRUPTER/EJECTOR

There are two types of interrupter/ejector: **Type 1** is the one-piece model, authentic to all Mosin-Nagants made prior to 1930 and to all Finnish models of whatever vintage. The **Type 2** is the two-piece model, introduced with the M1891/30 rifle and used on all models thereafter.

The ejector expels the empty cartridge case from the receiver. The ejector itself — whether integral with the interrupter or as a separate piece attached to the interrupter by a screw — is simply a small blade which protrudes through a slot in the side of the bolt head and expels the cartridge or cartridge case upwards and to the right when the bolt is drawn open and back.

The interrupter exerts pressure on the rounds in the magazine beneath the top cartridge to enable cartridges to feed smoothly from the magazine into the chamber. The interrupter prevents a cartridge from being fed from the magazine into the chamber until the preceding cartridge — or cartridge case — has been completely ejected, thereby eliminating 'double-feeding', a potential cause of jamming.

Type 1 Interrupter/Ejector

The **Type 1** interrupter/ejector is made of a single piece of blued steel 90 mm (3.54 in) long and 10 mm (0.39 in) at its widest point. The piece is flat, with protrusions on both ends and on the outer edge; the inner edge is slightly scalloped. Russian and Finnish interrupter/ejectors show arsenal logos. See Figure 1-53.

Type 2 Interrupter/Ejector
The **Type 2** interrupter/ejector is comprised of two pieces: the interrupter and the ejector. Both are made of blued steel and unmarked, refer to Figure 1-53.

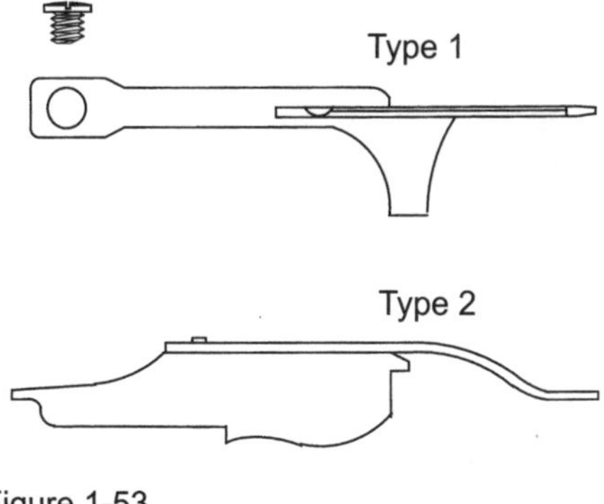

Figure 1-53

The interrupter is flat, with protrusions on both ends and on the outer edge; the inner edge is slightly scalloped. It is 60 mm (2.36 in) long and 10 mm (0.39 in) wide.

The ejector is flat, 65 mm (2.55 in) long, 13 mm (0.511 in) wide at the front end, and 7 mm (0.275 in) wide at the rear. There is a rectangular hole 5 mm (0.196 in) long and 2 mm (0.078 in) wide near the front edge; this mates with a nipple on the interrupter. There is a 3 mm (0.118 in) hole at the rear for the screw which secures the interrupter/ejector assembly to the receiver. The screw is 5 mm (0.196 in) long and the head is 5 mm in diameter.

Chinese, Hungarian and Polish interrupter/ejectors are unmarked.

RECEIVER

The receiver is a tube-like piece of machined steel which holds five parts of the Mosin-Nagant: 1) barrel which is threaded into the front end, 2) ejector/interrupter which is fitted into a slot on its left side, 3) the trigger which is attached to a lug on the underside of the receiver by a steel pin 17 mm (0.669 in) long, 4) the sear which is screwed to the receiver just forward of the trigger, 5) the bolt assembly which rides on a track within the receiver. See Figure 1-54.

Although Mosin-Nagant receivers are commonly thought to have been manufactured only in two variations — hexagonal and round — there are

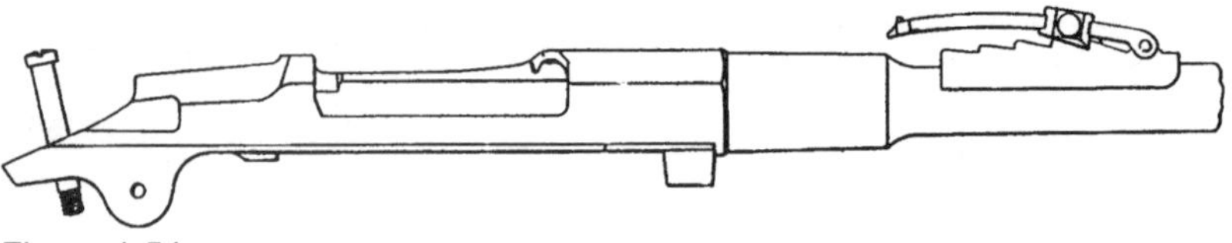

Figure 1-54

actually at least four distinct types. Not only have these four types not been identified in the literature before, but there are no official designations known. Accordingly, the author has identified them as Types 1 through 4, in order of manufacture.

Note: All Mosin-Nagant receivers, of whatever type, were milled from steel blanks and blued; all have the same basic dimensions.

The **Type 1** Mosin-Nagant receiver (see Figure 1-55A) was the form found on all original Mosin-Nagant rifles manufactured from 1891 to 1930 and is commonly referred to as "hexagonal", although a more accurate term is "polygonal." The chamber area is hexagonal (Arrow 1), the area around the clip guide is squared (Arrow 2) and the scalloped area at the left extends virtually to the stock (Arrow 3).

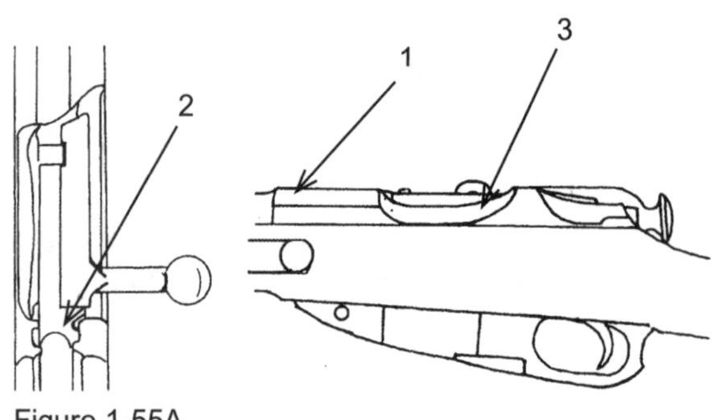

Figure 1-55A

The **Type 2** receiver (see Figure 1-55B) was designed for the M1891/30 rifle in 1930. It differs from the Type 1 in that the area around the clip guide is noticeably more rounded. The scallop is like that of the Type 1, extending down virtually to the stock. The chamber area is round, as in all subsequent varieties (Arrow). The receiver was machined round to reduce costs and simplify production.

The Type 2 is found on all Mosin-Nagant types made after 1930, except for Finnish rifles, almost of all which were reworked from the earlier hexagonal Type 1. It was replaced from 1942 to circa 1945 by the Type 3 but reappeared in post–World War II M1944 carbines.

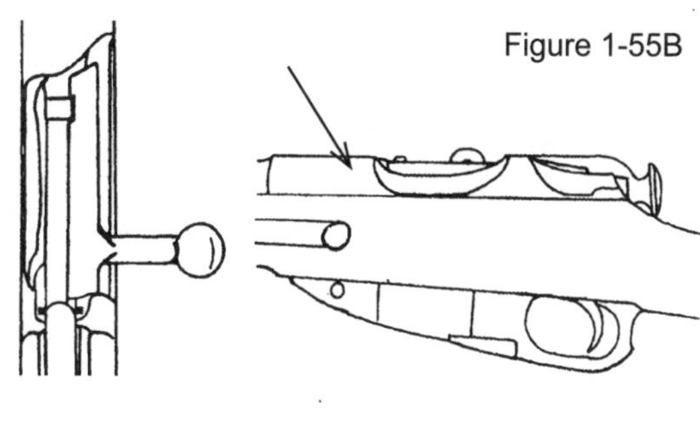
Figure 1-55B

The **Type 3** receiver (see Figure 1-55C) replaced the Type 2 starting in 1942 on the M1891/30 rifle, the M1938 carbine and some M1944 carbines made during the war years. It was almost certainly a war emergency expedient dictated by material shortages and manufacturing shortcuts. There are minor variations in the degree of roundness in the clip area, but all observed specimens fit the general pattern. The scallop is distinctive in that it is slight and ends ± 8 mm (0.31 in) above the stock, rather than extending down to the wood line as in the Types 1 and 2 (Arrow).

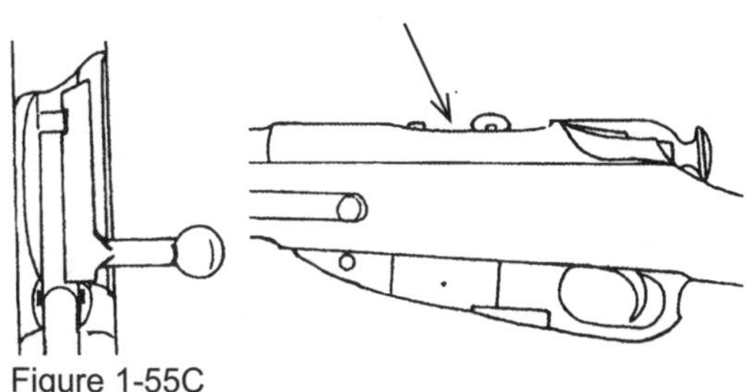
Figure 1-55C

The **Type 4** Mosin-Nagant receiver is unique to Poland's M1944, see Figure 1-55D. The scallop is so slight as to almost constitute a sloping plane from the inner edge of the

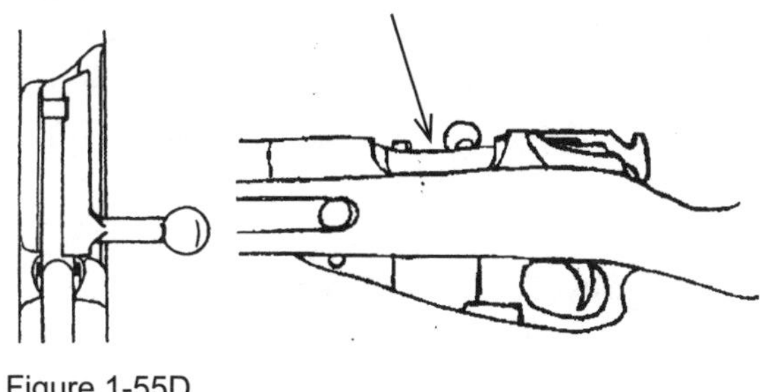
Figure 1-55D

receiver wall to the wood line of the stock.

Note: The Soviets continued to use the Type 1 hexagonal receivers remaining in inventory after the change to the Type 2 round receiver. They can be found on some M1891/30 rifles made as late as mid-1936.

With the exception of the Polish Type 4 receiver, those made by various other nations which used or produced the Mosin-Nagant series are identifiable only by their markings. See Appendix C.

RUSSIAN RECEIVERS

Russian receivers are always are marked with the maker or arsenal logo on the interior of the rear tang, behind the screw hole. If the logo is missing it was almost certainly machined off during refurbishing in Finland.

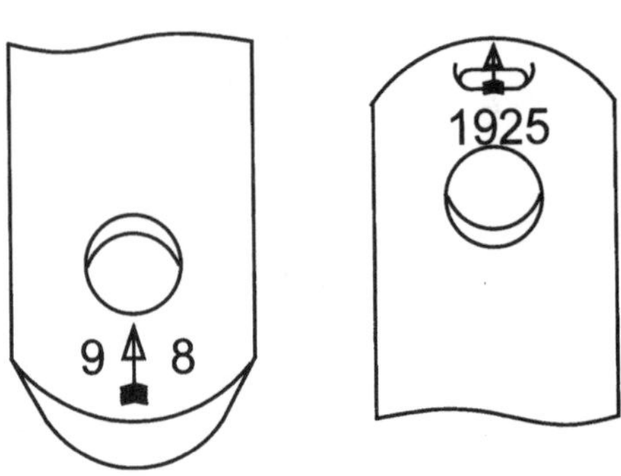

Figure 1-56

Russian-made receivers also show the year of production on the interior of the rear tang: for 19th-century production only the last two digits of the year are given, sometimes followed by the Cyrillic letter Г *(geh)* — the abbreviation for the Russian word *god*, meaning 'year'. Some examples also have the production month stamped on the tang, such as 6.99, indicating June 1899. On 20th-century production, the date can be either the last two digits or the last three, or all four, followed in some instances by Г *(geh)*. See Figure 1-56, which shows the receiver tangs of two rifles, from Sestroryetsk (1898) and Izhevsk (1925).

Type 1 Hexagonal Receiver

Machined from a single steel billet, the top of the receiver includes three rectangular facets, 13 mm (0.511 in) wide and varying in length from right to left from 47 mm to 57 mm (1.85 in to 2.24 in), refer to Figure 1-55A.

The underside of the receiver is flat, and the sides between the bottom and the faceted top are rounded. The underside has a bottle-shaped opening 90 mm (3.54 in) long to accept the cartridge from the magazine and has a milled hole for the trigger.

The tang screw hole is drilled and threaded at the rear of the receiver. The tang screw enters through the bottom of the trigger guard, passes through the stock and threads into the tang screw hole.

The bottom stock screw threads into a screw hole drilled into a 15 mm x 15 mm (0.59 in x 0.59 in) lug on the underside of the receiver at the barrel-end.

An alignment mark on the front end of the receiver should match an index mark on the underside of the barrel's receiver ring. If it does not, have the rifle checked for headspace before firing.

On pre-Revolution receivers the two-headed imperial eagle was stamped on the center facet on top of the receiver near where it meets the receiver ring.

Under Soviet rule the Imperial Eagle was defaced on the Tsarist era receivers.

Various inspection marks in the form of Cyrillic letters and numbers will be observed on Russian receivers, particularly on the underside.

The hexagonal receiver is authentic to the M1891 Infantry rifle, Dragoon rifle, Cossack rifle, and M1907 carbine. It is also found on *some* M1891/30 rifles made — probably of preexisting parts — at least as late as mid-1936.

Type 2 Round Receiver

The round receiver design was part of the extensive overhaul of the standard rifle undertaken by the Soviets which resulted in the M1891/30 rifle and its offspring, the M1938 and M1944 carbines. The round receiver was simpler to manufacture than the hexagonal variety and required less time, resources and expense. There are two distinct types as described above. Refer to Figures 1-55B and C.

FINNISH RECEIVERS

The Finns did not manufacture a Mosin-Nagant receiver as they had huge stocks of Russian receivers on hand. To all intents and purposes only Type 1 Hexagonal receivers were used on Finnish rifles, as these were the only ones in stock up to the Winter War of 1939–40. Even after Russia attacked Finland on November 30, 1939, there remained sufficient quantities of the hexagonal receivers in the Finnish inventory to preclude the need to manufacture any.

Note: Some Finnish m/91-30s — and, reportedly, a few m/39s — were fabricated with rounded receivers captured from the Russians, but these are the exception.

AMERICAN RECEIVERS

Those receivers manufactured by New England Westinghouse and Remington Arms are identical to those Type 1 receivers manufactured in Russia and France, except for the markings, refer to Figure 1-55A. The maker's logo is found on the exterior of the rear tang, behind the screw hole. The year of manufacture is not indicated. All dimensions and finishes are identical to Russian Type 1 receivers.

POLISH RECEIVERS

Poland manufactured the Type 4 receiver only for their M1944 carbine, refer to Figure 1-55D. It can be distinguished — in addition to its markings — by the slight scallop that slopes from the inner edge of the receiver wall to the wood line of the stock.

HUNGARIAN RECEIVERS

Only Type 2 receivers were manufactured in Hungary for the Hungarian variation of the M1944 carbine. They are marked on the carbine with the Hungarian communist government's symbol, a crossed hammer and stalk of wheat, surmounted by a five-pointed star and surrounded by a wreath of wheat. The symbol is directly beneath the year of manufacture and above the serial number. Refer to Chapter 3 for further information.

ROMANIAN RECEIVERS

Romanian M1944 carbine receivers were the Type 3, described above. They are marked on the underside of the rear tang with the Romanian arrowhead in a triangle used to mark parts, below which is a rectangle enclosing the last three digits of the year of manufacture. Refer to Chapter 3 for further information.

Figure 1-57A

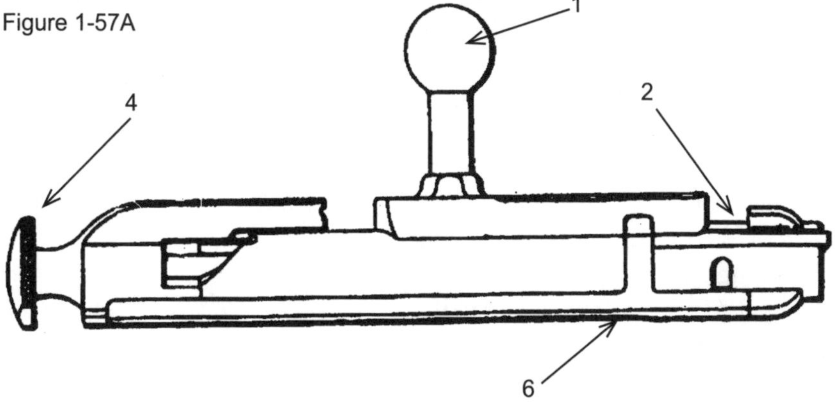

BOLT ASSEMBLY

All parts of the bolt are made of steel, finished in-the-white with the exception of the extractor, which is sometimes blued, and the mainspring, which often appears blue, black or straw color from the tempering process, unless polished white.

The bolt assembly consists of seven pieces: 1) bolt handle, 2) bolt head, 3) extractor, 4) cocking piece, 5) firing pin, 6) firing pin guide or connecting bar, and 7) mainspring (not pictured). See Figures 1-57A and B. The bolt, bolt head, firing pin, firing pin guide and cocking piece are always marked. The extractor is sometimes marked. The mainspring is, for obvious reasons, unmarked. Almost without exception, all bolt parts are interchangeable regardless of the manufacturer or country of origin.

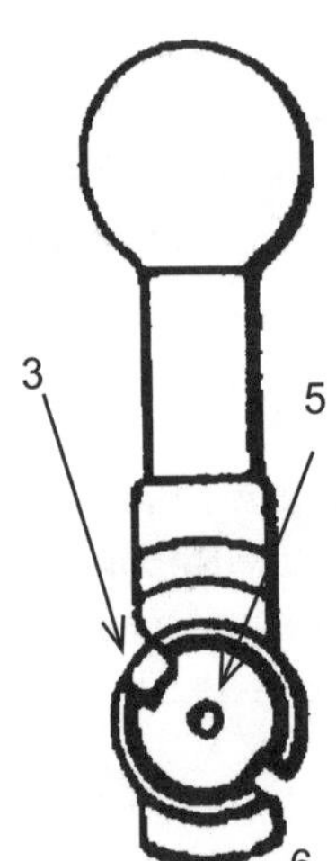

Figure 1-57B

Caution: Although Mosin-Nagant bolts and their components are mostly interchangeable (with the exceptions described below), because of differences in headspace a rifle whose bolt has been interchanged with that of another should NOT be fired without having first been checked by a competent gunsmith.

There are four types of bolts used. The original M1891 bolt assembly (**Type 1**) has a straight bolt handle projecting at a 90-degree right angle to the bolt body; it was used on all Mosin-Nagants of whatever variation with the exception of those models listed below:

Sniper Rifles

The M1891/30 *snayperskaya*, Finnish scoped rifles, etc., all used the **Type 2** bolt with the elongated, turned-down bolt handle. See Figure 1-58. Except for the bolt handle, the rest of the assembly is identical to that used on all other Mosin-Nagants. The Type 2 bolt handle is 98.42 mm (3.875 in) long from root to the tip of the ball. The right-angle bend began at 7.93 mm (0.3125 in) from the root and bent sharply down at an 80-degree angle from the root. The sniper bolt cannot be used on a standard rifle unless a relief cut is made for the handle on the right side of the stock.

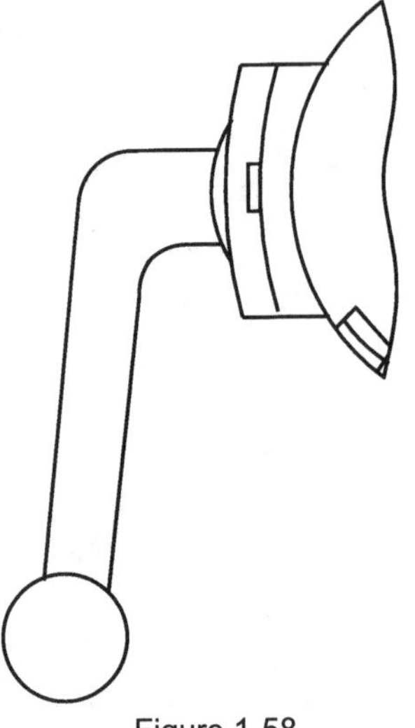
Figure 1-58

Finnish m/27 Carbine
This Finnish carbine used a distinctive **Type 3** turned-down bolt handle. Figure 1-59. It cannot be installed on a standard Mosin-Nagant without a relief cut on the right side of the stock.

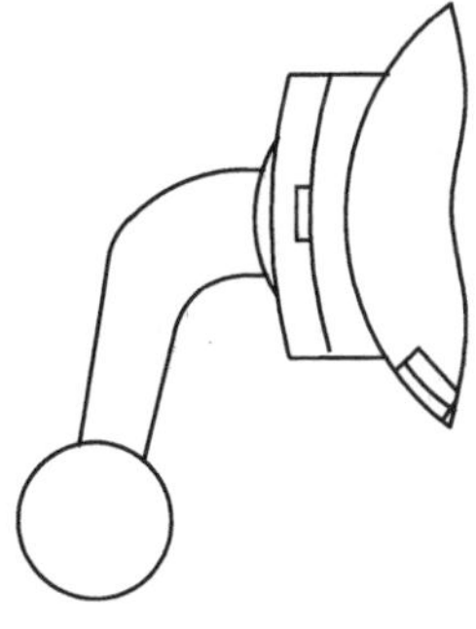
Figure 1-59

Polish wz. 91/98/25 Rifle
This Polish rifle used the **Type 4** Mosin-Nagant bolt. Its bolt face was altered to accommodate the 7.92 x 57 mm Mauser cartridge. The rimmed Mosin-Nagant cartridge will not snap onto the face of this bolt. Otherwise, it is the same as the Type 1.

BOLT
The bolt is milled from a single piece of steel and is 120 mm (4.72 in) long. It is comprised of the bolt handle, cocking cam, primary extracting cam, safety notch, safety lug, bolt body through which pass the firing pin and mainspring. The bolt is connected to the bolt head by the connecting bar. See Figure 1-60.

Bolt Head
The bolt head is milled from a single piece of steel. It is 38 mm (1.496 in) long and 15 mm (0.590 in) in diameter, excluding the lugs. An 8 mm (0.314 in) wide hole is bored completely through it to accommodate the firing pin and mainspring. It contains the extractor, which is seated in a groove milled into the bolt head. There are two locking lugs on the bolt head, which secure the bolt assembly to the receiver. See Figure 1-61.

Extractor
The extractor is 40 mm (1.57 in) long and 5 mm (0.196 in) wide, and is seated in a groove milled into the bolt head. Its purpose is to extract cartridges from the rifle, which it does by means of a small claw on the bolt-face side which seizes the rim of the cartridge case, thus allowing the ejector to engage and eject it. See Figure 1-62.

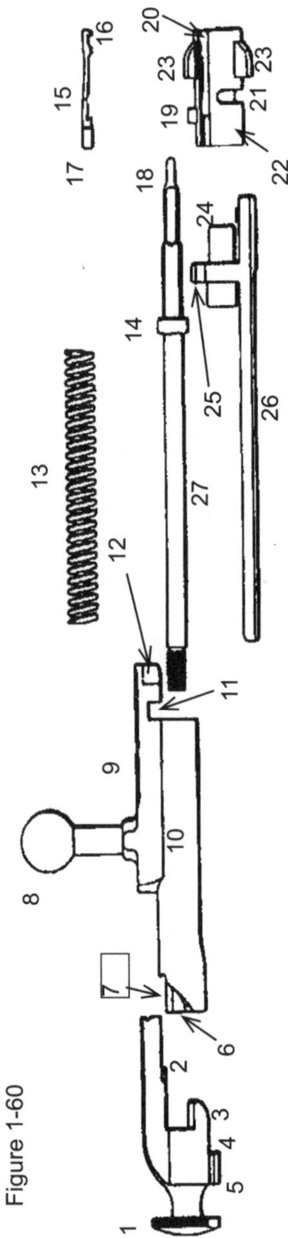

Figure 1-60

Bolt Assembly	
1. Cocking Knob	15. Extractor
2. Safety Catch Finger	16. Extractor Hook
3. Cocking Cam	17. Extractor Base
4. Cocking Piece	18. Striker Point
5. Cock Notch	19. Alignment Lug
6. Cocking Cam	20. Extractor Slot
7. Safety Lug	21. Retaining Slot
8. Bolt Handle	22. Bolt Head
9. Rib	23. Locking Lugs
10. Bolt	24. Barrel
11. Retainer Slot	25. Retaining Lug
12. Alignment Slot	26. Connecting Bar
13. Mainspring	27. Firing Pin
14. Collar	

To remove the extractor — and this should be done only to replace it — first disassemble the bolt assembly (as described later in this section), then secure the bolt head firmly in a padded vise. Using a punch or similar tool, and a hammer, gently tap the extractor towards the rear of the bolt head and off. Clean the extractor groove of accumulated oil, grease and dirt, then oil very lightly. Install the new extractor by gently tapping forward from the rear.

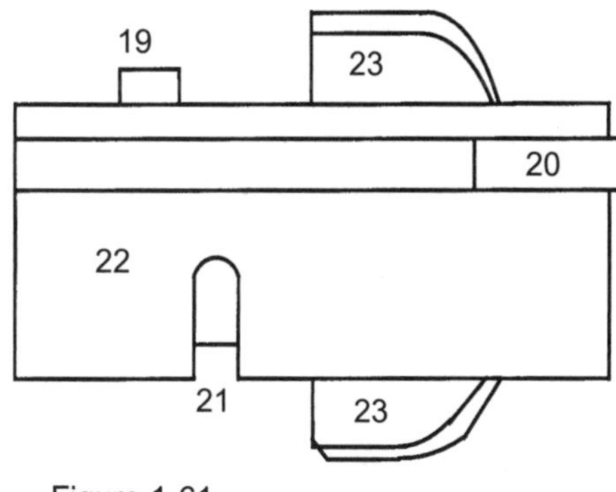

Figure 1-61

Cocking Piece

The cocking piece is 70 mm (2.755 in) long and terminates in a head that has a slightly flattened bottom. The rim is knurled and is 30 mm (1.18 in) in diameter. A hole 6 mm (0.236 in) in diameter is bored through the cocking piece to accommodate the firing pin. The rear end of the firing pin is flush with the back of the cocking piece. Note that, in contrast to the usual design of a bolt action cocking piece, the cocking piece of the Mosin-Nagant turns with the bolt. See Figure 1-63.

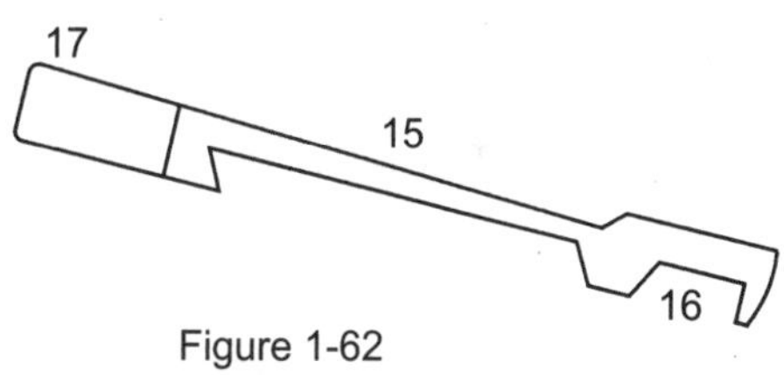

Figure 1-62

The cocking piece is used to re-cock the rifle in the event of a misfire without working the bolt by pulling back until the sear is heard to engage, then releasing it.

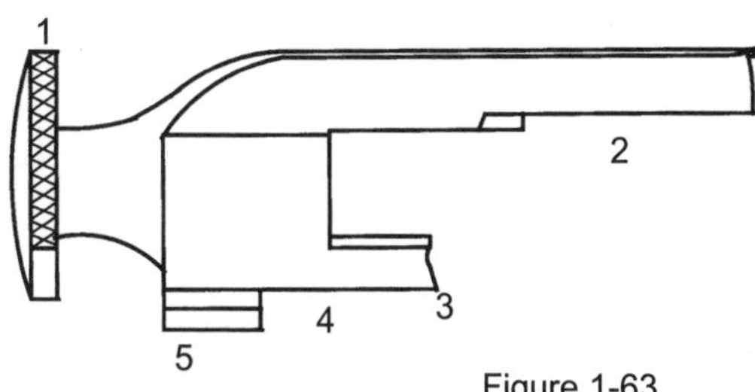

Figure 1-63

The cocking piece also serves as the safety. Though sturdy and reasonably reliable, it is also clumsy and difficult to manipulate; anyone who uses it will instantly un-

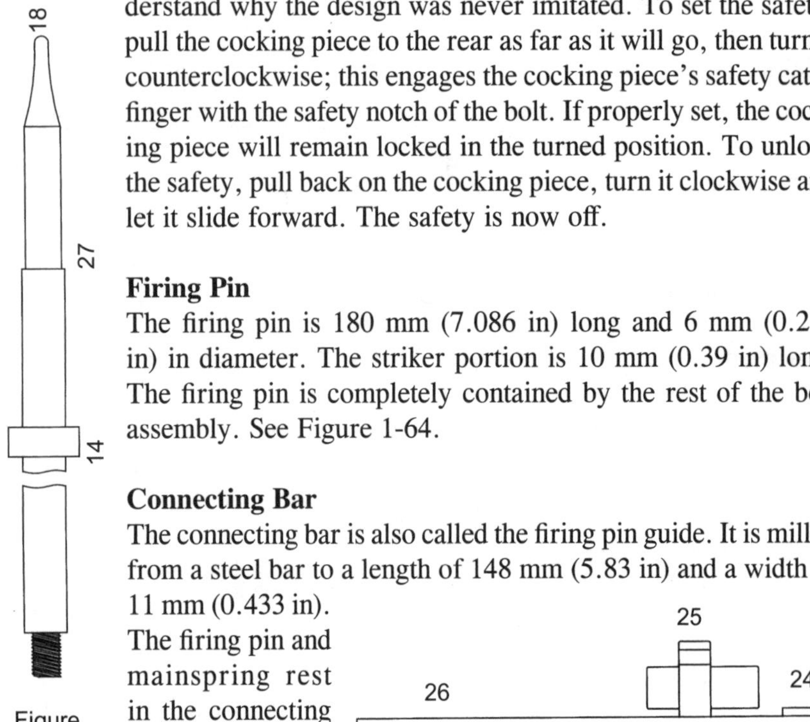

Figure 1-64

derstand why the design was never imitated. To set the safety: pull the cocking piece to the rear as far as it will go, then turn it counterclockwise; this engages the cocking piece's safety catch finger with the safety notch of the bolt. If properly set, the cocking piece will remain locked in the turned position. To unlock the safety, pull back on the cocking piece, turn it clockwise and let it slide forward. The safety is now off.

Firing Pin

The firing pin is 180 mm (7.086 in) long and 6 mm (0.236 in) in diameter. The striker portion is 10 mm (0.39 in) long. The firing pin is completely contained by the rest of the bolt assembly. See Figure 1-64.

Connecting Bar

The connecting bar is also called the firing pin guide. It is milled from a steel bar to a length of 148 mm (5.83 in) and a width of 11 mm (0.433 in). The firing pin and mainspring rest in the connecting bar's concave interior. The cylinder and stop which hold the bolt head are integral parts of the bar. The rear of the guide is slotted to engage the bolt. See Figure 1-65.

25
24
26

Figure 1-65

Mainspring

The mainspring (Figure 1-66) is a steel coil spring nominally 95 mm (3.74 in) long and 10 mm (0.39 in) wide. It slides over the firing pin.

Figure 1-66

The Mosin-Nagant Rifle

Barrels

General Remarks

Mosin-Nagant barrels were made of ordnance steel and blued. The breech end is threaded to screw into the receiver. The barrels vary greatly in length from model to model. See Table 1-5 for Russian and Finnish barrel specifications and Figure 1-67 for an overall view of the Mosin-Nagant barrel.

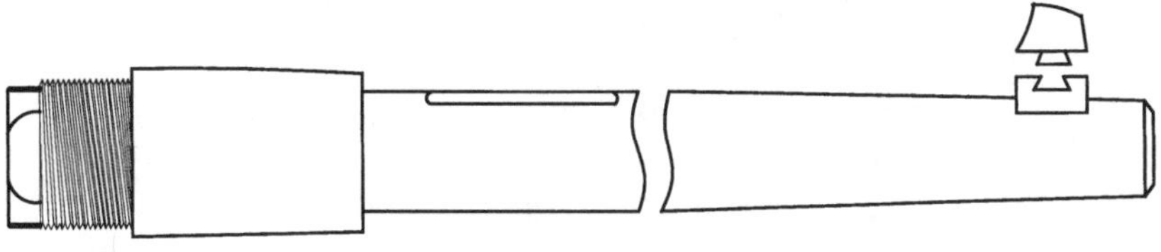

Figure 1-67

Mosin-Nagant barrels show a profusion of markings, many of which are the key to determining the origin and model of the weapon. Because of their importance, barrel markings are illustrated and described in Appendix C.

Russian Barrels

All Mosin-Nagant barrels have 4-groove, concentric right-hand rifling; the grooves are 0.007 in deep, with one turn every 9.5 in. The bore diameter of Russian rifles and carbines made before the adoption of the D cartridge in 1930 is nominally caliber 0.300; thereafter it is 0.310 — often 0.311 — for all Russian and Russian-derived models, although diameters as great as 0.314 inch are known.

Finnish Barrels

The Finnish barrels differ substantially among themselves in bore diameters as the figures in Table 1-6 show.

Table 1-5
Mosin-Nagant Barrel Lengths, Russian Models
Table 1-3 Specifications for Russian Mosin-Nagant Models

Model	Rifle M1891	Cossack Rifle	Dragoon Rifle	Rifle M91/30	Carbine 1907	Carbine 1938	Carbine 1944
Barrel Length	803 mm 31.6 in	732 mm 28.8 in	732 mm 28.8 in	729 mm 28.7 in	510 mm 20 in	510 mm 20 in	520 mm 20.47 in

Mosin-Nagant Barrel Lengths, Finnish Models

Model	Rifle m/27	Cavalry Carbine m/27	Rifle m/28	Rifle m/28-30	Rifle m/39		
Barrel Length	685 mm 27 in	610 mm 24 in	685 mm 27 in	685 mm 27 in	685 mm 27 in		

Table 1-6, Finnish Rifle Bore Diameters	
Bore Diameter	**Model**
0.3095 in	m/91/24, m/91 ("P" series), m/91 (1925-27), m/91 (World War II series)
0.3082 in	m/28
0.308 to 0.314 in	m/39, m/91-30

The Finnish company Tikkakoski produced 10,000 M1891 barrels in the years 1925–1927, of which 7,000 are unstepped and 3,000 are of the heavier, stepped type. The term "step" refers to the increase in the exterior diameter of the barrel a few inches behind the front sight. The step allowed these Finnish barrels to accept the original M1891 socket bayonet. Existing stocks had the barrel channels recut to accept the new barrels. See Figure 1-68.

The m/91s produced by Tikkakoski in 1925–27 reportedly had three different bore diameters, represented by the letters "A", "B" or "C" stamped on the receiver ring below the serial number. The author has also observed several barrels stamped with the letter "F" but this is not mentioned in the reference literature and *may* stand for the Swedish company, Fagersta. The bore measurements of the three types are not divulged in the literature. The most common diameter is alleged to be 0.3095.

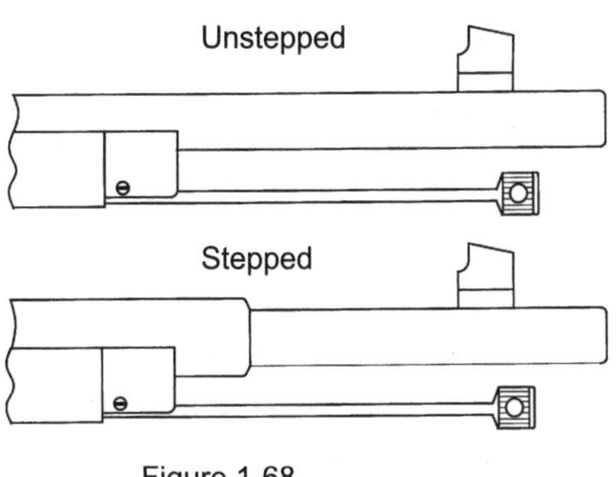

Figure 1-68

Note: The name Tikkakoski means "Woodpecker Falls" or "Woodpecker

Rapids." The company was established in 1893 to make wood and metal products and began producing firearms parts in 1918. The firm underwent several ownership and name changes before becoming Tikkakoski Oy in 1930.

In 1923 the Finns purchased 8,000 new m/1891 barrels from the Swiss firm Schweizerische Industrie Gesellschaft (SIG) of Neuhausen, Switzerland — the maker's name is stamped on the right side of the barrel forward of the chamber. An additional 18,000 barrels were furnished by the German firms Oskar Will AG, Venuswaffenfabrik, and Römerwerke AG. Barrels made by these three manufacturers are marked BÖHLER-STAHL (German for "Böhler Steel": Gebrüder Böhler, i.e., Böhler Brothers, was the Austrian steel maker) on the underside, just in front of the receiver.

Use of the Swiss and German barrels — almost all of which are stepped, rather than tapered like the original Russian variety — required recutting the barrel channel of reused Russian stocks to fit the new barrel contour, as for the Tikkakoski barrels previously mentioned. These barrels are significantly heavier than the originals and are fitted with a 2-inch-long aluminum sleeve near the front barrel band, allowing the barrel to "float" which increased accuracy.

Another Finnish barrel mark, "B", is found on the top of chambers and is considered controversial. According to one theory the barrels were made in Belgium and assembled by VKT. Some of the barrels have Belgian proof marks — such as small stars and the letters "K" and "EL" — on the underside of the chamber, together with the Tikkakoski logo. All reported "B" barrels have been seen on rifles dated 1942, but that does not exclude the possibility that they were made before or after then as well. VKT received an order of 8,500 m/91 barrel blanks from Belgium as late as September 1944, but Finland surrendered before the blanks could be used. It is possible, even probable, that they were made into finished rifles of some kind as late as January 1945 and for years after the war. See Chapter 3: The World War II Jalkaväenkivääri m/91, for a more complete discussion.

VKT reportedly also made 92 m/91 barrels in February 1944, which are marked with a capital "V". The significance of this marking is unknown.

To a considerable extent identification of various Mosin-Nagants by country and model can be made by examining the barrel markings stamped on the weapon's chamber. A list of markings is found in Appendix C.

FRONT SIGHTS

There are three basic types of front sight which, for purposes of convenience, we will call **Type 1** Blade (or 'barleycorn'), **Type 2** Hooded Post, and **Type 3** Finnish which occurs in several variations which are described below.

TYPE 1 BLADE SIGHT

The **Type 1** blade sight is made of blued steel. It is 10 mm (0.39 in) from base to apex, and 10 mm x 10 mm at its base. It rests in a grooved sight base and is not protected by a sight hood. This sight is used on the M1891 Infantry rifle, Dragoon rifle, Cossack rifle, and M1907 carbine. Inspectors' marks are common on Russian-made blade sight bases, though not on the blades. See Figure 1-69.

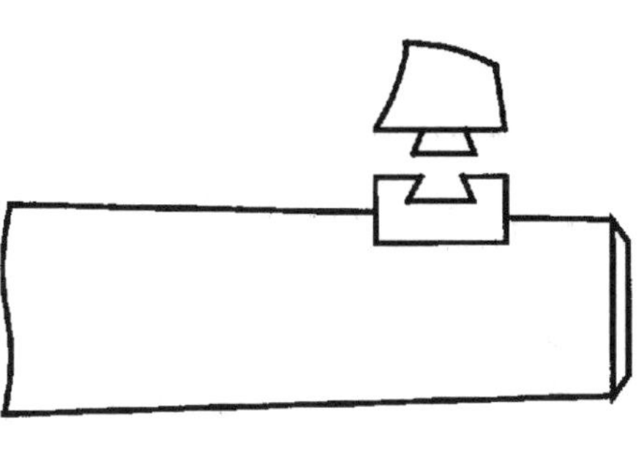

Figure 1-69

Type 2 Hooded Post Sight

There are three variations of the Type 2 hooded post sight. The **Type 2A** front sight consists of a blued metal post 2 mm (0.078 in) in diameter rising 8 mm (0.314 in) above its base. The post is protected by a metal hood 10 mm (0.39 in) wide, 25 mm (0.98 in) from base to top; its exterior diameter is 17 mm (0.67 in), and interior diameter is 14 mm (0.551 in).

The hood rests in a 10 mm x 10 mm (0.39 in x 0.39 in) base identical to that of the earlier blade sight. There is a small hole 4 mm (0.157 in) in diameter on the top of the hood, which admits light to aid in sighting and provides access for removal, replacement and adjustment of the sight post. Unlike the post sight used on the carbines it has no ring around the barrel. This sight first appeared on the M1891/30 rifle and has been used in only slightly modified form on all Russian and Russian-type models developed since then, including the SKS and Kalashnikov. This type of sight assembly is unmarked except for the sight-alignment vertical scribe on the front of the sight and its base. See Figure 1-70.

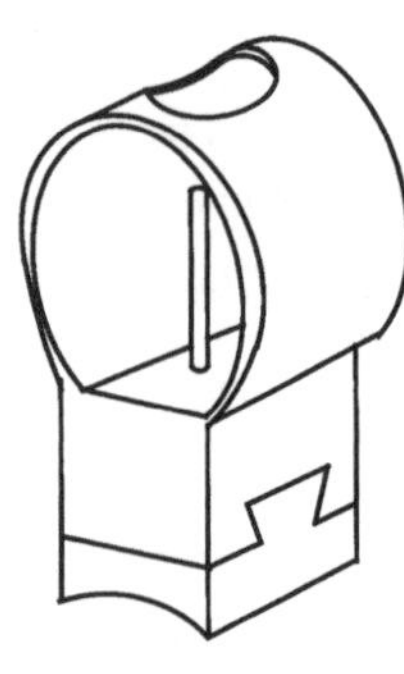

Figure 1-70

M1891/30 Rifle — Uses the Type 1 hooded post sight described above.

M1938 Carbine — The M1938 carbine uses the **Type 2B** sight post and hood. It is similar to the Type 2A but is lower — 20 mm (0.787 in) — from base to top. It also has a slightly larger base which measures 12 mm x 12 mm (0.472 in x 0.472 in) mounted on, and integral to, a ring fitted around the muzzle 9 mm (0.354 in) back from the crown. The sight assembly is unmarked except for the alignment slash on the front, see Figure 1-71.

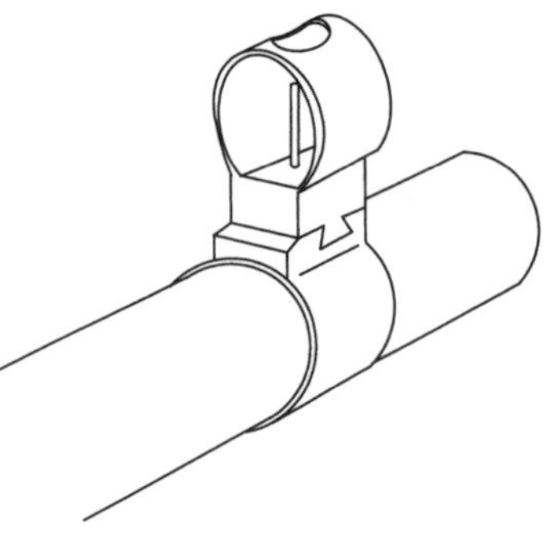

Figure 1-71

M1944 Carbine — The M1944 carbine uses the **Type 2C** hooded post sight. During the first few years' production the Type 2B front sight was used but starting circa 1946 new hood bases and sight bases 20 mm (0.787 in) wide were produced and fitted to Russian, East Bloc and Chinese M1944s made — or retrofitted — from 1945 or 1946 through the end of production in the early 1960s. See Figure 1-72.

Type 3 Finnish Sight

Finnish front sights are variations of the blade sight used by the Russians, but redesigned to produce a cleaner and clearer sight picture. There are 3 variations of the Type 3 Finnish Front Sight.

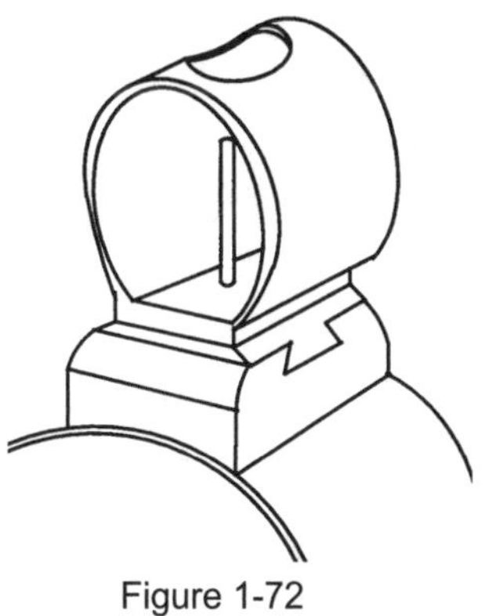

Figure 1-72

Finnish m/27 Rifle – The **Type 3A** blade sight is 10 mm (0.39 in) tall from base to apex. See Figure 1-73. The base is 10 mm x 20 mm (0.39 in x 0.787 in), the longer side parallel to the barrel. The bottom of the base is flat. The sight assembly differs noticeably from all preceding models in that it is protected by two 'ears' which are part of a single unit which slides over the muzzle. Apparently these 'ears' were a source of some amusement to the Finns, who nicknamed the rifle *Pystykorva* ("Pomeranian" or "Spitz", as in the dogs). The sight base is attached to this unit by a single screw whose head is 3 mm (0.118 in) in diameter; the screw is located at the front end of the base platform and helps to secure the sight assembly to the barrel. This unit is 35 mm (1.377 in) high and 20 mm (0.787 in) wide. Each ear has a hole 10 mm (0.39 in) in diameter. The entire sight assembly is made of blued steel and is unmarked.

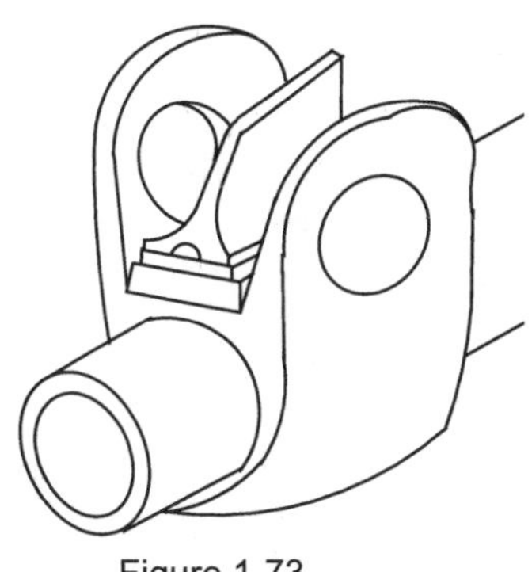

Figure 1-73

Finnish m/28 Rifle. Uses the same Type **3A** sight as that of the m/27.

Finnish m/28-30 Rifle – The Type **3B** sight is an improved version of the Type 3A. See Figure 1-74. It is also is 35 mm (1.377 in) high and protected by 'ears', but is 20 mm x 20 mm (0.787 in x 0.787 in) in width and length and the 'ear' portion is somewhat more angular than the earlier model. The sight base is secured to the barrel by a screw whose head is

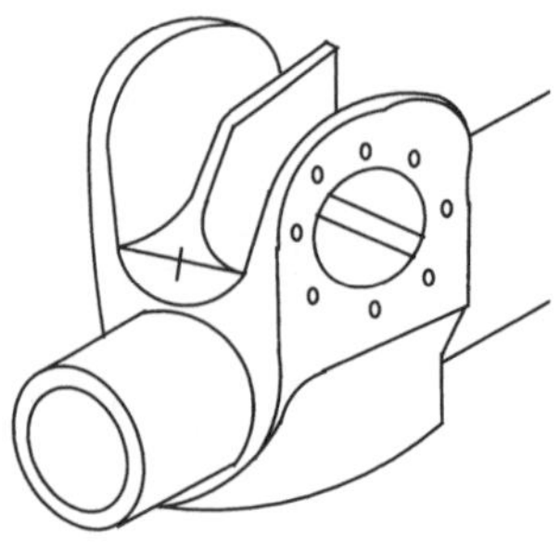
Figure 1-74

2 mm (0.078 in) in diameter. The bottom of the sight-blade base is rounded rather than flat like that of the earlier model.

The Type 3B sight assembly is held together by a screw passing from ear to ear through the sight base. Like its predecessor this sight has a small screw connecting it to the barrel; unlike the earlier model, however, the screw is at the rear of the base platform. The screw on the left side is also used to adjust the windage — a first for the Mosin-Nagant. The screw head is surrounded by eight dots punched into the ear. Each dot represents a windage adjustment of 50 mm (1.968 in) at 100 meters (109.3 yards). The sight base is marked with the SAKO logo: an "S" in a cogwheel crowned with three evergreen sprigs.

Finnish m/39 Rifle — uses the same Type 3B sight as the m/28-30. Some m/39s are marked atop the sight blade and/or immediately behind the sight base with a two-digit number between 60 and 90 which represents the height of the blade measured in tenths of millimeters, e.g., 70 = 7 mm (0.275 in).

Finnish m/91-30 Rifle — uses the **Type 3C** front sight which has a unique blade. Between the sight base and the blade, common to the original Russian M1891 models, is an additional level or base fastened in place by dovetails to the blade and the base. The blade is unprotected. See Figure 1-75.

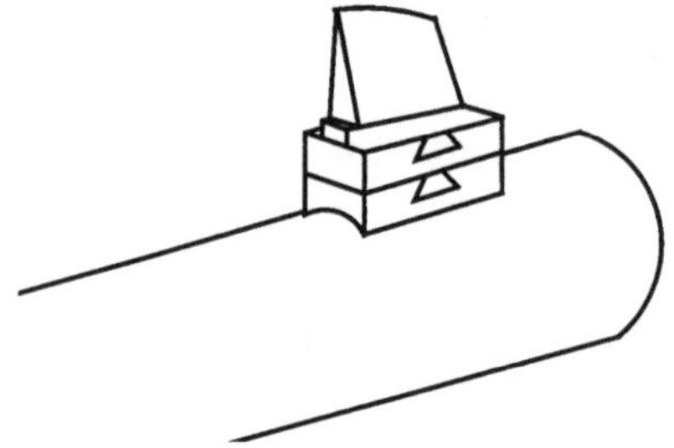
Figure 1-75

REAR SIGHTS

RUSSIAN REAR SIGHTS

Five basic types of rear sights were

used on all Russian Mosin-Nagant rifles, three prior to the redesign of the rifle in 1930. The original three types were graduated in *arshini* (the plural of *arshin*), an old Russian measurement equivalent to 711.2 mm (28 in). The Russians themselves usually referred to the measurement as a *shag*, meaning 'pace' or 'step'. All rear sights were made of steel and blued.

The original M1891 Infantry, Dragoon and Cossack rifles had a flat tangent sight (**Type 1**); this was changed to a leaf-and-ramp sight after adoption of the M1908 *spitzer* bullet (**Type 2**). The M1907 carbine had a unique sight which was never changed (**Type 3**). After 1930 the new M1891/30 rifle (**Type 4**) and the M1938 and M1944 carbines had a redesigned rear sight, all of which were tangent and graduated in meters (**Type 5**).

Note: The Cossack model rear sight was graduated differently from Infantry and Dragoon rifles. It was not zeroed with a bayonet attached, as they were, since Cossacks did not normally fight on foot where the bayonet could be used to advantage.

Beginning in the later 1920s the Finns made several major improvements in the rear sight resulting in entirely new configurations. All the rear sights are discussed in detail below.

M1891 Infantry Rifle

The original **Type 1** rear sight was a tangent leaf type common to the era, secured to the barrel by two screws. See Figure 1-76. Range graduations were marked on the left side of the sight base from 200 to 1000 *arshini* in increments of 200. The leaf was marked with additional graduations up to 2600 *arshini* in increments of 100. The bar at the top of the leaf has a V-notch to aid in sighting. The sight bar is adjusted up or down by first pressing the buttons on the side. Adjustments are held by notches on the leaf's sides. The maximum distance was an optimistic 2,700 *arshini* (2,100 yards).

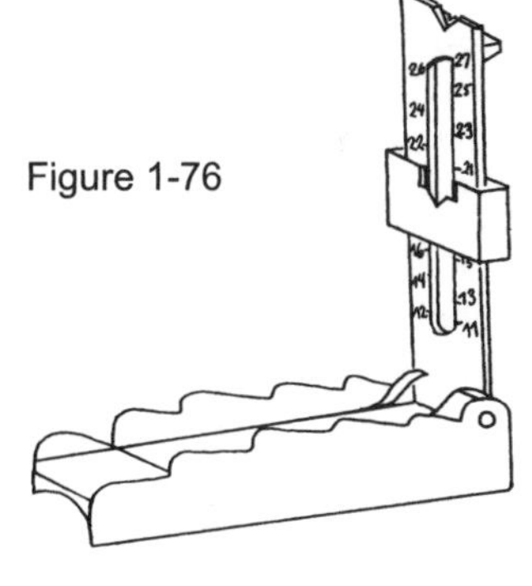

Figure 1-76

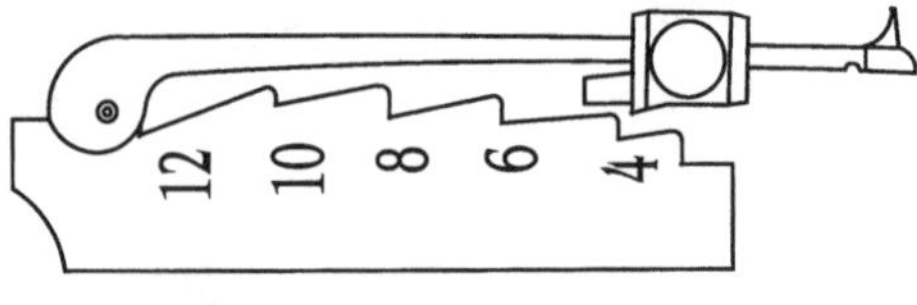

Figure 1-77

The first rear sight was replaced after adoption of the M1908 *spitzer* bullet with the **Type 2** rear sight of a wholly different configuration. See Figure 1-77.

Like the Type 1, the new rear sight had no provision for windage adjustment. It was held in a dovetail slot on the barrel and was made up of 9 pieces (Figure 1-78): 1) sight base, 2) joint pin, 3) base spring, 4) base spring screw, 5) sight leaf, 6) slide, 7) slide catch cap, 8) slide catch spring, and 9) slide catch.

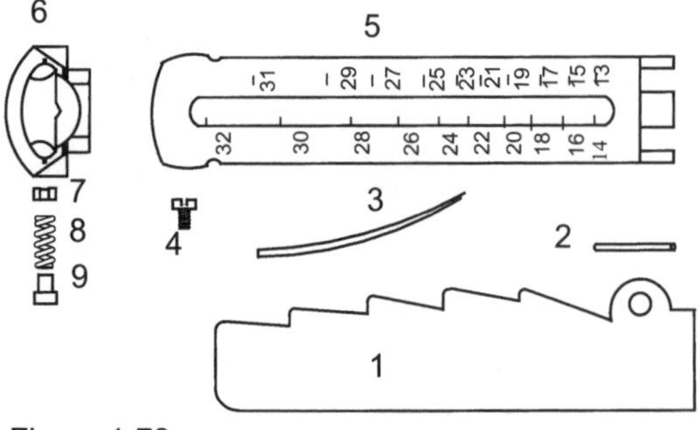

Figure 1-78

The sight base had a saw-toothed ramp on either side and the leaf was attached at the front of the base by a pin through two lugs. The sight was marked in hundreds of *arshini* (4, 6, 8, 10, 12) on the left side, and on the inside of the leaf from 13 through 32, inclusive. Across the front face of the leaf is the rear sight slide cut with a V-notch used for sighting in the 400 to 1,200 *arshini* range. The slide is moved up and down the leaf by pressing the buttons on each side, and is locked at each gradation by parallel ribs across the leaf face. The sight leaf and base are marked with the arsenal's or manufacturer's logo.

The rear sights of rifles captured or purchased by Finland were updated by stamping metric equivalents to the *arshini* on the base in the series 2, 3, 4, 5 1/2, 7, 8 1/2. Some sights may lack numeral "2." Many, but by no means all, sights 'metricized' by the Finns have an **M** in block or script, upper or lower case, stamped on the metric side. The *arshini* measurements on the left side of the base almost always have slashes through them.

Dragoon Rifle

The Dragoon rifles used the Type 1 or Type 2 rear sight.

Cossack Rifle

The **Type 1** rear sight was installed on the Cossack rifle. It was stamped Каз (i.e., Kaz. in Cyrillic letters, for *kazach'ya*, Cossack). Early production rifles had a tangent rear sight similar to that of the Infantry and Dragoon rifles but with slightly different graduations. After adoption of the *spitzer* bullet in 1908 the sights were changed to the **Type 2** but with slightly different range markings. Cossack model rear sights are marked on the underside of the leaf in graduations of hundreds of *arshini* from 13 to 32, inclusive; they are not marked on the left side.

M1907 Carbine

The **Type 3** sight, unique to this model, is a tangent, L-shaped rear sight which raised and lowered on a rear hinge. See Figure 1-79. The sights were arsenal-marked and the elevation settings were in hundreds of *arshini* from 4 through 20, inclusive on the top of the sight leaf. Range was adjusted by moving the rear sight slide up and down the leaf, which had a V-notch open aperture (400 *arshini*). In 1910 the rear sight was changed slightly as the result of the adoption of the M1908 bullet.

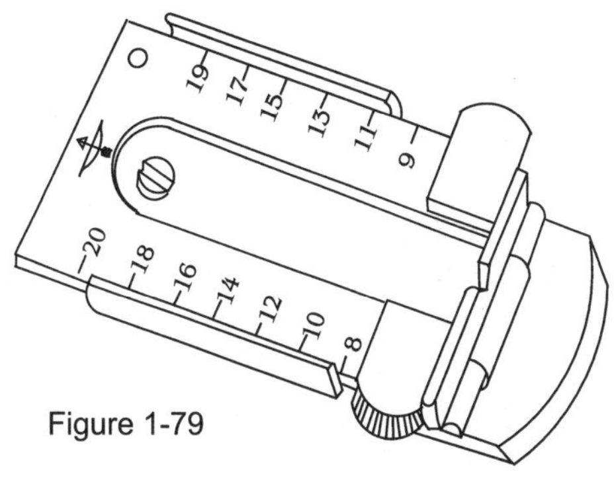

Figure 1-79

The rear sight protruded through a hole in the handguard approximately 1 in forward of the receiver ring and was secured to the barrel by a single screw. The sight base was 15 mm (0.59 in) wide and 40 mm (1.57 in) long. This sight was unique to the M1907 carbine.

M1891/30 Rifle

The **Type 4** rear sight, a new and simplified variation, was introduced

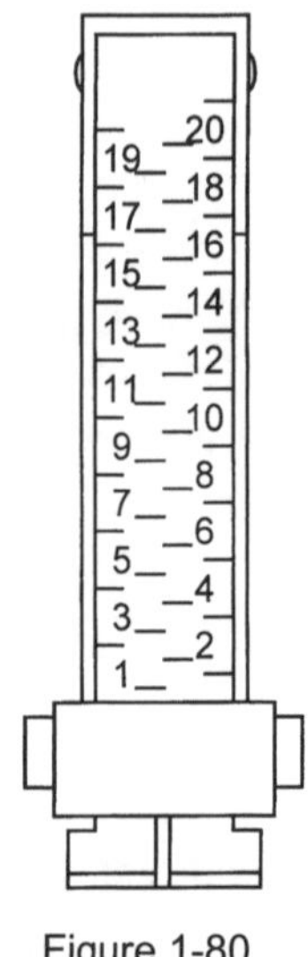

Figure 1-80

with the M1891/30. The sight is tangent, with a curved ramp, and somewhat resembles the original Type 1 M1891 rear sight. As with the previous types there is no provision for windage adjustment. The sight is graduated in hundreds of meters, from 1 through 20, inclusive. See Figure 1-80.

M1938 Carbine

The **Type 5** rear sight, see Figure 1-81, for the M1938 carbines is a smaller and simplified version of the tangent leaf sight used on the M1891/30. The sight base is 55 mm by 18 mm (2.165 in by 0.708 in), and the leaf 60 mm by 13 mm (2.36 in by 0.51 in). The leaf is hinged at the front by a pin and can be adjusted for range by a V-notched slide which is moved by pinching and holding the serrated tension button on its sides. The slide is held in position by an internal spring and by grooves machined into the leaf. The sight leaf is graduated in 100s of meters from 1 through 10, inclusive.

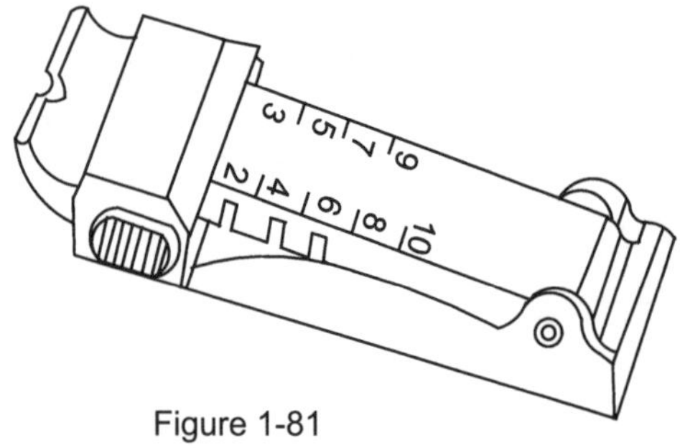

Figure 1-81

M1944 Carbine

Also uses the **Type 5** rear sight.

FINNISH REAR SIGHTS

Finnish m/27 Rifle

Finnish Mosin-Nagants used the original Russian rear sights until the advent of the m/27 rifle. A new rear sight was developed for the *spitzer*-induced modernizations of 1909.

The **Finnish Type 1** rear sight is a ramp-and-leaf similar in appearance to the Russian Type 1, though the saw-toothed ramp is somewhat flatter. The leaf has a separate aperture-bar which is attached to the top of the leaf by two small screws. The rear sight slide is moved up and down the leaf by pressing the tension buttons located on both sides of the slide. The bar is locked at the selected range by a groove on the leaf, and is elevated by the sight bar resting on the saw-teeth of the ramp. See Figure 1-82.

The base is 74 mm (2.91 in) long, 18 mm (0.70 in) wide, and 14 mm (0.55 in) tall. The sight leaf is 80 mm (3.15 in) long and 23 mm (0.90 in) wide. There are 10 distance-adjustment notches for the slide on the new sight-leaf, as opposed to 11 on the old one. The groove at the front of the top side of the leaf is much more ogival than that of its predecessor.

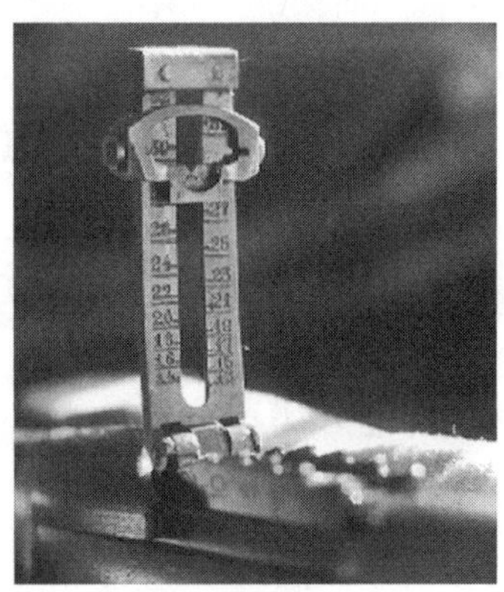

Figure 1-82

Although introduced well into the metric era the sight is still marked in *arshini* (4, 6, 8, 10, and 12) on the left side of the base, as well as metric graduations (3, 4, 5 1/2, 7, and 8 1/2 — preceded by an **M**) on the right. The underside of the leaf is marked in *arshini*, in increments of 100 from 13 through 32, inclusive, indicating that the leaf was probably 'recycled' from earlier rifles. An *arshin* equals 2.333 feet.

As parts of the Type 1 rear sights were scavenged from Russian rear sights and used either 'as is' or with slight modifications, many components will show tsarist-era arsenal marks.

Finnish m/28 Rifle
The m/28 used the **Finnish Type 1** rear sight.

Finnish m/28-30 Rifle
The **Type 2** rear sight was developed for the m/28-30 rifle. This ramp-and-leaf sight was 90 mm (3.54 in) long, 25 mm (0.98 in) wide, and 27 mm (1.06 in) at its maximum height. The graduations are marked to 2,000

meters in hundreds of meters (2, 3, 4, 6, 8) stamped on the left side of the base. On the top of the leaf, 1.5, 2, 3, 4, 5, 6, 8, 10 are marked and on the underside of the leaf, the ranges for 12, 14, 16, 18, and 20 are marked, all indicating hundreds of meters. The rear sight slide is moved by pinching the serrated tension buttons located on either side of the bar. See Figure 1-83

Figure 1-83

Finnish m/39 Rifle

The m/39 rifles used the **Type 2** rear sight.

CLEANING RODS

The following general remarks apply to all Mosin-Nagant cleaning rods with the exception of the rods used for the Finnish m/39 rifle and the Chinese Type 53 carbine.

General Remarks

All Mosin-Nagants were issued with a steel cleaning rod (*bannik*, in Russian), often blued. They were threaded on one end and the other had a pierced, barrel-shaped head. Cleaning rods may have maker or arsenal marks on the shaft or top of the head and some are serial-numbered. Any such markings are uncommon.

To aid in gripping it the head is grooved — vertically or diagonally — though some are knurled. Vertically grooved heads are the most common, see Figure 1-84.

Chinese cleaning rods have smooth heads.

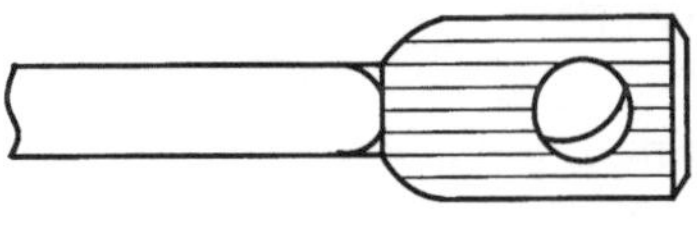

Figure 1-84

A hole 5 mm (0.196 in) in diameter is drilled through the head and is used to hold the punch from the cleaning kit to form a handle for the cleaning rod. The threaded end of the rod is used to secure it within the stock or to attach a cleaning jag or bore brush, see Figure 1-85.

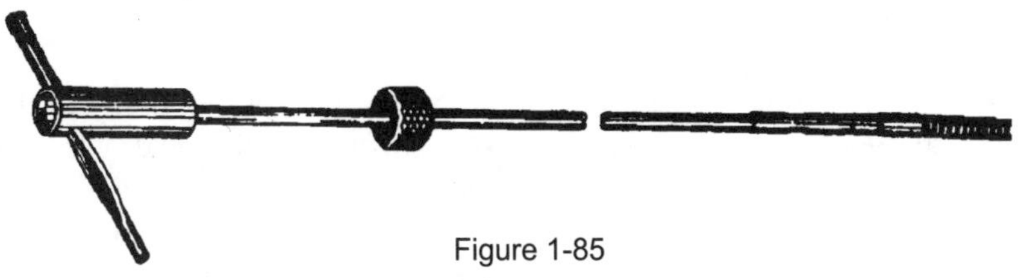

Figure 1-85

The cleaning rod is carried in a groove on the underside of the stock and is secured by screwing into a threaded metal retaining nut sunk flush in the bed forward of the receiver cut.

There are five basic types (plus one Chinese) of Mosin-Nagant cleaning rod:

Infantry Rifle Cleaning Rod — The M1891 Infantry rifles had two types of cleaning rod. The **Type 1** cleaning rod was 475 mm (18.7 in) long, which was inadequate given the length of the barrel. These were replaced by the end of the 1890s with the **Type 2** cleaning rod which was nominally 735 mm (28.93 in) long (actual length can vary by 52 mm — 2 in — or more) and 5 mm (0.196 in) in diameter. The head is 8 mm–10 mm (0.314 in–0.39 in) long and 10 mm in diameter, and the hole is 5 mm in diameter. The threaded portion is 10 mm long.

Dragoon Rifle Cleaning Rod — This **Type 3** cleaning rod was nominally 650 mm (25.59 in) long, but can vary in length by up to 15 mm (0.590

in), and more. The head is 8 mm (0.314 in) long and 5 mm (0.196 in) in diameter; the hole in the head is 4 mm (0.157 in) in diameter. The rod is 5 mm in diameter. The threaded portion of the end is 10 mm long. This cleaning rod was used on all Dragoon, Cossack and M1891/30 rifles, and on the Finnish m/27, m/28 and m/28-30 rifles.

Carbine Cleaning Rod — The **Type 4** cleaning rod used for the M1907 and succeeding carbines (except the Chinese Type 53) was 450 mm (17.71 in) long. The head is 8 mm (0.314 in) in both diameter and length; the threaded tip is 8 mm long. Unlike other varieties, Polish carbine cleaning rods are not blued.

m/39 Rifle Cleaning Rod — The **Type 5** cleaning rod is unique to the Finnish m/39 rifle. The cleaning rod is recognizable by the head, which is cylindrical rather than barrel-shaped. See Figure 1-86. The resemblance to a Mauser cleaning rod is probably not accidental, and its adoption may have been influenced by the large number of Swedish and German Mausers in Finnish military service at the time.

The rod is 620 mm (24.40 in) long overall and 5 mm (0.196 in) in diameter. The head is 20 mm (0.787 in) long from front end to the shaft; the head is diagonally grooved and its top is concave. The head has a slot for the cleaning rod handle, rather than a circular hole. The slot is 10 mm (0.39 in) long and 3 mm (0.118 in) wide. The threaded section is 7 mm (0.275 in) long and fits the bore-brush and jag accessories of the Mosin-Nagant military-issue cleaning kit.

Chinese Carbine Cleaning Rod — The **Type 6** cleaning rod was used only on the Chinese Type 53 Mosin-Nagant carbines. It was 430 mm (16.93 in) long, with a threaded tip 7 mm (0.275 in) in length. At 6 mm (0.236 in) in both diameter and length the head is quite small; the hole is 3.5 mm (0.137 in) in diameter. This cleaning rod is somewhat lighter in weight than its East Bloc counterparts.

This rod is also the type found on Chinese-made SKS carbines and AK-47s, and it is probable that the original Type 53 cleaning rod was identical to the Soviet version, being replaced with newer rods as original ones wore out, broke or were lost.

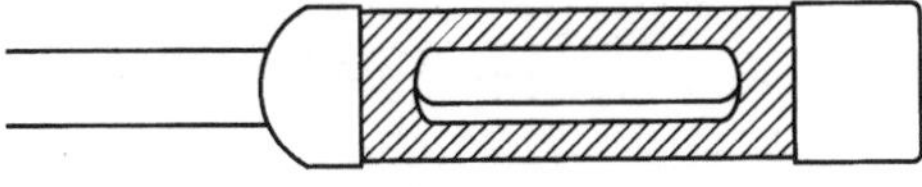

Figure 1-86

Chapter 2
Development of the Mosin-Nagant

The Franco-Prussian War of 1870–71 provided many lessons for European military and political leaders. Some of those lessons were learnt and remembered: that military talent in the Bonaparte family began and ended with Napoleon I, for example. Other lessons were learnt but not long remembered, such as the unfortunate consequences of sending infantry or cavalry charging into the enemy's machine-gun fire, and the high cost in human life demanded of would-be owners of the larders and vineyards of Alsace-Lorraine; both of which lessons would be forgotten or ignored in 1914 and again in 1939. For our purposes, however, the significance of the Franco-Prussian War is its impetus for the development of modern infantry small arms. Once the machine gun proved itself on the battlefield the need for increased firepower for the infantry rank and file became apparent, and the armies of Europe began to look for weapons to replace the single-shot rifles of the day.

Tsarist Russia's decision to join the search for a modern rifle came about during the Russo-Turkish War (1877–78), when Russian troops armed with single-shot rifles (Berdan Models 1 and 2, the Karle, and the Krnka — all designed by foreigners) came under fire from Turkish units armed with Winchester Model 1873 repeating rifles. In 1882 Russia's Main Artillery Administration (*Glavnoye artilleriiskoe upravleniye*), the bureau responsible for all military armaments, undertook to develop a magazine-fed, multiround weapon from the Berdan design. The project failed and was abandoned.

As the decade wore on, smokeless gunpowder was developed in France which significantly reduced fouling, produced less smoke and permitted the use of smaller-caliber bullets, allowing more ammunition to be carried by soldiers. Germany produced the Reichs-Commissions rifle of 1888 and the 7.92 mm Mauser cartridge, while the French developed the 8 x 50.5 mm cartridge for the Lebel Model 1886.

The Mosin-Nagant Rifle

The year 1889 was particularly fruitful for the new generation of infantry rifles — Great Britain adopted the Lee-Metford, Austria-Hungary the Mannlicher, Switzerland the Schmidt-Rubin and the United States the Krag-Jørgensen. The Russians formed a "Special Commission for the Testing of Magazine[-fed] Rifles" (*Osobaya komissia dlya ispitaniya magazinnikh ruzhei*) under the direction of General-Major N. I. Chagin which tested a number of designs, including those of Mauser, Lebel, Lee, and Mannlicher. Among the lesser lights in this competition was a young Russian army captain named Mosin.

Sergei Ivanovich Mosin (1849–1902) was born in Ramon, a village in the Voronezh district south of Moscow. He was educated at the local military secondary school and thereafter at the Alexandrovsky Military College in Moscow and the Mikhailovsky Artillery Academy in St. Petersburg.

After graduation in 1875, Mosin began work at the Tula Small Arms Factory (*Tulskii Oruzhenie Zavod*) as an assistant to the director, attaining more important posts there during a tenure which would last almost a quarter of a century. In 1894 Mosin became director of the Sestroryetsk Small Arms Factory (*Sestroryetskii Oruzhenie Zavod*) near St. Petersburg, where he remained until his death in 1902.

The Model 1891: From Alexander III to Stalin

Beginning in about 1883, Mosin experimented with a number of rifle designs in 10.6 mm caliber, submitting designs for 8-round, internal magazine rifles to the Chagin Commission in 1884 and 1885.

Despite the secret nature of the projects word of Mosin's experiments evidently reached beyond the Russian borders: according to papers found after his death Mosin turned down an offer of 6,000,000 francs from the French firm H. Richter for the rights to his 8-round magazine design, which would have been incorporated into a new model of the Gras (Mavrodin, *Iz istorii otechestvennogo oruzhiya: Russkaya vintovka*).

This may have been the first time a Russian firearms innovation generated any interest in the West, and the last until Kalashnikov developed his AK assault rifle in the late 1940s.

The Mosin-Nagant Rifle

Between 1887 and 1889, working with the smaller calibers then coming into general use among European armies, Mosin developed a 5-shot, straight-line magazine prototype in 7.62 mm; employing the antediluvian Russian measurements of the era it was designated 3-line caliber. The *liniya*, or line, is equivalent to 0.10 in or 2.54 mm; therefore, 3 *linii* equals 7.62 mm or .30 in.

Once more, Mosin presented a design to the Chagin Commission. In October 1889 the Belgian weapons designer Léon Nagant (1833–1900) — probably still smarting over his homeland's adoption of the Mauser in preference to his own rifle — submitted his 3.5 line (8.89 mm) rifle and 500 rounds of ammunition for testing by the Russian government.

Both designers' weapons were tested between December 1890 and March 1891 by the officers and men of the Izmailovskii, Pavlovskii, and 147th Samarskii Regiments, and the First Guards Battalion. At the end of the trials all of these units expressed a preference for Nagant's rifle, and on 19 March 1891 the Commission voted 14 to 10 to approve the Belgian's design. General Chagin voted with the majority, but stated that he did so only because of the test results and not because *he* believed Mosin's design to be technically inferior to Nagant's. Fortunately for Mosin other forces were at work in the selection process, and the timely intervention of certain highly placed military and academic figures persuaded — if that is the word — the Commission to recommend Mosin's design instead of Nagant's. The decisive nudge may have come from General-Lieutenant P.L. Chebyshev, a professor at the Mikhailovsky Artillery Academy, whose report stated that the "domestic model" ("*otechestvennii obrazets*") was better than the foreign one ("*luchshe zagranichnovo*"). Reading between the lines of the post-testing goings-on one cannot avoid the feeling that the real reason Mosin's rifle was chosen over Nagant's was that Mosin was a Russian and Nagant was not.

A compromise of sorts was reached by the adoption of the Mosin model with a Nagant-designed feed system. Considerable difference of opinion remains as to the extent of Nagant's contribution to the final product, but his influence is generally recognized in the design of the magazine follower, the bolt and the charger clip. As an aside, the Russians must have been impressed with Nagant's clip: his Belgian factory produced tens of millions of them for the Russian Army during the 1890s.

The final rifle design was approved and designated *Russkaya trekhlineinaya vintovka obrazets 1891-ago goda* (Russian 3-line rifle, Model 1891) by the committee and submitted to Tsar Alexander III in April 1891. For an unknown reason, he removed the designation *russkaya* for the name before approving its adoption. In an unusual departure from the normal custom of naming a rifle after its inventor, Mosin's name was not included in the designation until well into the Soviet era when he was honored posthumously by the rifle being renamed the "Mosin-system 7.62 mm Magazine Rifle, Model of 1891" (*7.62 mm magazinnaya vintovka sistemi Mosina obrazets 1891-ogo goda*). In view of Léon Nagant's contributions to the weapon's design the designation "Mosin-Nagant," commonly used in the West, would have seemed fairer.

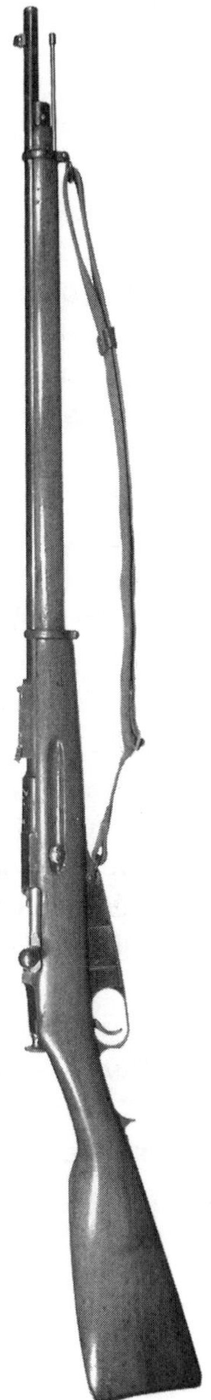

The Model 1891 Infantry Rifle
(*Pekhotnaya vintovka obrazets 1891-ogo goda*)

Manufacture of the rifle began in 1892 in the imperial ordnance factories at Tula, Sestroryetsk and Izhevsk, with an initial production goal of 3,290,000 weapons, see Figure 2-1. Due to a lack

Fig. 2-1. Model 1891 infantry rifle made 1893 at Châtellerault, France. Early features: no handguard, flat rear sight, finger rest behind the trigger guard, early sling attachment to the magazine and the front band. Karl-Heinz Wrobel collection.

of machine tools and skilled labor generally, and at Izhevsk in particular, an order for 500,000 rifles was placed with a French arms company, Manufacture Nationale d'Armes de Châtellerault, in 1891; the first sample rifle was made in the last week of July 1892, and presented to the Russian delegation for approval on August 9th. The first arms delivery was made on October 31st. This is the cause of some controversy among firearms enthusiasts, some of whom believe that the rifles were made in Belgium and others, in France.

Fig. 2-2. Two Imperial Army Russian soldiers armed with Mosin-Nagant Dragoon rifles during the Russo-Japanese War. Photo courtesy of Ralph Denton.

Approximately 500,000 rifles were made by Châtellerault by the time the contract ended in 1895; these can be identified by the inscription containing the word ШАТЕЛЬРО ("Châtellerault") in Cyrillic, stamped on the receiver ring with the date, 1892, 1893, and 1894. The last arms shipment, a case of seventeen rifles (the others contained twenty), was sent to Russia on April 25, 1895. (See Appendix C: Identification and Attribution.) The new rifles were issued to troops in what was regarded as the most threatened area at the time: along the German border in Russian Poland.

Problems soon developed with the Châtellerault rifles — inordinate wear on the rifling and at the muzzle, initially attributed to substandard barrel steel. The problem was eventually diagnosed as — partially, at least — the result of improper cleaning techniques by the soldiers who were accustomed to cleaning their Berdan rifles vigorously from the muzzle end (Underhill, "Under the Red Star").

Production did not begin in earnest in the three Russian arsenals until late in 1893; domestic output in the period 1892–1896 totaled 1,470,470 combat rifles and 32,443 suitable for training purposes. By the time the Russo-Japanese War broke out in 1904 approximately 3,800,000 rifles had been manufactured.

A number of changes were made to the M1891 in the years up to about 1910; so many, in fact, that a number of Western sources erroneously refer to the M1907 carbine as the M1910. Many of these changes were the result of Russia's adoption of the M1908 *spitzer* bullet whose ballistics required or made advisable certain changes to the entire weapon. Whether the changes occurred in 1909 or 1910, or both, is still uncertain. The steel finger rest behind the trigger guard was eliminated in 1894. Circa 1909 new barrel bands were introduced which fitted flush with the underside of the stock rather than protruding below the stock as the earlier type did. Another of these changes was the consistent addition of a handguard.

In 1908 (some sources say 1910) a convex rear sight leaf designed by V. P. Konovalov, a technician at the Sestroryetsk Arms Factory, was substituted for the original flat leaf; oddly, the flat leaf sight returned twenty-two years later with the adoption of the Model 1891/30. The original rear sight had graduations marked on the left side of the sight base from 200 to 1000 *arshini* (1 *arshin* = 711.2 mm, or 2.33 feet or 28 inches or 0.777 yard). In the 1920s, after the Soviets adopted the metric system, the sights were re-marked in meters as well, in increments of 200. See the description of Rear Sights in Chapter 1. Also in 1909 or 1910 a metal bolt was added through the rear of the finger groove to strengthen the stock against the effects of recoil.

The Berdan-style sling swivels, originally attached under the forward barrel band and at the front end of the magazine, were replaced beginning around 1910 by slots cut through the stock between the barrel bands and midway between the butt and the trigger guard and lined with metal washers. Finnish reworks of Russian originals often have sling swivels mounted in the sling slots.

The conversion to sling slots entailed using a cumbersome and somewhat eccentric sling assembly consisting of two leather straps — resembling a dog collar — and the sling itself, see Chapter 6: Accessories.

The M1891's first blooding came in the Russo-Japanese War (1904–1905), in which it proved sturdy and reliable under the harsh and primitive field conditions of northeast Asia, but somewhat inaccurate even at short ranges due to poor sighting. The M1891's round-nosed 7.62 bullet, though inadequate at long ranges, was serviceable enough until Russia upgraded its ammunition by adopting the 150-grain pointed (*spitzer*) bullet in 1908 as part of an improved cartridge (described in Chapter 7: Ammunition).

In the years between 1892 and 1908 the Russian Army took delivery of 313,375 M1891 Infantry rifles and an additional 54,235 training rifles (Komarov, *Istoriya vintovki ot pischchali do avtomata*).

The Dragoon Rifle

The dragoon (*dragunskaya*) model Mosin-Nagant

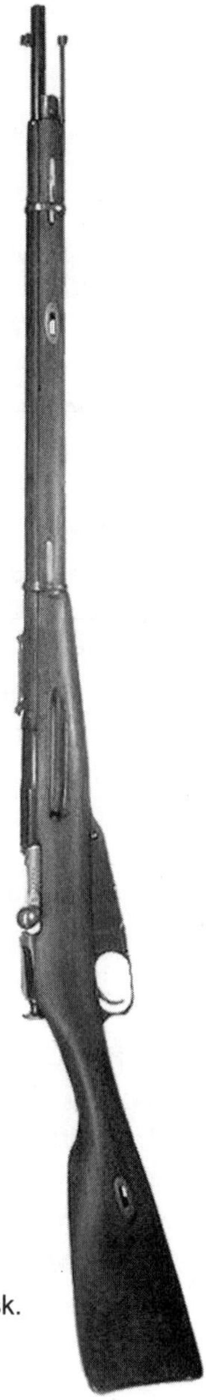

Fig. 2-3. Mosin-Nagant Dragoon Rifle made 1904 at Izhevsk. Early features: long handguard with sight graduations, first flat rear sight. Karl-Heinz Wrobel collection.

was 2.5 in shorter and 0.9 lb lighter than the infantry rifle. It was developed during the 1890s for use by mounted infantry and closely resembled the post-1894 infantry model but was less bulky, see Figure 2-3. The author has no specific reference to the date the Dragoon model was first produced. The Mavrodins (see the Bibliography) state that both the Dragoon and Cossack models were accepted — or adopted: they use the word *prinyati*, which has both meanings — by the Russians in 1891. Aside from its length and weight the dragoon model varied noticeably from the infantry rifle only in having different barrel bands — solid and secured by flat retaining springs along the stock. It was made without a handguard until 1910. The new rear sight and recoil bolt were also added at about the same time. Between the beginning of production and 1908 the Russian Army received 421,025 Dragoon rifles.

The Cossack Rifle

The "Cossack" (*kazach'ya*) version was introduced for those horseborne gentlemen in the later 1890s. It was almost identical to the dragoon model but originally had a flat rear sight leaf similar to that of the M1891/30, see Figure 2-4. This sight was changed with the adoption of the M1908 *spitzer* bullet, and was thereafter a sawtooth ramp-and-leaf sight almost identical to that of the Dragoon. Unlike the Infantry and Dragoon models, the Cossack rifle was sighted to be used without a bayonet as they were not issued with this weapon. The cossacks were traditionally

Fig. 2-4. Model 1891 Cossack rifle, made 1896 at Izhevsk. Early features: shortened long handguard, first flat rear sight, the only M1891 Cossack rifle with those early features known worldwide. Karl-Heinz Wrobel collection.

armed with sabers.

One report states that the Cossack model was originally produced fully stocked, as was the M1907 carbine, but the author has been unable to find any evidence for this claim. The Cossack rifle was initially made without the reinforcing bolts in the stock, but rifles made in and after 1909 did have the reinforcing bolts. It is also a possiblity that older weapons were retrofitted with the bolt after adoption of the new cartridge.

One source states that the Cossack rifle had a slightly different cleaning rod from the dragoon and infantry models, but the author has been unable to substantiate this report.

A true Cossack rifle is easily recognized by the letters "Каз." (i.e., Kaz. in Cyrillic lettering, for *kazach'ya*, Cossack) stamped on the receiver ring just below the serial number. The *kazach'ya* model was not produced in large numbers and saw little distribution. Manufacture was largely curtailed in 1905 and was discontinued altogether in 1914 (some sources say 1915). Between the mid-1890s and 1908 the Russian Army received 187,572 Cossack rifles.

One source reports that the reason for the near-ending of production after 1905 was that the weapon had given a disappointing performance in the war against Japan, but as it is almost identical to the dragoon model such an explanation is baffling. The dragoon model, however, was eminently successful and was the basis of the Model 1891/30.

The Model 1907 Carbine

Despite its virtues the M1891 was too long and too heavy for engineers, artillerymen and signalers to carry. Cavalrymen found the 51-inch-long rifle awkward on horseback. As early as 1895 a carbine (*karabin*) prototype was developed, reportedly by altering the dragoon rifle. Introduced in 1907 the carbine, at 40 in and 7.5 lbs, was 11.37 in shorter and 2.12 lbs lighter than the infantry rifle (*pekhotnaya vintovka*). The carbine was stocked almost to the front sight and thus did not take a bayonet, see Figure 2-5. The M1907 carbine has a rear sight with graduations of 400 to 2,000 *arshini* (311 to 1,555 yards).

Note: The M1907 carbine is often mistakenly referred to as the M1910 Carbine. While a number of changes were made to the carbine circa 1910, there is no evidence to indicate that the carbine was ever redesignated the M1910.

Production of new carbines was undertaken at the Izhevsk factory, and existing Dragoon and Cossack rifles were altered to carbines at Sestroryetsk using a system developed by N. I. Yurov. It was also in 1907 that, at an early stage in his distinguished career, Feodor Vasilievich Tokarev (1871–1968) attempted to develop a semiautomatic rifle from the M1891. The attempt would prove unsuccessful.

It is thought that production of the M1907 was discontinued early in World War I. Rumor has it that the weapons were still being manufactured in the 1920s.

Caution: There are Soviet-era, arsenal-reworked carbines on the market which have tsarist-era-dated hexagonal receivers, and which are advertised — through honest mistake, ignorance, or otherwise — as M1910 carbines (the usual misnomer for the M1907). These are referred to sometimes — and perhaps more accurately — as M91/38s. [See the section on the M1938 carbine later in this text.] Genuine M1907s are quite rare, and collectors are advised to examine the weapon *very* carefully before buying, paying particular attention to the rear sight, front sight, handguard, and stock.

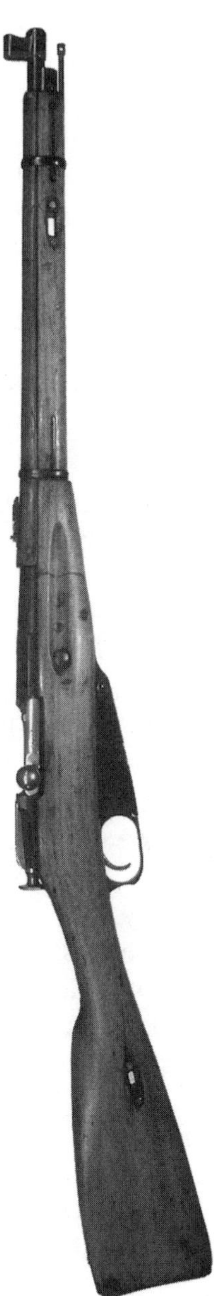

Fig. 2-5. Model 1907 carbine made in 1909 at Izhevsk. Early features: first rear sight graduated to 1900 *Arshini* only, and Izhevsk-made front sight hood. Karl-Heinz Wrobel collection.

WAR, REVOLUTION AND FOREIGNERS

The beginning of the First World War found Russia seriously short of most of the weapons and supplies necessary for conducting modern large-scale military operations. Production of the M1891 continued to the end of Russia's participation in the war, and thereafter, but was confined to the dragoon and infantry models; the Cossack rifle was dropped from production very early in the war, as was the M1907 carbine.

Stockpiles of small arms were wholly inadequate to equip Russia's huge armed forces, and domestic industry was unable to meet the increased demand for weapons, thus forcing the Russian government to acquire arms from abroad. Because of the desperate shortage of rifles, in November 1914 the war ministry authorized procurement of foreign arms regardless of caliber. Subsequently, some 600,000 Arisaka Type 30 rifles in caliber 6.5 x 50 mm were purchased from Japan in 1914–16. In 1913 the Mexican government defaulted on a contract for Arisakas in 7 x 57 mm Mauser, and the Japanese were later able to sell about 30,000 of those weapons to Russia. An additional 128,000 6.5 x 50 mm Type 38 Arisakas were purchased by Russia in 1916 from the British, who had declared them obsolete after buying them for the Royal Navy and Royal Flying Corps only a year before.

As the war dragged on, enormous numbers of M1891s were destroyed, lost or captured — as many as 240,000 per month. Many captured weapons were reissued by the Germans to their rear-echelon military units and navy.

The Austro-Hungarians received large numbers of the M1891s from their German ally in addition to those which their troops captured on the Eastern Front, and issued them to their own military. Like Germany, Austria-Hungary was well-supplied with captured Russian ammunition, but when those supplies ran low the Austrians reworked some of their M1891s to accept the Austrian 8 x 50 mm round; some of this was done at the Wiener-Neustadt armory near Vienna. Some Russian M1891s have been found which bear the marking **OE WG** for Oesterreichische Waffenfabrik Gesellschaft ("Austrian Weapons Co.," the Steyr arsenal) which may be the origin of the rumor that

Mosin-Nagants were manufactured in Austria. There was certainly refurbishing work done, and Steyr may have made some new barrels, although this latter proposition remains hypothetical.

The Austrians sold many of their captured Russian rifles to Finland in the 1920s; they can be recognized by the Austrian marking **AZF** (*Artillerie-Zeugs-Fabrik* = Artillery Ordnance Factory), indicating that they had been inspected before being issued to Austrian troops.

While their enemies shot at them with Russian rifles, many of the hapless Tsar Nicholas II's soldiers went into battle armed only with clubs or knives — or unarmed altogether — and were expected to pick up a rifle from their fallen comrades. Although they captured about 700,000 rifles from enemy troops and obtained some 2,461,000 from foreign sources, the Russians remained chronically short of firearms throughout the First World War.

FROM MOTHER RUSSIA TO UNCLE SAM — AND BACK

In November 1914, the Russian government contracted with the Winchester Repeating Arms Co. to supply what would eventually reach a total of 293,816 Winchester Model 95 rifles (in Russian nomenclature *Vintovka Vinchestera obrazets 1915-ago goda*, i.e., Winchester Rifle M1915) chambered for the standard Russian 7.62 x 54 mm Rimmed round. Winchester also furnished the bayonets for these arms and tens of millions of rounds of ammunition.

The Russian government also ordered 1.5 million M1891 infantry rifles and 100,000,000 rounds of ammunition from Remington Arms-Union Metallic Cartridge Co. Another American firm, New England Westinghouse, received a similar order for 1.8 million rifles, with both companies to provide the traditional socket bayonets as well. These rifles are described in Chapter 3.

The Model 1891/30 Rifle (*Vintovka obrazets 1891/30-ogo goda*)

Russian production of the infantry and dragoon models continued through World War I and the Civil War which followed. Weapons manufacture declined drastically during the period 1917–1925, as is reflected in the average production figures for the Izhevsk arsenal (54,000 rifles per month in 1916 compared to 15,000/month in 1918), and Tula (60,000 rifles/month in 1916 but down to 10,000/month in 1918). Sestroryetsk produced 14,545 infantry rifles — no dragoons — at the beginning of 1918. When fighting between Reds and Whites threatened the arsenal it was closed and its workers conscripted to fight the White Army; it never produced Mosin-Nagant rifles again. A few Feodorov automatic rifles were made at Sestroryetsk before production halted altogether, and for a few years during the 1920s and '30s the factory made farm equipment. In 1940 weapons production recommenced with the SVT-40, but this was halted the following year when the factory was abandoned at the approach of the Finnish army in July 1941. The Germans overran the factory in September.

Production was further disrupted during the Civil War by the various evacuations and occupations of Izhevsk by Red and White forces; the Tula arsenal, however, remained in Bolshevik hands and operated throughout the period.

After the Revolution the Soviets adopted the metric system, and one noteworthy and highly visible post-Revolution change in the Mosin-Nagant is the metric distance measurements stamped onto the rear sights of Soviet-era weapons. The rear sights of tsarist-era rifles carry the old measurements in *arshini (*1 *arshin* equals 711.2 mm or 2.33 feet or 28 inches or 0.777 yard*)*, from 400 to 3,200 (roughly 311 to 2,489 yards).

On 3 October 1922 the *Revvoensoviet* (Revolutionary Military Council) of the Workers' and Peasants' Red Army (*Raboch'ye-Krestyanskaya Krasnaya Armiya*) issued a decree to the effect that only one type of rifle was thereafter to be manufactured for the military: the "3-line dragoon rifle, Model 1891, with [its] bayonet" ("*3-linaya dragunskaya vintovka, obrazets 1891g., so shtikom*"), see Figure 2-6. Because supplies of M1891 parts (barrels, receivers, stocks, etc.) still existed the Soviets decided to continue fabrication of both the infantry and dragoon models until such time as the stockpiles were exhausted. Some M1891/30s were still being made with hexagonal receivers as late as mid-1936. Meanwhile, a shorter hybrid rifle based on the dragoon version was also fabricated with both existing and new parts, having a 730 mm (28.75 in) barrel and an overall length of 1,232 mm (48.5 in).

Manufacture of the new rifle began at Izhevsk in 1923 and at Tula the following year. Production of the M1891/30 ceased at Tula in the spring or summer of 1939 in favor of the ill-fated SVT-38 but resumed somewhat later: it was being made there in 1942, but probably not before.

There is a brief mention in a French intelligence report the author has seen (undated, but from the mid-to-late 1920s judging by its file) of rifles and carbines being manufactured in Omsk, but no further details were given. Moreover, a U.S. Army G-2 (Military Intelligence) report from Warsaw, dated February 13, 1933, states that the M1891/30 was being made in Kharkov, at the Kirov Factory in Leningrad, a bicycle factory in Moscow, the Frunze Memorial Bicycle Factory in Penza, a factory in Poltava, and the Niezamoznik Factory in Nikolayev. This may mean that the rifles were being assembled in those places, or it may mean exactly what it says; there is no elaboration.

Early in 1924 a committee consisting of, among others, Ye. K. Kabakov and I. A. Komaritskii, began work on modernizing the M1891, using the dragoon model as a basis. The first trial rifles were made in 1927 and by 1930 a new design had been agreed upon, which was standardized on 28 April as the "Rifle Model 1891/30" (*vintovka obrazets 1891/30 goda*). On 10 June 1930, Ieronim Petrovich Uborevich, head of the Red Army's armaments production department, issued the order to proceed with production of the new rifle.

The Model 1891/30 differed from its predecessors in several significant features: the rear sight,

Fig. 2-6. Model 91/30 Dragoon. Author's collection.

concave and saw-toothed on the earlier infantry and dragoon models (but, curiously, flat on the 19th-century originals) was now flat. As noted above, owing to the adoption of the metric system by Soviet Russia the sight was now graduated in meters rather than the traditional *arshini*. Metric measurements are stamped, in 100s of meters, on the top of the rear sight, as indicated by the numerals from 1 through 20, inclusive.

The hexagonal receiver was replaced by a cylindrical one, thus both simplifying production and reducing its cost; the blade sight was changed to a hooded post; and the barrel was shortened by 5 mm (0.196 in). On the new rifle the barrel bands were held in place by barrel band springs inletted into each side of the stock.

A new bayonet was developed for the modernized rifle by Kabakov and Komaritskii which substituted a spring-loaded catch for the archaic locking ring on the traditional socket bayonet.

The Russians concocted a number of experimental variations of the M1891/30 during the 1930s, some of which were outwardly similar to the improved designs the Finns were producing during the late 1920s and throughout the 1930s; none of them succeeded in replacing the model adopted in 1930. Various new types of blade as well as spike bayonets were also considered, but the Kabakov-Komaritskii pattern was retained.

The Soviets produced more than twenty million rifles and carbines during the "Great Patriotic War" (June 1941–August 1945), of which approximately 11,145,000 were made at Izhevsk. In the spring or summer of 1939 the Tula ordnance factory ceased production of Mosin-Nagants in favor of the poorly designed Model 1938 Tokarev semiautomatic rifle (the SVT-38). Although never actually deserted, as the German onslaught neared Tula in 1941 the factory was shut down and its equipment moved to the Urals, where production resumed. The M1891/30 production resumed at Tula beginning sometime in 1942 but ceased in 1944. Rifles made on the Tula machinery at Izhevsk continued to be stamped with the Tula factory logo.

Thanks to its location in the northern Urals, safely away from the high-water mark of the German invasion, the Izhevsk arsenal replaced mighty Tula as the Soviets' principal small-arms factory for the remainder of the war.

The arsenal at Sestroryetsk was abandoned in the summer of 1941, at the approach of Finnish troops — the Germans actually did occupy the place in September, 1941 — and the personnel and their equipment were relocated to the quaintly named "Red Toolmaker" factory at Leningrad (the once and future St. Petersburg), where they set about making submachine guns and other useful things.

The M1891/30 rifle was produced in huge quantities. From an initial output of 102,000 in 1930 annual production had increased to 1,396,667 in 1938; by 1945 some 17,475,000 of these rifles had been manufactured. The day of the bolt-action rifle as the principal infantry weapon of modern powers was drawing rapidly to a close, however, and after combat trials toward the end of World War II showed great promise a new, self-loading (i.e., semiautomatic) rifle was adopted by the Soviets: the *Samozaryadnii karabin Simonova obrazets 1945 goda* (Self-loading Simonov carbine, Model 1945) or SKS-45. Developed initially to make use of the 7.62 x 39 mm Model 43 cartridge (*patrona obrazets 1943 goda*) the Russians had derived from the German 7.92 x 33 mm *kurz* (i.e., short) round, the SKS-45 was soon replaced by the *Avtomat Kalashnikova*, known to much of the world — though not to the Russians — as the AK-47. The Russian designation is AK, AKM, AKS, etc., but not AK-47.

Interestingly, the M1891 in a sense did double-duty during the Great Patriotic War. In 1942, when the Germans were besieging Leningrad, a young armaments technician named Alexei Ivanovich Sudayev (1912–1946) invented a submachine gun which could be manufactured with the limited industrial facilities and materials then available in the city. His creation, the Sudayev Machine-pistol Model 1942 (*Pistolet-pulemet Sudayeva obrazets 1942-ogo goda*, or PPS42) and its successor, the PPS43, were made principally of sheet-metal stampings; the barrels of many of these arms, however, were not newly fabricated but were simply taken from old M1891s and sawn-off to fit. This may also have been done during the manufacture

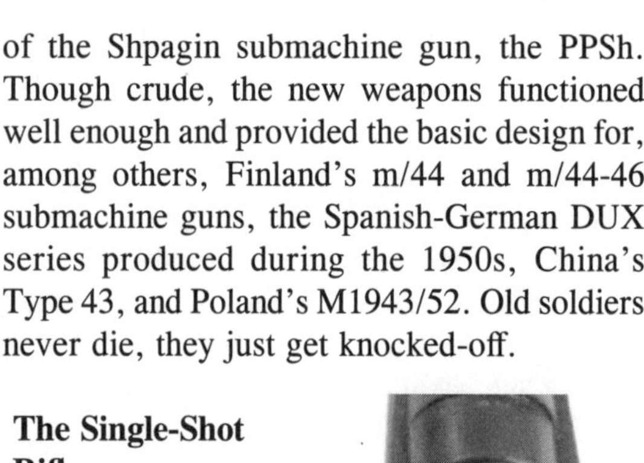

of the Shpagin submachine gun, the PPSh. Though crude, the new weapons functioned well enough and provided the basic design for, among others, Finland's m/44 and m/44-46 submachine guns, the Spanish-German DUX series produced during the 1950s, China's Type 43, and Poland's M1943/52. Old soldiers never die, they just get knocked-off.

The Single-Shot Rifle

A single-shot version of the Mosin-Nagant exists which is quite similar in appearance to the M1891/30, and which is probably a military training rifle; it was produced at least as late as 1952 at Izhevsk and, possibly, at the other Russian arsenals as well, see Figures 2-7 and 2-8. In common with other members of the Mosin-Nagant family, this rifle is caliber 7.62 x 54R.

Fig. 2-8. Receiver marking on this single-shot training rifle show that it was manufactured at the Izhevsk Arsenal in 1952. Steve Kehaya collection.

The single-shot rifle can be distinguished from the M1891/30 principally by its stock, which has no sling slots or other provisions for the attachment of a sling, nor is there a hole for storing a cleaning rod. The stock has no cutout

Fig. 2-7. The single-shot version training rifle of the Mosin-Nagant Model 91/30. Steve Kehaya collection.

below the action for the five-round magazine found on almost all other Mosin-Nagants; a metal plate fastened within the magazine well prevents more than one cartridge from being inserted at a time.

This model should not be confused with a prototype single-shot rifle developed by Mosin in the late 1880s, which is virtually identical to the M1891 Infantry rifle but lacks the external magazine.

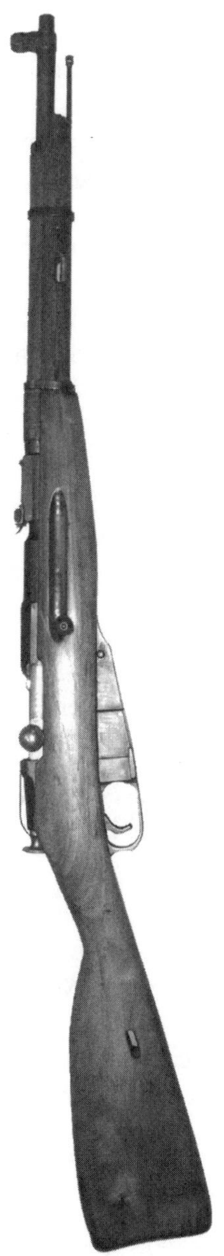

The Model 1938 Carbine (*7,62 mm Karabin obrazets 1938-ogo goda*)

As cavalry, artillery, signalers, etc. still required lighter, shorter shoulder arms, the Soviets adopted a new carbine, the "7.62 mm carbine model of the year 1938" (*7,62 mm karabin obrazets 1938-ogo goda*) by decree dated 26 February 1939, see Figure 2-9. This model differed from the M1907 in that it was not fully stocked and utilized the new hooded-post front sight of the M1891/30 rifle. The M1938, like its predecessor, did not accept a bayonet, but this is due to the annulation under the front sight rather than to the presence of a M1907-type full stock; a bayonet for the M1938 was in fact tested but rejected. See Chapter 5, Bayonets.

The M1938 had an improved rear sight graduated in 100s of meters, indicated by the numerals 1 through 10, stamped on the rear sight leaf.

The M1938 was produced from 1939 to 1944 when it was replaced by the M1944. There are a few, quite rare, dated 1945. The M1938 was made at both Tula and Izhevsk, though production

Fig. 2-9. Model 1938 Carbine. Author's collection.

at Tula was limited and does not seem to have continued past 1941.

Among recent imports to the United States, are firearms which appear to be arsenal-refinished M1938 carbines but which have octagonal receivers with manufacture dates from the 1890s and early 1900s. These may be newly cannibalized M1907 carbines fitted with M1938 stocks and sights, cobbled together for the export market, though it is more probable that they are authentic Soviet or other East Bloc reworks from past decades. In the mid-to-late 1960s, for example, some East German border guards who defected to the West brought with them an odd hybrid weapon in the form of M1891/30s professionally cut-down and refinished into close copies of the M1938 carbine. The opinion in *Bundeswehr* (West German Army) circles at the time was that the work had probably been done in East Germany or, possibly, Czechoslovakia, although there were no reported markings to indicate where the conversion was performed. Post-1989 research indicates that the source was, indeed, Czechoslovakia. This hybrid is referred to (though perhaps not officially styled) as the M1891/38.

The Model 1944 Carbine (*7,62 mm Karabin obrazets 1944-ogo goda*)

Battle experience during the Second World War demonstrated that the M1891/30, though significantly shorter and lighter than its infantry-model predecessor, was still uncomfortably long — especially when fitted with a bayonet — and awkwardly balanced for use in the cramped confines of buildings, trenches and bunkers; in street fighting; and in environments such as forests and ruins which abounded in obstructions and protrusions. The number of requests (reported in Bolotin, *Soviet Small-Arms and Ammunition* — you have to wonder how much attention the Soviet government paid to the "demands" of its citizens) from the front for a more convenient weapon prompted a survey which revealed a significant demand for an improved carbine and, specifically, one which could accept a permanently attached, folding bayonet. The concept of the folding bayonet was certainly not new: it had been used by the Italians on the Mannlicher-Carcano and the Japanese on the Arisaka carbines for years, and dates to at least the end of the 18th century, when it appears on English guns.

In May of 1943 tests were conducted with eight prototypes of bayonet pursuant to development of a new carbine model (Datig, "Russian Military Firearms," etc., Bolotin, *Soviet Small-Arms and Ammunition*). The design eventually selected for serious consideration was submitted by N. S. Semin. Battlefield testing of the Semin bayonet was conducted in November 1943 and January 1944. In some texts, December 1943 is omitted from the test period; this may have been an error in the original source or the weapon may actually not have been tested in December for whatever reason.

Some 50,000 M1944 carbines were manufactured in 1943 for trials. On 17 January 1944 Semin's model was approved by the State Defense Committee *(Gosudarstvennii Komitet Oboroni*) for inclusion on a new carbine to be issued to infantry, cavalry, and engineers. The bayonet is made of steel with a military-grade bluing; it is 383 mm (15.1 in) long, inclusive of the barrel-sleeve and locking bracket, both of which are integral to the bayonet assembly. This bayonet retains the cruciform style and flathead-screwdriver tip of its predecessors. The blade folds along the right side of the weapon when not in use and rests in a groove routed into the stock. Unlike the M1891 and M1891/30 bayonets the M1944 is not serial-numbered; some examples have the usual arsenal marks, and others are unmarked altogether.

The new weapon was officially styled "7.62 mm carbine model of the year 1944" (7,62 mm *karabin obrazets 1944-ogo goda*) and was sup-

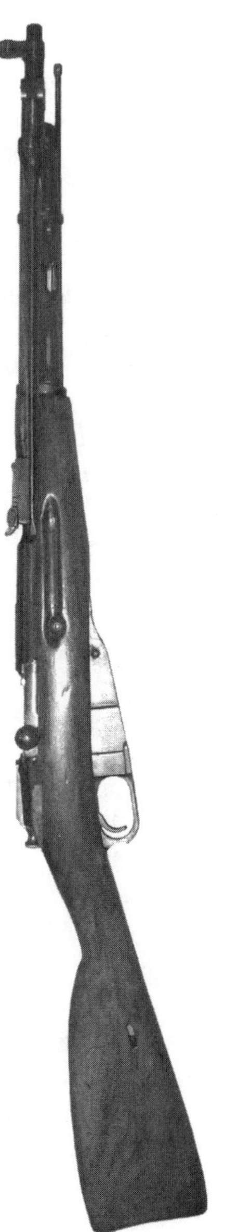

Fig. 2-10. Model 1944 Mosin-Nagant Carbine with folding bayonet. Author's collection.

plied to the Red Army beginning in February 1944, see Figure 2-10. Soviet M1944 carbines were produced at Izhevsk, and have the usual markings. Some, however, were produced at Izhevsk but are stamped with the Soviet-era Tula "star-and-arrow" logo: these are M1938 carbines altered to the M1944 configuration as part of the latter weapon's development and are dated 1943. They are quite uncommmon.

Aside from its folding bayonet the M1944 is virtually identical to the M1938 carbine, although the M1944's barrel is 10 mm longer and the weapon weighs 0.75 kg (1.65 lbs) more, almost all of which is the bayonet. The new carbine, though very muzzle-heavy because of the bayonet and thus clumsy to handle, was successful enough to be manufactured in the Soviet Union until at least 1948, and in several other countries for many years after the end of World War II.

Some minor modifications can be found on late- and post-World War II carbines: a wider base for the front sight and a more elaborate folding bayonet assembly being the principal items. Sometime around or shortly after the end of World War II — possibly as early as late 1945, and certainly by the 1946 production year — the Russians improved the M1944 bayonet by adding an "ear" to the front end of the bracket like that already mounted on the rear. The end of the sleeve was also altered, with two cams replacing the notched indentations of the earlier model which fitted over the "ears" when the bayonet was folded back along the stock. The muzzle ring was changed to include a cutout which helped secure the bayonet to the muzzle when in use, see Figure 5-7 in Chapter 5. All of these modifications will be found on Chinese and East Bloc M44s as well as on the later Russian production.

The M1944 is believed to have been in production from 1944 to at least 1948, although there are indications that some were manufactured as late as 1956. The author has been unable to verify the latter date. Test versions were also produced with 22- and 24-inch barrels, and a few test carbines were also manufactured for the 7.62 x 39 mm cartridge. None of these tests led to new series of carbines. Further work on these prototypes was abandoned in favor of the SKS carbine.

The M1944 was still in active service with impoverished guerrilla groups, and as a reserve weapon in other Communist and Third World countries, at least as late as the 1980s and probably thereafter. During the Soviet occupation of Afghanistan in the 1980s, M1944s were issued to conscript soldiers of the Soviets' quisling Afghan government. When United States forces intervened against the Marxist regime in Grenada in October 1983 they captured 2,432 M1944 carbines, reportedly furnished by Cuba as they have markings in Spanish on the stocks. Interestingly enough, some Spanish-language marked M1944 carbines are now being sold in the United States. The story usually goes that they were captured in Grenada. In fact, they were sold by Cuba to Canada for badly needed hard currency, and then resold in the United States. Federal law makes it illegal for weapons captured by American military forces to be resold to civilians.

M1944 carbines are seen in photographs of Palestinian guerrilla trainees in the 1980s. Nicaragua issued M1944s to its troops.

The Soviet Union furnished various models of Mosin-Nagants by the tens of thousands to its satellites, clients, and various guerrilla and terrorist groups. The practice seems to have begun with Lenin's order to ship M1891 rifles to Afghanistan early in the 1920s as a cheap foreign aid gesture and, perhaps incidentally, a means to annoy and disconcert the British in neighboring India. Because of this widespread diffusion of weaponry it is possible to find Mosin-Nagant rifles and carbines with all manner of interesting and exotic markings from places as remote from each other as Cuba and Syria. The full story of the peregrinations of these firearms will probably never be known.

The M1891/30 Rifle Sound Suppressor

Mention will be made at this point of the sound suppressor (also referred to as a "muffler", in U.S. Army parlance) produced during the Second World War for the M1891/30. The Soviet device is 235 mm (9.25 in) long and weighs 0.5 kg (1.1 lbs); it is 32 mm (1.259 in) in diameter. The suppressor is attached to the muzzle by means of a socket quite similar to that of the standard Mosin-Nagant bayonet. There are two rubber plates in the suppressor, each of which is 15 mm (0.59 in) thick. The baffles typically lasted for about 100 shots, after which they had to be replaced and the device thoroughly cleaned. The suppressor was used only with the ammunition produced for it, which had a green case and was sometimes called the "partisan round".

Chapter 3
Foreign Variations of the Mosin-Nagant

The dozen or so Mosin-Nagant system weapons produced outside Russia owe their existence largely to the fact that the countries which made them share a common border with her. These nations were subjected to considerable Russian influence — tsarist and Soviet, and largely unwanted — for many years. In most instances there is no other reason why any of the following weapons would have been produced.

Austria-Hungary

Despite their mostly lackluster military performance on the Eastern Front throughout World War I the Austro-Hungarians managed to capture thousands of Russian rifles. Some of these they gave to their Turkish ally, others they converted to their own use. The Austrians altered some of the rifles to fire the standard 8 x 50 mm round used in their Mannlichers. Refurbishment and conversion work was done by Oesterreichische Waffenfabrik Gesellschaft (Austrian Arsenal Company) at Steyr (which marked the rifles OE WG), and at Berndorf. Berndorf reworks are stamped with a picture of a bear: this is an old pun on the town's name, which sounds like Bärendorf, "Bears Town", to German speakers. Similar bear puns are also used for Berlin and Bern, though none of the places' names are actually derived from Bär (bear). The Austrians sold many — perhaps all — of their remaining M1891s to Finland during the 1920s.

Bulgaria

Russia furnished an indeterminable number of Mosin-Nagants (mostly, if not exclusively, M1891 Infantry rifles) to Bulgaria during the various local wars in the late 19th and early 20th centuries in which Bulgarians fought Turks, Romanians, and other Balkanites. The Serbs were also beneficiaries of this Russian largesse; this proved awkward in 1913, during the Second Balkan War, when the Serbs and Bulgarians were

Figure 3-1. Model 1891/59. Author's collection.

on opposite sides. This Russian foreign aid accounts for the Mosin-Nagants circulating in places such as Albania and Yugoslavia, which sold the weapons to Finland in the 1920s.

There is an alleged Bulgarian Mosin-Nagant mutant designated the Model 1891/59, see Figure 3-1, the details of which are reportedly as follows: sometime after World War II the Soviets persuaded (or forced) the Bulgarians to acquire surplus ex-Russian M1891/30s in addition to the M1891s already in inventory, and to convert them into slightly more modern weapons somewhat like M1938 carbines. This work was undertaken at the Bulgarian arsenals in Tarnovo and Kasanlak in the later 1950s, and the result was Bulgaria's Model 1891/59. The weapon was fabricated largely by shortening existing M1891 and M1891/30s. The barrel on the new weapon is 20.5 in long, and the total length is 39.75 in. It weighs 7.5 lbs. Total production of this carbine is supposedly 35,000.

The author cannot confirm the origin of this weapon and it is reported only for the reader's information. In my opinion, the M1891/59 is a Russian product made of parts salvaged from otherwise scrappable Mosin-Nagants and meant as a reserve weapon in the event of invasion by the West — always a consideration for Soviet planners, especially in the 1950s when the Cold War was very frosty indeed.

Reportedly, these M1891/59 carbines were used in the Soviet Union by the *VoKhr* (*Voiska Vnutrennie Okhrani*, i.e., Interior Guard Troops) in the 1960s, while guarding lower-level facilities such as railroad bridges, warehouses, etc.

Whatever its background, the M1891/59 is outwardly quite similar to the Soviets' M1938 carbine and consists principally or exclusively of Russian parts. It can be immediately distinguished from the M1938 carbine by the marking "1891/59" on the chamber below the date and above the serial number.

The stock is similar to the that used on the M1944 carbine, but it does not have the bayonet groove routed into the top right of the forearm; it is serial-numbered to the weapon with the number stamped on the left side of the butt. The butt plate is also serial-numbered on the top tang, behind the screw. The sling slots are fully lined with metal; the escutcheons do not have screws but are inletted into the stock instead. This carbine uses a cut-down M1891/30 handguard, rather than the standard carbine handguard, as the M1891/30 rear sight was installed.

The M1891/30 rear sight has been machined to remove the metric markings beyond 10 leaving two shallow grooves along the top of the leaf. The M1891/59 is commonly found with the earlier of the two types of carbine front-sight base.

Communist-era Bulgarian arms in general are marked with Bulgaria's East Bloc country code: the numeral "10" in the center of two concentric circles. There is also a Bulgarian identification mark which looks like a pinecone. These two marks, or either of them, might be present on some 1891/59s — if indeed they are Bulgarian — but the author has never seen one so marked. Some of these carbines reportedly have been 'sanitized' by the removal of all Russian markings, but all of them that I have seen have been well-marked with the usual Russian stampings.

With respect to the supposed origins of the Bulgarian 1891/59, it is interesting to note that in the mid-to-late 1960s some of the East German border guards who defected to the West brought with them a curious hybrid weapon in the form of M1891/30s professionally cut-down and refinished into near-copies of the M1938 carbine. The opinion in *Bundeswehr* (West German Army) circles at the time was that the work had probably been done in East Germany or, possibly,

Czechoslovakia, although there were no reported markings to indicate where the conversion was performed. Given the number of similar weapons starting to appear in the West with the T-in-a-circle Czech refurbishment mark, it appears that the East German border guard carbines may have had the same source.

PEOPLE'S REPUBLIC OF CHINA

Communist China began production of its version of the M1944 carbine in May 1953, hence its designation as "Type 53". The Chinese characters for "Type 53" (See Figure 3-2) are stamped on the receiver above the date of manufacture; on late-production weapons (post-circa 1959) the model designation is omitted and there are no Chinese ideographs at all. It is probable that the Chinese carbines were made on machinery supplied by the Russians in the early 1950s during the height of Sino-Soviet friendship, as is the case with China's first TT-33 (Tokarev) pistols and the Type 56 carbine (the Chinese version of the SKS, which succeeded the Type 53).

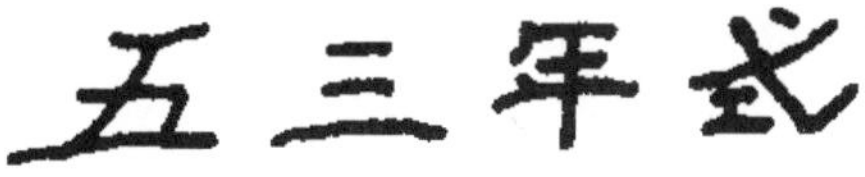

Figure 3-2.

Note: The Chinese characters in Figure 3-2 mean literally "53 Year Type". The third character shown, meaning year, is omitted on some examples. The standard Chinese for 53 are the following three symbols, Figure 3-3a which literally mean 5 [x] 10 [+]3. Deleting the character for ten, Figure 3-3b, can and does occur without changing the meaning of the number group.

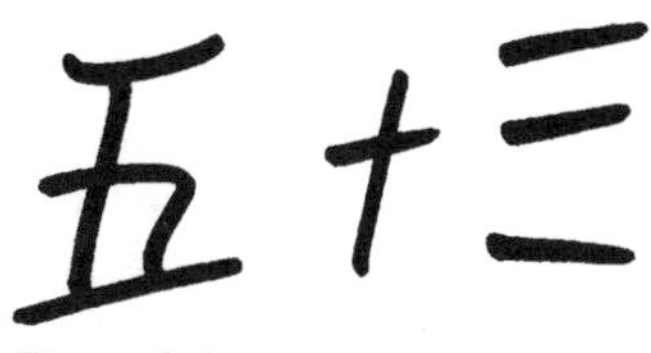

Figure 3-3a.

Some carbines have the production-year date followed by a period and an additional one or two numbers indicating the month of manufacture: e.g., May 1954 is 1954.5 and August 1954 is 1954.08. The numbers below the date are the code number of the factory where the weapon was made, e.g., 296 or 26, indicating State Factory No. 296 at Chonqing (formerly Chunking); note, however, that on some carbines the factory number is located above the date. (Note also that the number 6 in the code group indicates an armaments factory.)

Figure 3-3b.

On carbines produced during most of the 1950s the range numbers on the rear sight are quite small: only 2 mm (0.078 in) tall; by 1960 they had been increased in height to a more readable 3 mm (0.118 in).

The Chinese carbines differ little from their Soviet counterparts, most noticeably in the use of local wood or woods for the stock. On some later production carbines (circa 1960) the heel of the stock (the top of the comb, at the rear) is flattened.

An interesting feature of the Type 53 is the profusion of inspectors' markings stamped on many stocks; though unlike the Russians the Chinese did not mark most metal pieces. Some stocks have a serial number stamped on the left side of the butt which, if original, should be identical to that on the receiver.

The Type 53's cleaning rod is shorter than the Russian variety by about 0.5 in (12.5 mm), and the head is plain rather than grooved or knurled; the screw-end differs somewhat as well. The bolt, magazine floorplate and butt plate are serial-numbered to the individual carbine. Unlike many Russian and East Bloc M1944s, the Chinese type will generally have an inspector's mark on the bayonet mounting bracket.

There is one report that mentions Type 53s being fitted with a folding bayonet ending in a spike point rather than the usual flathead-screwdriver tip, but the author is unable to verify its existence. The bayonet in question may have simply been repaired.

Chinese slings for the Type 53 are very similar in appearance to their Russian counterparts, but are somewhat narrower (1.25 in) as compared to the typical Russian sling width of 1.75 in. They are generally a darkish green or greenish khaki. Some Chinese slings will be found without the Russian-style buckle "dog collar" on the sling; a leather strap tied with leather or cotton cord was used instead. Chinese slings are sometimes marked with the ideograms for "Type 53".

The Type 53 was produced as late as 1961, and possibly later, although as a military arm it was gradually replaced after 1956 when the Chinese began making copies of the Soviet SKS carbine and AK-47 assault rifle. The Type 53 remained in service with provincial militia and rear-echelon units well into the 1970s, and probably thereafter.

Although they did not produce them the Chinese were supplied with — or, perhaps, purchased — M1891 Infantry rifles at some point between about 1920 and about 1950, the obvious source being the Soviet Union. The author has examined two unusual M1891s — a New England Westinghouse produced in 1915, and a 1917 Tula — in two entirely different (and uncatalogued) U.S. government collections. Both rifles had the two Chinese ideographs (Figure 3-4A) — "sun" and "moon" which, when taken together, mean "bright" or, in some contexts, "tomorrow" or "future", and pronounced, approximately, "ming", above the ideograph meaning "big" or "great", and pronounced, approximately, "dah" (Figure 3-4B). Each of the ideographs is approximately 2.0 in tall; they are neatly painted — possibly stenciled — identically on the buttstock of both rifles; they are oriented lengthwise to the rifle, the tops of the ideographs towards the muzzle. The paint was probably white when new but has mellowed to a yellowish-ivory. Both, either, or neither of these rifles may be Korean War captures; there is no documentation for them and their provenance is unknown. The significance of the inscription is as baffling as it is intriguing.

Figure 3-4A.

Figure 3-4B.

Note: "Ming" also means Ming Dynasty. The last ethnic Chinese dynasty, the Ming was overthrown by the Manchus, or Ch'ing Dynasty, in 1644. The Ch'ing was officially terminated by the Chinese republic's constitution in 1912.

CZECHOSLOVAKIA

A Czech-made weapon vaguely resembling the M1938 carbine was recycled from M1891s; it is referred to as the M91/38. This piece typically has the early polygonal receiver, a cut-down rifle barrel, M1938 tangent rear sight, and the post–World War II wide-base carbine front sight base. The M1944 stock was used. The Czech "T-in-a-circle" rework mark is stamped on the receiver. This "carbine" is very similar to the supposed Bulgarian M1891/59.

In the early 1950s Czechoslovakia briefly produced a sniper rifle based on the M1891/30 which was designated the ZG 51/91/30. A second sniper rifle, the *Odstřelovaci puška vz.54* (sniper rifle model [19]54), was manufactured by the Czechs from 1954 to 1957, on original M1891/30 actions. See Chapter 4 for further details.

The Czechs, like the East Germans, refurbished arms for the East Bloc and Soviet-influenced countries and groups during the Cold War. These were marked with a "T" or 11 within a circle.

FINLAND

Prior to 1917, Finland was part of Russia and the Tsar ruled as the Grand Duke of Finland. After Russia's Bolshevik Revolution of November 1917 Finnish Bolsheviks seized power in Helsinki and southern Finland. A brutal Red/White civil war broke out immediately. The White Guard anti-Communist forces were organized and commanded by Baron Carl Gustaf Emil Mannerheim (1867–1951), a Finnish aristocrat and former tsarist general. His troops were largely trained by German soldiers (and included a few German troops) and in fierce fighting Mannerheim largely crushed the Communists by mid-1918, although sporadic fighting went on until 1920. Finland maintained a precarious independence until the Soviets grew strong enough to trample it in the Winter War of 1939–40 which began with a sneak attack on Helsinki by Russian bombers on November 30, 1939.

The Jalkaväenkivääri m/91

Note: Jalkaväenkivääri means "infantry rifle" in Finnish.

The Mosin-Nagant Rifle

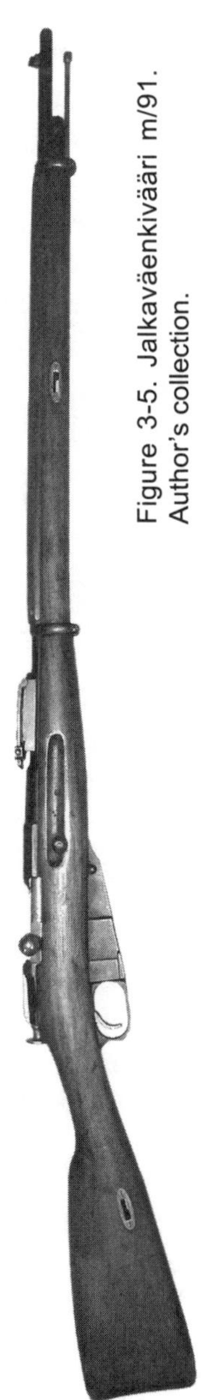

Figure 3-5. Jalkaväenkivääri m/91. Author's collection.

Finland's new army and the Civil Guard were, at first, armed mostly with various models of the M1891 taken from the imperial arsenal at Helsinki when the 1917 Russian Revolution began. The Civil Guard (*Suojeluskunta)* was a quasi-official national militia from the 1920s to 1944 when it was, at the insistence of the Soviet Union, disbanded after the Finns surrendered. Finland fought against the Soviet Union in the Winter War (November 1939 to March 1940), and again in what was called the Continuation War, 1941 to 1944.

During the 1920s, in an effort to standardize their military small arms, the Finns purchased (or, in some instances, traded other weapons for) an additional 18,400 M1891s from Albania, Czechoslovakia, Hungary and Poland; others were acquired from France, Italy, Germany and Austria. Some of these rifles were retained in their original forms, though most were modernized during succeeding years.

The French had a large number of Mosin-Nagants which had been surrendered by the Germans in 1918. Some were given as souvenirs to members of the Allied military delegations to the Versailles Treaty Conference in 1919, and some made their way to Finland. In 1939, the Finns purchased an additional 56,500 M1891s from Yugoslavia, some of which required significant refurbishing.

The first of the Finnish modifications was designated simply *Jalkaväenkivääri m/91* ("Infantry Rifle, Model 91"), and was the basic M1891 with improvements such as a new handguard (on some examples), refurbished or new barrels, etc., see Figure 3-5.

These rifles are usually found with a rear sight graduated in both meters (on the right) and *arshini*, the original Russian old-style measurements (on the left). The *arshini* are marked 4, 6, 8, 10, and 12; usually there is a slash through each numeral. The metric measurements are often indicated by an "M" in either block-letter or script. The metric numerals are 2, 3, 4, 5 1/2, 7, and 8 1/2. Sometimes these numerals begin with 2 1/2, and sometimes with 3. Metricization of the rear sights began about May 1926. Although metric measurements are standard on the outside right side of re-marked rear sights, the inside of the leaf always retains the old measurements in *arshini*.

Some of this upgrading from 1919 until the early 1920s was done by *Suomen Ampumatarvetehdas* (Finnish Ammunition Factory) at Riihimäki, which also manufactured about 200 new barrels for Infantry as well as Dragoon M1891s. These weapons, marked with the letters SAT in a circle surmounting the place name Riihimäki, are very rare.

The Finnish company Tikkakoski produced 10,000 M1891 barrels in the years 1925–1927, of which 7,000 are unstepped and 3,000 are of the heavier, stepped type (refer to Figure 1-12). Barrels produced in 1925 and 1926 have the dates stamped on the underside, while the 1927 run is found with the date atop the chamber; the Tikkakoski "T-in-a-triangle" symbol is stamped on the chamber of all three years' production of barrels. These barrels were reportedly made in three different bore diameters, designated "A", "B" and "C", and are marked as such. The "A" barrels are "considered inferior" according to a statement in *Rifles of the Snow,* but no reason is given; the "B"-marked ones should not be confused with the "B" variety which means the barrel was made in Belgium; and the "C" barrels are the commonest. The author has observed barrels marked "E", "F" and "G", but has not been able to find references to them.

The large number of M1891s available to the Finns encouraged them to experiment with various methods of salvaging otherwise unusable barrels. Capitalizing on Italian success with the Salerno process of barrel relining (sleeving the barrel and recutting the rifling), the Finns rebored about 13,000 M1891 barrels at the government's Arsenal No.1 (*Asevarikko-1*, or *AVK-1*) at Helsinki during 1925–1927. This is the so-called "P" series, from *Suomessa putkit tehttu* ("[rifle] bores made in Finland"), the rifles being identifiable by the capital P on the chamber followed by a dash and the numerals 25, 26 or 27 designating the year. As part of the "P" process old markings were removed and the barrels renumbered. Those barrels not used at the time were placed in storage and used a decade and a half later as part of the World War II production of the m/91.

In 1939, emboldened by his non-aggression pact with Hitler and the USSR's virtually unopposed annexation of eastern Poland and takeover of military and naval bases in the Baltic states, Stalin demanded substantial territorial and political concessions from Finland, some, but not all, of which the Finns were willing to make. To settle the matter the USSR invaded Finland on November 30, 1939, without a declaration of war. On December 14, 1939, in a display of principle and resolve unique in its otherwise pusillanimous history, the League of Nations expelled the Soviet Union from its membership for the unprovoked aggression against Finland.

The Finns fought skillfully and bravely but were unable to match the vast Soviet resources of men and matériel. Rather than suffer the complete devastation of their country — a foretaste of which the Soviets demonstrated by savagely bombing Helsinki on the first day of the invasion — the Finns surrendered in March 1940, ending what has become known as the Winter War.

When Germany attacked the Soviet Union on June 22, 1941, Finland, by then a German co-belligerent, reoccupied the lost areas of Karelia. Finland was not, technically, a German ally and it did not declare war on the United States, although it was legally at war with Great Britain and the Soviet Union, which were allies of the United States. Even though the Finns had been preparing for further Russian attacks after the 1940 surrender, it is reported they only had 507,601 military rifles in 1941.

Showing more integrity than either their Nazi co-belligerents or Communist foes, the Finns halted their advance after reaching their pre-1939 borders. Fortune was reversed yet again in September 1944 and Finland once more lost its eastern border areas to the USSR; they have never been returned.

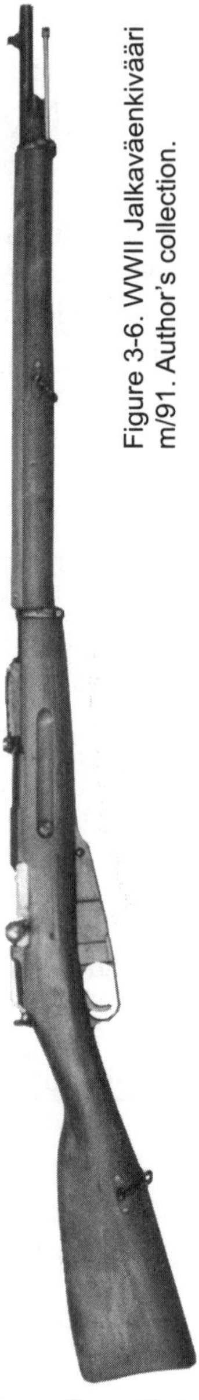

Figure 3-6. WWII Jalkaväenkivääri m/91. Author's collection.

The World War II Jalkaväenkivääri m/91
The Finns began their own production of the original M1891 infantry model in 1940. The work was undertaken by Tikkakoski between June 1940 and January 1943, and VKT *(Valtion Kivääritehdas* — State Rifle Factory) between September 1941 and January 1945. Tikkakoski made some 33,000 M1891s, and VKT about 45,000. See Figure 3-6.

There is also a barrel mark "B" about which considerable controversy exists. According to one theory the barrels were made in Belgium and assembled by VKT, with the stocks being made at *Asevarikko*-3 at Kuopio. Some of the barrels have Belgian proof marks — such as small stars and the letters "K" and "EL" — on the underside of the chamber, together with the Tikkakoski logo. The "Belgian" barrels were, according to this theory, furnished as military aid by Germany: Belgium had been under German occupation since May 1940. Five thousand barrels — or barrel blanks — are alleged to have been exported to Finland, of which 2,000 were used on m/91s and the remainder on m/39s.

Note: *Asevarikko*-2 was located at Viipuri, also called, in Swedish, Vyborg, which was near the pre-1940 Finnish/Soviet border. This factory was closed in 1942 because it was too near the fighting at Leningrad. The area was surrendered to the Soviet Union in 1940 and again in 1944, and remains Russian territory today.

All reported "B" barrels have been on rifles dated 1942 (see Figure 3-7), but that does not exclude the possibility that they were made before or after then as well. VKT received an order of 8,500 m/91 barrel blanks from Belgium as late as September 1944, but Finland surrendered before the blanks could be used. It is possible, even probable, that they were made into finished rifles of some kind after the war. Palokangas reports that VKT made 8,500 B-marked m/91 barrels as late as January 1945.

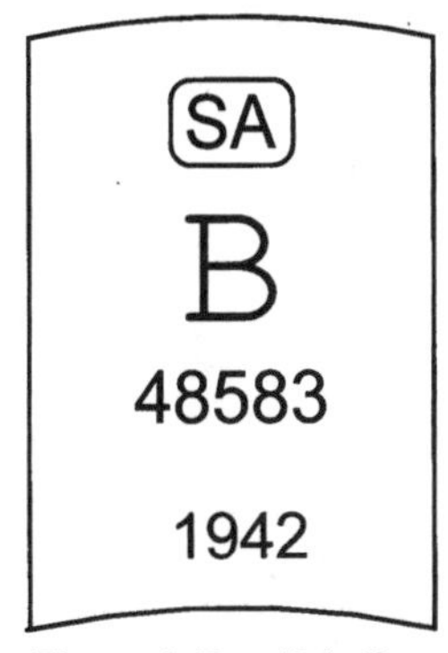

Figure 3-7. m/91 rifles with receivers marked "B" were dated 1942.

Another theory supposes that the "B" indicates barrels or blanks produced by the Swedish firm Bofórs, makers of the famous antiaircraft guns. Tikkakoski had used Bofórs steel in some of its production after 1932, but the Tikkakoski m/39 barrel production took place in the late 1960s and early 1970s.

Having set forth the more common theories of the "B" barrels' origin, the author will note that Markku Palokangas, the highly knowledgeable curator of Finland's premier arms museum, states that the "B" barrels were made of steel purchased from Belgium in 1939 and 1940 for use in Finnish production of m/91 barrels, with some of the barrels eventually being altered for, and actually made into, m/39s. This would account for the absence of Belgian proof marks on so many "B" barrels and, in my opinion, is most likely to be the solution to the mystery.

The World War II "Belgian B" barrels ought not to be confused with the "Tikkakoski B" barrels made in the 1920s: the "Belgian B" is stamped atop the chamber in the usual place for a manufacturer's logo, above all other markings; the "Tikkakoski-barrel B" is also found on the chamber, but below the serial number.

Finland continued to purchase M1891s from Germany — and Bulgaria — during World War II. Many of these were used solely as sources of parts for Finnish m/91s.

VKT reportedly made 92 m/91 barrels in February 1944, which

are marked with a capital "V". The significance of this marking is unknown.

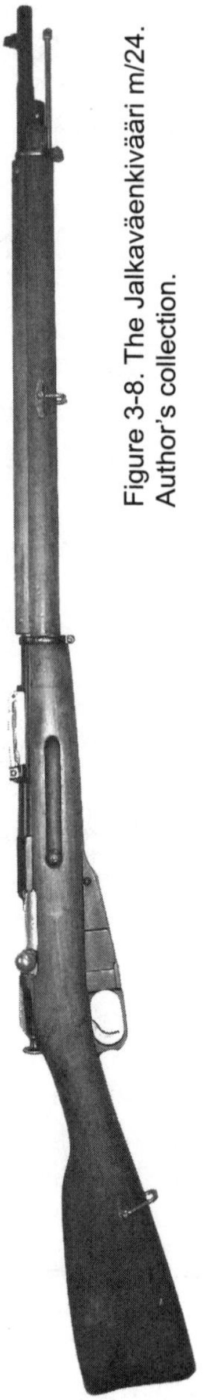

Figure 3-8. The Jalkaväenkivääri m/24. Author's collection.

The Jalkaväenkivääri m/24

In 1924, a domestically designed rifle was produced which the Finns designated Jalkaväenkivääri m/24 (m/91-24, according to some sources) and which reportedly was originally intended for the Suojeluskunta (the Civil Guard). Some of these pieces were undoubtedly issued to the Civil Guard as they bear a Civil Guard serial number in addition to the manufacturer's serial number; the two numbers are not identical except by coincidence and, in any event, mean two different things. See Figure 3-8.

The m/24 is simply the old M1891 reworked by the Civil Guards arms repair shop in 1923 with new barrels, 8,000 of which were purchased from the Swiss firm Schweizerische Industrie Gesellschaft (SIG). These arms can be easily recognized by the maker's name and factory town, "Neuhausen," stamped on the right side of the barrel forward of the chamber, under the wood line of the stock.

An additional 18,000 barrels were furnished by the German firms Oskar Will AG, Venuswaffenfabrik, and Römerwerke AG. Barrels made by these three manufacturers are marked **BÖHLER-STAHL** (German for "Böhler Steel": Gebrüder Böhler ["Böhler Brothers"] was the Austrian steel maker) on the underside, just in front of the receiver. Use of the Swiss and German barrels — almost all of which are stepped, rather than tapered like the original Russian variety — also required recutting the bed of reused Russian stocks to fit. These barrels are significantly heavier than the originals and are fitted with a 2 in-long aluminum sleeve near the front barrel band which allowed the barrel to "float," both of which innovations helped to increase accuracy.The Swiss and German markings on these barrels are probably the source of the rumors that Mosin-Nagants were manufactured in those two countries.

The m/24 was produced at the Civil Guard arsenal in Helsinki from 1923 to 1927. The arsenal had been established for the Civil Guard in 1919, and on June 1, 1927 it became a limited liability company under the name *Suojeluskuntain Ase- ja Konepaja Osakeyhtiö* (Civil Guard Arms & Machine-shop Co., Ltd.), better known as SAKO. It is sometimes referred to by its Swedish name *Skyddskärernas Vapen och Mekaniska Aktiebolag* as Swedish as well as Finnish are the official languages of Finland. In 1927 production was moved to Riihimäki, north and somewhat west of the Finnish capital. This model was nicknamed the "*Lotta*" rifle after the *Lotta Svärd*, the women's auxiliary of the Civil Guard. The organization was named for the heroine of a famous Finnish patriotic poem by Rüneberg. By 1941, there were about 100,000 women in the group (from a total population of a little over 3.5 million). It was disbanded in 1944. In 1924 the *Lotta* ladies raised funds to purchase or refurbish 10,000 of the weapons.

The m/24, of which between 25,000 and 38,000 may have been made, is equipped with the same modified rear sight as the m/91 described above. A quick and simple way to identify these rifles is by the early Civil Guard logo on the chamber: a capital **S** crowned by three fir sprigs, enclosed in a shield.

Six hundred and fifty m/24s were shortened in 1932–34 by the State Rifle Factory (VKT) in Jyväskylä either as an experiment or, possibly, for use by cavalry and other forces traditionally armed with carbines.

Ratsuväenkivääri m/91

After Finland gained independence from Russia in 1918, Finnish cavalry units were initially armed with M1891 Infantry rifles, then with German-made Mauser 98a carbines. Beginning in 1924, these carbines were replaced with some Russian Dragoon and Cossack rifles which had been left in the country after the Civil War. Both these rifles were considered to be one model as their differences are negligible — the

Dragoon was sighted with the bayonet attached, the Cossack model was not. The rifles were designated *Ratsuväenkivääri m/91* (Cavalry Rifle m/91).

Between the rifles in Finland, those purchased abroad (principally from Italy) and those captured from the Soviets during the Winter War, the total of m/91 cavalry rifles in Finnish service reached approximately 5,500 by 1940, although this rifle was already being phased out by 1935 in favor of the m/27 cavalry carbine. At the late date of 1944 the Finns purchased an additional 4,000 ex-Soviet Model 1891 cavalry rifles from Germany.

The *Ratsuväenkivääri m/91* is usually found with only minor modifications from the Russian originals: the usual metric graduations added to the rear sight and, occasionally, Finnish-style two-piece stocks. Some examples also were modified by having the Mauser-type sling indentation routed into the right side of the buttstock, identical to that of the m/27 cavalry carbine. The standard Russian Model 1891 cruciform bayonet was used with these weapons, but was shortened for cavalry use. They are described fully in Chapter 5.

Fewer than 19,000 of these rifles survived the war. The Finns modified 1,500 m/91 cavalry rifles for use as bayonet-training weapons in 1959, and the remaining 17,358 were sold as surplus in the United States and Canada the following year.

Civil Guard Serial Numbers

The Civil Guard assigned its own serial numbers, sequentially numbered and running as high as six digits; they are not the same as the rifle's *serial number*, which was assigned by original manufacturer. Tables in Appendix I, I-1 and I-2, provide lists of serial numbers used by units of the Civil Guard. There are unexplained overlaps and gaps in the available literature.

A Civil Guard number is always preceded by a capital **S** and can be found on any model. It is usually stamped on the chamber, but it is not uncommon to see them on the side of the receiver and on the flat of the bolt. On some examples the last two digits of the Civil Guard number are also stamped on the bolt head. A rifle may have several

Civil Guard numbers, indicating a passage through various Civil Guard districts, regiments and even battalions; prior numbers are struck through with a line. Some Civil Guards rifles also have rack numbers indicating their location within an individual unit, though this is not especially common. These rack numbers are usually one to three digits and will seem 'out of place' as they appear on the chamber or behind the front sight. Rack numbers are also found on some Civil Guard bayonets and are meant to be identical to the rack number of the rifles with which they were issued. See Chapter 5, Bayonets

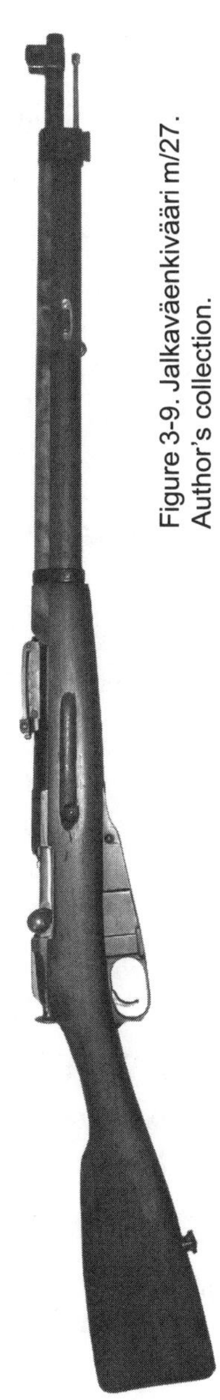

Figure 3-9. Jalkaväenkivääri m/27. Author's collection.

The Jalkaväenkivääri m/27

The *Jalkaväenkivääri m/27* is essentially a short m/24, see Figure 3-9. It was the first model to have the new hinged nosecap. The hinge was on the right and the securing machine screw on the left, although the author has observed one m/27 with the screw on the right. The screw was parallel to the bore. Refer to Figure 1-33. The nosecap also carries the bayonet and because it tended to rotate when the bayonet was used, cracking the stock, two parallel metal braces, one on each side, were added in 1935 and retrofitted to existing rifles through 1937. The braces are 75 mm (2.95 in) long by 10 mm (0.39 in) wide and fit into grooves milled in the stock. A bolt enters the brace on the right, penetrates the stock and screws into the left brace. Refer to Figure 1-34.

The m/27's sling is attached to one swivel mounted on the underside of the buttstock and one through the sling slot in the for end; the rear sling slot is retained on some rifles and filled in on others; some examples lack the swivel under the buttstock. Refer to Figures 1-41, 1-42 and 1-43.

A few experimental m/27s were produced with the so-called "committee stock," similar — but not identical — in appearance to the pistol grip stock eventually developed for the m/39.

The rear sight on some examples is an aperture, rather than a notch as on earlier models, and is graduated to 800 meters. The front sight is a blade (or 'barleycorn') protected by metal 'ears'; apparently these 'ears' were a source of some amusement to the Finns, who nicknamed the rifle *Pystykorva* ("Pomeranian" or "Spitz", as in the dogs). Refer to Figure 1-73.

The nickname was also applied to the m/27 cavalry rifle, the m/28 and the m/28-30, for the same reason. Some of the rifles had a brass disc inset into the buttstock showing the type and number of the unit to which they were issued, and the individual rack number of the rifle; these were ordered removed in 1941, probably for military security reasons.

Approximately 60,000 of the rifles were manufactured during the period 1927–1934 by Tikkakoski within the serial number range 20,000 to 81,000. VKT produced about 3,000 rifles with serial numbers ranging from 0001 to 3000; 1,000 to 2,600 are reported to have been produced in the period 1932–35, and the model continued in production until 1940. The m/27s were intended for the regular army rather than the Civil Guard, and were gradually replaced in service during and after 1940 by the m/39.

During the 1930s, the Finns also developed a sniper rifle based on the Mosin-Nagant and equipped with the *Physica* 3x telescope, produced by Physica Oy, an optics company in Helsinki. Sniper Rifles are discussed in detail in Chapter 4.

Between 1934 and 1945 1,400 m/27s were produced that were barreled and chambered for the .22 long rifle and .22 short cartridges, presumably as target rifles. The Finnish designation was Pienoiskivääri m/27.

Ratsuväenkivääri m/27

The Finns produced a cavalry version of the m/27 which was 1,110 mm (43.70 in) long, had a barrel length of 610 mm (24.01 in), and weighed 4.1 kg (9.02 lbs). It was thus 75 mm (2.95 in) shorter and 0.13 kg (about 4 oz.) lighter than the standard rifle.

The bolt handle was turned-down and the stock recessed to allow it to close. The carbine had a versatile sling-mounting system, consisting of a side-mounted sling bracket in a concave area on the right side of the buttstock based on the sling mounting system of the Mauser 98a (refer to Figure 1-43) and swivels on the underside of the buttstock and on the bottom and left side of the rear barrel band (refer to Figure 1-44). This system is somewhat similar to that used on the m/39 rifle.

Like the standard m/27 and other Finnish rifles some of the cavalry carbines had a brass unit-identification disk set into the buttstock. The cavalry disk markings are: URR (Uusimaa Dragoon Rgt.), RvAUK (Cavalry N.C.O. School), HRR (Häme Cavalry Rgt.),VEsk (Signal Squadron) and RatsPtri (Mounted Artillery Battery).

Approximately 2,500 m/27 cavalry rifles were produced by Tikkakoski in 1933–34, with serial numbers between 72800 to 74900; VKT produced an additional 200 barrels in 1937. For reasons which are obscure this project was soon scrapped, and the model is very rare.

Jalkaväenkivääri m/28

Similar to the m/27 is the *Sk. Y. Jalkaväenkivääri m/28* , adopted in August 1927 and first issued during the following year. The m/28 is a slightly heavier (at 4.18 kg, or 9.20 lbs) version of the m/27 with differently pitched rifling, an improved trigger, a somewhat different stock and a rear sight re-graduated to 850 meters, see Figure 3-10.

It also has a shorter barrel, 20,000 of which were made by SIG. "Schweizerische Industrie Gesellschaft" is stamped on the right side of these barrels, but is hidden by the stock; they were made in 1926 and 1927, and the year of manufacture can be seen as a "26" or "27" enclosed in a square stamped on the underside of the barrel just forward of the receiver.

The Tikkakoski factory made 13,016 barrels for this weapon, but

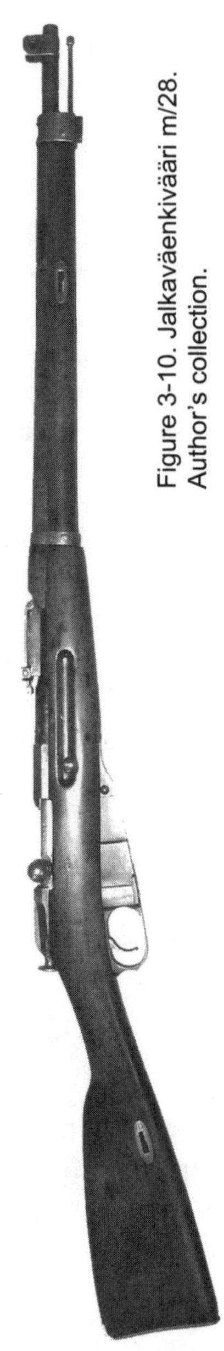
Figure 3-10. Jalkaväenkivääri m/28.
Author's collection.

these are undated. The m/28 can be instantly recognized by the letters SY (an early *Suojeluskunta* abbreviation) stamped on the receiver ring.

Occasionally one will find an m/28 with two sling slots in the buttstock, one about 1.5 in above the original Russian-placed slot. These were intended for use by ski-troops and the second sling slot provided better balance for the rifle.

Experience with nosecap problems led the Finns to develop a simplified nosecap for this model. It had a lug which accepted all the domestically developed knife-type bayonets: the m/27, m/28, m/28-30, m/35 Sk. Y., and m/39. There are two versions of this nosecap: the first is of two pieces (refer to Figure 1-35), and the second is a single-piece unit (refer to Figure 1-36) which was used on a succeeding model, the m/28-30, as well.

Some 30,000 m/28 rifles were fabricated — of existing Russian M1891 actions and the new barrels—between 1928 to 1933 at the Civil Guard's arsenal at Riihimäki, an enterprise which had recently (June 1, 1927) become SAKO (*Suojeluskuntain Ase- ja Konepaja Osakeyhtiö* , i.e., Civil Guard Arms & Machine-shop Co., Ltd.).

There was a transitional model between the m/28 and m/28-30 which is, to all intents and purposes, identical to the m/28 but has the m/28-30 type of rear sight. An unknown number were made, but they are not especially rare.

A Sniper Rifle version was developed from the m/28 but only nine were produced. Even so, the m/28 established the sniper rifle in Finnish military lore when Simo Hähya, a farmer in civilian life, became a national hero when he accounted for more than 500 Soviet soldiers with his m/28 during a 15-week period. See Chapter 4 for further details.

Jalkaväenkivääri m/28-30

A further variant of the m/27 is the *Jalkaväenkivääri m/28-30*. It was made for and used by the Civil Guard (*Suojeluskunta*), see Figure 3-11. This weapon has a Mauser-style tangent rear sight graduated to 2,000 meters and a somewhat heavier, SAKO-made barrel of Finnish-made Lokomo steel, with a 25 mm long aluminum sleeve around the barrel 90 mm behind the muzzle, enabling the barrel to "float" and thus improve accuracy. It weighs an additional 0.25 kg (0.55 lbs) but is otherwise like its predecessor except for an improved front sight, adjustable for windage, in the form of a circle of eight dots on the left side of the sight protector; each dot represents a gradation of 50 mm (1.96 in) at 100 meters (109.3 yards). Adjustments are made by using a slotted screwdriver or similar tool to turn the slot in the center of the dots. Refer to Figure 1-74.

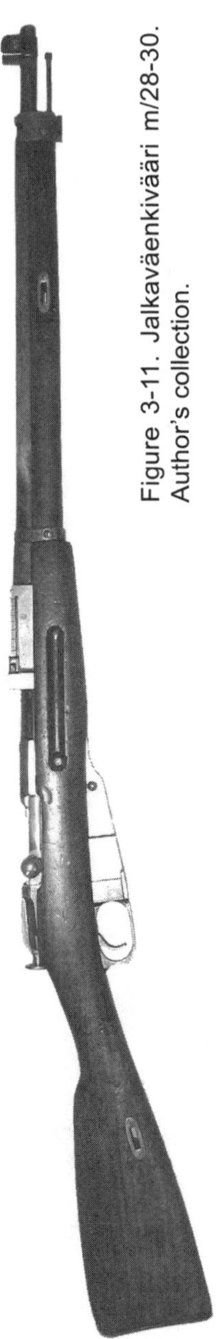

Figure 3-11. Jalkaväenkivääri m/28-30. Author's collection.

Approximately 36,000 m/28-30s were produced from 1933 to 1940. In 1938, SAKO changed its name to *Oy SAKO AB* and began to manufacture stocks for the first time. The m/28-30 was the first with SAKO-made stocks (serial number range: 34,000–70,000). During the years 1934–41 between 2,000 and 5,000 m/28-30s (reported totals vary significantly) were manufactured for the civilian market; these rifles are characterized by serial numbers in the 100,000 to 105,000 range. These rifles have a unique logo on the receiver: a capital "S" crowned with three fir sprigs, all in a

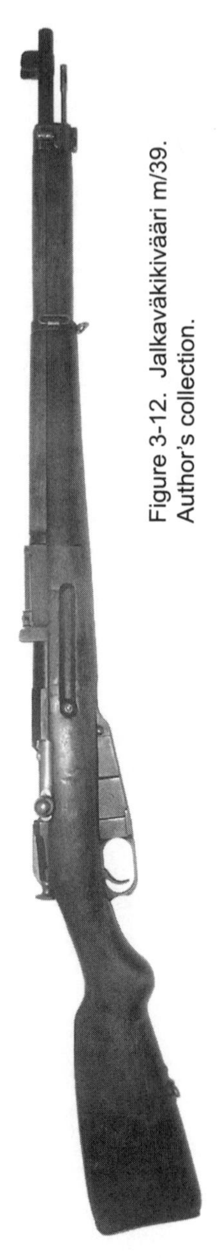
Figure 3-12. Jalkaväkikivääri m/39. Author's collection.

gear wheel, below which are the words, "SAKO RIIHIMÄKI". See Appendix C. Twenty-five m/28-30 rifles were adapted for sniping with the addition of German telescopic sights from the firms of Zeiss, Hensoldt and Busch. See Chapter 4.

The Jalkaväkikivääri m/39

Significant changes in the Finnish Mosin-Nagant occurred as a result of extensive redesign undertaken in 1938 by a committee consisting of consultants from the Finnish army, Civil Guard and Department of Defense. The new weapon was formally approved in 1939 and designated *Jalkaväkikivääri m/39* (Infantry Rifle M1939). See Figure 3-12. It was nicknamed the *Ukko-Pekka* ("Old Man Pekka") after Finnish President P.-E. "Pekka" Svinhufvud. This rifle differs from earlier models in having a pistol-grip stock (the first 5,000 or so were reported to have been made with a straight-wrist stock in 1940 and 1941) with a somewhat higher comb than earlier models, a feature which helps to reduce recoil. This model also has a wider chamber to accommodate the new Russian-designed "D" cartridge adopted in 1930. The Finns later captured huge quantities of this cartridge during both the Winter- and Continuation Wars. Thus, most Finnish-Mosin Nagants will be marked with a "D" on the receiver and, often, the stock indicating that the chamber was widened to accommodate the Finnish D166 bullet. The new "D" bullet weighed 11.82 gm (182 gr). Finnish rifle bores were tighter at 0.3082 to 0.3095 inch than Russian bores at 0.310 to 0.311 inch and there was a possibility of dangerously high pressures if the larger-diameter round was used in the tighter Finnish bores.

The new rifle also used a Soviet M1891/30-type two-piece interrupter-ejector. The front sight remained the same as in the m/28-30 but the aluminum barrel-sleeve was abandoned.

The m/39 was manufactured by SAKO, VKT, and Tikkakoski. The Tikkakoski rifles are, possibly, made from m/91 barrels shortened for the m/39 configuration, but this is unconfirmed. The smallest number of pre-1960s m/39s are those made by SAKO for the Civil Guard and marked "Sk. Y."

Some m/39s have a capital "B" stamped on the chamber in the usual place for a maker's logo. The significance of the "B" is a matter of controversy, with some proponents arguing that it signifies a Belgian-made barrel or barrel-blank, with others supporting the theory that it represents a product of the Swedish firm Boförs. The Belgian theory postulates that the barrels were from Russian weapons captured by the Germans and refurbished, probably at Fabrique Nationale in Liège. The more probable answer is that the barrel blanks were of new Belgian manufacture and made as barrels for Finland.

The forward barrel band is hinged with an improved version of that used on the m/27, but it differs in being hinged on the *left* and secured by a screw on the right running *perpendicular* to the stock — the opposite of the m/27 arrangement (refer to Figure 1-37). The rear barrel band is mounted with two sling swivels: one on the bottom and one on the left side, with corresponding hardware on the buttstock permitting the user to carry the rifle slung in two different ways. Refer to Figure 1-44.

In order to save weight a lighter barrel was developed, but the new weapon was nonetheless now up to a hefty 4.54 kg (10 lbs) — .44 kg (0.97 lb) more than the m/27, though the same length.

The m/39 continued in production until the Finns surrendered to the Russians in September of 1944, but some 1945-dated m/39s exist. Remarkably, about 5,500 m/39s were produced (probably assembled by SAKO, and largely from preexisting SAKO parts) from about 1967 until about 1972, reportedly as highly accurate target rifles for use in

Finnish military officer training.

The approximate serial number ranges for the m/39 are as shown in Table 3-1.

Table 3-1
m/39 Infantry Rifle Serial Number Ranges

Manufacturer	Serial Number Range
SAKO	200,000 to 259,278
VKT	28,690 to 67,680
B	35,814 to 48,703
Sk. Y.	500,000 to 510,588
Tikkakoski	26,999 to 67,680 (?)
SAKO 1967–73 (?)	300,800 (?) to 306,051

Note: In 1945 — not 1944 as is often reported — a controlling interest in SAKO was donated to the Red Cross, possibly to exempt the company from confiscation by the USSR as part of Finnish war reparations. SAKO then began to produce innocuous civilian goods for a brief period. In 1946 SAKO began manufacturing the L 46 rifle and the P 46 small bore rifle, and has continued in the arms business ever since. In 1962, the Red Cross transferred its shares to Suomen Kaapelitehdas Oy.

Jalkaväenkivääri m/91-30

The Finns captured over 28,300 Soviet M1891/30s in the Winter War of 1939–40, as well as thousands of battlefield pickups of varying degrees of preservation which were then used primarily for spare parts. After the Finns entered the war against the USSR in mid-1941, they acquired many thousands of additional rifles.

During 1943–1944 the Tikkakoski factory produced some 24,000 copies of the Soviet M1891/30 rifle in serial number range circa 50,000 to 74,000. The rifles consisted of Tikkakoski-made barrels and, mostly, new Finnish birch stocks and handguards. Other parts came from captured Soviet rifles bought from Germany in 1944; these were castoffs suitable only for cannibalizing for parts.

These rifles, according to one source (Bowser, *Rifles of the Snow*), were never issued and remained unused until they were sold as surplus in 1986. That being said, however, the author has seen numerous Finnish m/91-30s with considerable wear consistent with field use. The matter of whether or not they were issued during wartime remains open to debate. The apparent field wear may have stemmed from Finnish military service and training during the postwar years.

The Finnish m/91-30s are a stereotypical Finnish conglomeration of recycled receivers, magazines, and other parts, mated with new or recycled stocks and new, Finnish-made barrels. They can be identified not only by the usual Tikkakoski logo but by the front sight, which differs from the Soviet M1891/30 in that it is not hooded and is a blade (rather than a post). The sight and its base consist of three pieces interlocked one atop the other (refer to Figure 1-75). In keeping with Finnish preference the m/91-30 has sling swivels (identical to those of the other Finnish models) rather than slots. The stock is generally of the typical Finnish two-piece variety, although one-piece reused Russian stocks are encountered from time to time.

The m/91-30 is the only Finnish Mosin-Nagant model which employed a significant number of round — rather than polygonal — receivers. By 1944 the Finns had four years' worth of captured Soviet M1891/30s in inventory, which, presumably, had serviceable receivers but unusable barrels.

Like the Germans in both World Wars, the Finns captured a considerable number of weapons from the Russians during the Winter War (1939–1940) and the Continuation War (1941–1944) — an estimated 366,079 during the Continuation War alone, according to one source. At the same time, the flow could also work the other way. The author once observed an m/39 that had reportedly been captured by an American serviceman in Vietnam.

Thus, Finnish Mosin-Nagants of all models are commonly found today with Russian (tsarist or Soviet, or both) and Finnish markings, and are identifiable by the property stamp "SA" for *Suomen Armeija*

("Finnish Army"), enclosed in a rounded-corner square, on the receiver, barrel, etc. See Figure 3-13. It might be noted that the "SA" designation was introduced in 1942 to replace the earlier marking, "*Puolustuslaitos*", meaning "Defense Department", which was used briefly earlier that year.

Figure 3-13.

All rifles in the Finnish series are hybrids and consist of some combination of Finnish, Russian (both tsarist and Soviet), Swiss, German, Belgian, and even French or American parts from the original Châtellerault order and the World War I Remington-UMC and New England Westinghouse contracts. (See From Mother Russia to Uncle Sam—and Back in Chapter 2.)

Generally, Finnish-made items are of higher quality than their Soviet Russian counterparts. The stocks, for example, are often characterized by the reinforcing bolt placed neatly in the finger groove rather than sloppily installed off-center, Russian-fashion. On the subject of stocks, any stock made in two pieces, mortised with finger-joints on the underside forward of the receiver, is Finnish (though not *all* Finnish stocks are two-piece). This is one of several ways by which a Finnish original (or rework) can be instantly identified.

Another instant-identifier is the double-measurement rear sight found on derivatives of the M1891. This is the post-1908 tsarist-era sawtooth convex leaf sight with the original measurements in 100s of *arshini* stamped on the left side: 4, 6, 8, 10, and 12; these numerals almost always have a slash mark through them. On the right side of the sight, equivalents of the *arshini* are stamped in gradations of 100s of meters: 2, 3, 4, 5 1/2, 7, and 8 1/2; some altered sights begin their metric measurements with 2 1/2 or 3, rather than 2.

A block-letter capital "**M**," indicating metric, is stamped on this side of some of these rear sights. On some sights the "***m***" is lowercase, in script. Because of the expense and effort which would have been involved, the *arshini* graduations on the inside of the sight leaf were not altered.

The Finns did not manufacture receivers. They did not need to do so as they "inherited" enough rifles after independence, purchased enough in the interwar years and captured more than enough during their two wars with the Soviet Union.

Finnish Slings

Finnish Mosin-Nagant slings were made in both leather and webbing. The Finnish slings are narrower (1.0 inch) than the Russian slings (1.75 inches) and differ in color, the leather being gray, gray-green, black, or brown, and the webbing gray, gray-green, or khaki. The slings are usually marked with the Finnish military property stamp "SA" or the Civil Guard stamps "SY" or "Sk. Y." Finnish slings can also be easily recognized by the stud(s) securing one end of the sling around one of the "dog collars" or through a swivel. Russian webbing slings have a sewn end-loop through which the "dog collar" passes and do not require other fastenings. For a more detailed discussion of the various types of slings, see Chapter 6.

GERMANY

Although Germany did not produce Mosin-Nagants (Finnish-contract barrels excepted), the Russian warhorses did serve both Kaiser and Führer.

During the First World War enormous numbers of Russian M1891s were destroyed, lost or captured — as many as 240,000 per month. Many captured weapons were reissued by the Germans to their rear-echelon military units and navy. As early as November 6, 1914, 7,000 Russian rifles were already in German naval service, mainly for use by shore-based guards. An inventory of weapons at the Kiel naval facilities made in February 1918 lists 4,405 Russian rifles (Black, "Guns of the German Navy 1914–1918").

Early in World War I German U-boats and minesweepers destroyed floating mines by shooting at them with machine guns. As machineguns were more urgently needed in the land battles, beginning on 14 April 1915 they were replaced on U-boats by two captured Russian rifles per boat. By September the allocation for patrol boats was three Russian rifles per ship for minesweeping duties.

In order to adapt the large number of Mosin-Nagants they captured from the Russians to their own slings, bayonets, ammunition, etc., the Germans made a number of alterations to them in the form of different sling swivels, barrel bands, bayonet lugs, and so forth.

Some of these arms in German service were converted to fire standard German 8 x 57 mm ammunition, but the huge quantity of captured Russian cartridges made this largely unnecessary; nonetheless, as many as 30,000 rifles may have been so altered. In order to accommodate the different dimensions of the German 7.92 x 57 mm Mauser cartridge the converted weapons required alterations to the receiver, magazine box, charger-clip guide, etc. Rifles thus modified can easily be identified by the notch cut into the top receiver flat to accommodate the Mauser cartridge.

On some ex-Russian M1891s the front of the stock was cut away and a device with a bayonet lug installed in order that the German knife-type bayonet could be used in place of the Russian socket variety. This device was in the form of a blued steel sleeve 115 mm (4.53 in) long; the first 7 mm (0.275 in) section from the front is a tube 16 mm (0.629 in) in diameter, and the remainder of the sleeve was 20 mm (0.078 in) in diameter. The entire sleeve extends from approximately 2 mm (0.078 in) behind the muzzle crown to the point approximately 65 mm (2.56 in) from the front barrel band, where the stock and handguard have been cut to accommodate it. The sleeve was secured at its rear by a collar and two screws, one on each side of the barrel. There was a 10 mm x 10 mm (0.39 in x 0.39 in) cutout on top of the sleeve through which the front sight protrudes. On the right side of the sleeve, in front of the collar, was a bayonet lug 10 mm wide and 30 mm (1.18 in) long; it is marked on the underside with a crowned capital "S" in Gothic type, see Figure 3-14. The sleeve appears somewhat like that of Germany's *Reichs-Commissions* rifle (the *Gewehr* 88), see Figure 3-15.

A simpler adaptation was made in the form of a one-piece, Russian-style nosecap with a standard German bayonet lug as an integral part; the lug is located on the *left* side of the nosecap, unlike the lug on the sleeved adapter described above; there are other variations as well.

Russian Mosin-Nagants captured by the Germans were often marked "AZR" or "DEUTSCHES REICH" (the latter inscription usually accompanied by a German imperial eagle) on the stock or receiver or both. Most of these weapons which survived the War — and Versailles Treaty restrictions — in German hands were sold to Finland in the 1920s.

Figure 3-14.

As in World War I, during World War II the Germans captured many thousands of Russian weapons and reissued them to their allies and to police and other formations within the Reich. In conformity with the German system for designating captured and reissued weapons, the Russian arms were given assigned *Fremdgerät* ("foreign equipment") code numbers for administrative purposes. The Mosin-Nagant Infantry, Dragoon and Cossack rifles were designated *Gewehr* (rifle) 252(r), 253(r) and 254(r), respectively. The M1907 and M1938 carbines were styled *Karabiner* 453(r) and 454(r). Due to the late date of issuance of the M1944 carbine (February 1944) it may not have been given a separate code number although an unconfirmed report states that it was designated 457(r). In all instances the (r) identifies the weapon as *russisch* (Russian).

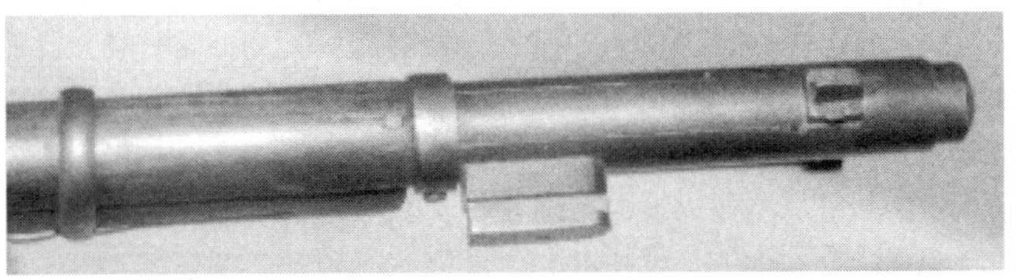

Figure 3-15. Model 1891 altered in Germany with a Mauser-type bayonet leg. Smithsonian Institution collection.

After World War II the M1944 continued in service with the Soviet-run East German regime; they can be seen, for example, in 1960s photographs of guards at the Berlin Wall and elsewhere. Some East German M1944s have the East German "1-in-a-triangle" proof mark stamped on the barrel, indicating a first-quality, or a similar "2" or "3" marking for inferior pieces. Refurbishing of these carbines was done at the Ernst Thaelmann works in Suhl.

In the mid-to-late 1960s some East German border guards who defected to the West brought with them a curious hybrid weapon in the form of M1891/30s professionally cut-down and nicely refinished into near-copies of the M1938 carbine. The opinion in *Bundeswehr* (West German Army) circles at the time was that the work had probably been done in East Germany or, possibly, Czechoslovakia, although there were no reported markings to indicate where the conversions were performed. The post-1989 consensus agrees on Czech origins.

HUNGARY

Good-quality copies of both the M1944 carbine and the M1891/30, including the receivers, were produced in Hungary in 1952–1955 and 1952–1954, respectively, by *Fémaru-Fegyver és Gépgyár* (FÉG) of Budapest. During this period the same company also manufactured a copy of the M1891/30 sniper rifle. Hungarian nomenclature for the M1944 was 44.M, and the M1891/30 was designated the 48.M. The company name in Hungarian translates to "Metal Goods, Weapon and Machine Factory."

Hungarian Mosin-Nagants are identifiable by the Communist-era national crest atop the receiver ring — below the date and above the serial number — but it is necessary to look carefully to distinguish it from a Soviet hammer-and-sickle. The Hungarian crest has a star at the top of a globe, a bar across the bottom, and a hammer — but no sickle: the object superimposed on the globe, crossing the hammer and facing right, is an ear of wheat. See Figure 3-16.

Figure 3-16.

Both the rifle and carbine may contain the occasional Russian part and are, generally, very well-made arms. Unlike their Russian counterparts the Hungarian M1944s have inspectors' marks on the bayonet bracket and the muzzle ring.

The stocks are marked with a "B" in a circle (for the Budapest arsenal) and may have "02" — the East Bloc code number for Hungary—as well; these markings are found on the right side of the butt. The bolt, magazine floorplate and butt plate are serial-numbered to the weapon.

These Hungarian-made rifles saw action in the hands of soldiers and civilians on both sides in the gallant but tragic Hungarian uprising against the Communist government and Soviet invaders during October-November 1956.

NORTH KOREA

North Korea allegedly produced an inferior copy of the M1891/30 rifle in the early 1950s, which is thought to have been designated the Type 30. In view of the industrial backwardness of the Hermit Kingdom and its lack of resources before, during and after the Korean War, however, it is unlikely that the North Koreans would have produced their own model of an obsolete rifle which had already been supplied to them in quantity by their Soviet and Chinese allies. That being said, the bizarre and overweening policy of *juche* ('consummate self reliance') conceived and brutally implemented by the late Great Leader Kim Il-Sung may well have prompted the North Koreans to undertake such an otherwise pointless project.

The North Korean rifles reportedly can be identified by a large bulky star in a circle preceding the serial number stamped on the left side of the receiver. Even if there are in fact no locally produced Mosin-Nagants this type of marking may have been applied to weapons furnished by the Soviets and Chinese.

At least as late as 1993, and probably thereafter, the M1891/30 *snayperskaya* rifle was a standard weapon in the North Korean military inventory, only gradually being replaced by the more modern Dragunov. From the very limited information and few photographs available it appears that both the M1891/30 sniper rifles and the Dragunovs are original Russian rifles rather than locally made products.

It has been alleged that a number of M1944 carbines were produced by Poland for the North Koreans, but were never shipped to them. Supposedly the Poles were able to recoup their losses on this contract by selling the weapons in the United States during the late 1990s.

Figure 3-17. Polish Model 91/98/25 rifle. Photo courtesy of 7.62x54r.net.

POLAND

Poland, with its common border and mostly unfortunate historical relations with Russia, produced a hybrid Mosin-Nagant during the 1920s. This weapon consisted of an original M1891, but with a new barrel in 7.92 mm caliber and the magazine and bolt-head reworked to permit use of the 8 x 57 mm rimless Mauser cartridge. The characteristic Mosin-Nagant sling slots were supplemented with swivels on the left side of the barrel band and buttstock, resulting in a configuration more German than Russian. The old-fashioned socket bayonet was dispensed with, an "H"-form nosecap and bayonet lug being fitted to accept Poland's wz.24 Mauser-type knife bayonet. The first of these altered rifles was designated the *wz. 91/98/23* from *wzor* ("model") 91 (the M1891 Mosin-Nagant) /98 (the 1898 Mauser Cartridge) and /23 (1923, the year the rifle was adopted). In some publications this rifle is called the "Polish Mauser *wz. 91/98/23*", but Poles regard that designation as incorrect. Not long thereafter, minor changes in the receiver, ejector and cleaning rod resulted in the *wz. 91/98/25* (one sees this model — though rarely — referred to as the *wz. 91/98/26*, but this appears to be erroneous, see Figure 3-17.

About 77,000 of these rifles were produced. They will have a prominent Polish eagle stamped on the chamber, together with the actual bore diameter (7.92, 7.93, etc.). These rifles were used principally by the gendarmeri, cavalry, and the horse-drawn artillery, and were soon replaced on active service by the M29 Mauser, after which they were issued to National Police, border guards and reserve units. At the outbreak of World War II in September 1939, there were approximately 76,400 Mosin-Nagants in the Polish government's inventory.

The M1944 carbine was manufactured in Poland for many years after the Second World War. Although production began under license in 1950, this carbine was being made in Poland somewhat earlier, at least by 1948; the Poles bgan to produce Mosin-Nagant ammunition in 1946. The M1944 carbine was produced in Poland until at least 1962, and only at the factory at Radom. One Polish source reports that M1944 bayonets of the first type were made there beginning in 1945, with the production of the second type starting in 1950. (See Chapter 5, Bayonets.) Polish-made M1944 bayonets are marked with the letter "y". The Polish M1944 carbine was in production at least as late as 1962 and can be identified by Polish factory markings on the barrel, receiver and stock. The principal identifier is a large numeral "11" — the Radom arsenal code number — within an oval on the receiver ring, and various marks (many of which are found within a diamond) on both the metal parts and the stock. Poland was still using the M1944 as part of military basic training in the early 1980s. See Figure 3-18.

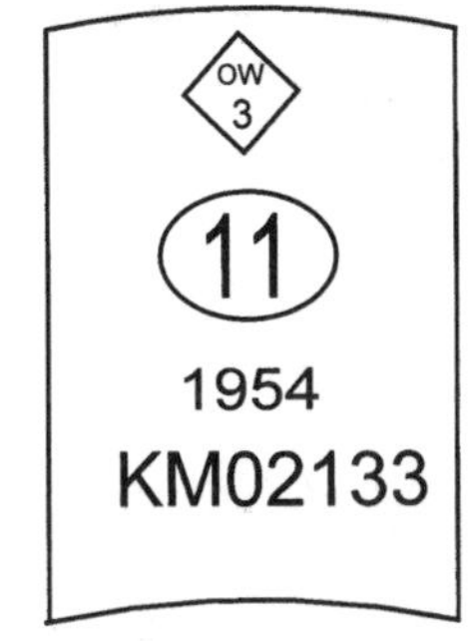

Figure 3-18.

It has been reported that a number of Polish M1944s were produced for North Korea but never delivered. It is believed that they were exported to the United States during the later 1990s.

The M1891/30 sniper rifle was used by the Poles, generally in the form of Soviet *snayperskaya* which they refurbished. Polish M1891/30 sniper rifles can be identified by the mounting rails which are serial-numbered to the scope.

Poland also produced a single-shot trainer in .22 Long rifle caliber, called the *5.6 mm karabinek sportowy wz. 1948* ("5.6 mm sport carbine M1948"). Although this rifle closely resembles a Mosin-Nagant in many external features — its stock, barrel bands, rear sight, ring-and-post front sight, etc., — it is actually not a Mosin-Nagant design at all,

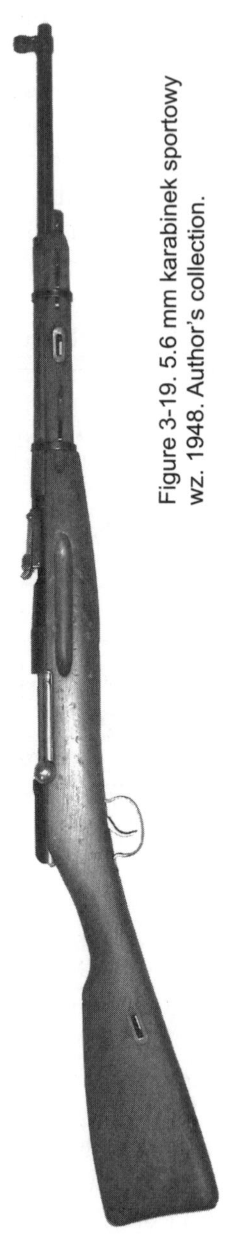
Figure 3-19. 5.6 mm karabinek sportowy wz. 1948. Author's collection.

but a simplified version of Poland's *karabinek sportowy wz. 1931* ("M1931 sporting carbine"). It is described here because it is usually mistaken for a member of the Mosin-Nagant family, see Figure 3-19.

The M1948 was used for training and sports by the Polish military, paramilitary untis, schools, and sport clubs. It appears to have been made from 1948 to 1958, and only at Radom.

On the left side of the top of the M1948 rear sight are gradations in meters, marked 25, 50, 75 and 100; to their right are three sets of four horizontal dashes indicating 5-meter increments. Specifications for the M1948: overall length 1,130 mm (44.49 in.); barrel length 630 mm (24.8 in.); weight 3.8 kg. (8.36 lb.): number of barrel grooves, 6; muzzle velocity, 350 m/sec. (1,148 ft/sec.).

Polish Mosin-Nagant "dog collar" slings are virtually the same as their Russian counterparts, but were also made of a synthetic material, somewhat like nylon, in a medium shade of green as well as the more familiar khaki webbing. During World War II the Soviet type of sling common to submachine guns was often seen on M1944s used by Polish army units. The reason is unknown, but the Poles evidently favored the idea as they continued to make and issue this sling well after the war.

ROMANIA

During the 1950s the Romanians manufactured their own version of the M1944 carbine, probably on machinery provided—in part—by the Soviets. It is possible, even probable, however, that the Romanian carbines are recycled Soviet M1944s refinished in Romania and containing some locally made parts.

This weapon is can be distinguished from Russian models by its markings, the most prominent of which is on the receiver: a small arrowhead in a triangle below a laurel wreath containing the letters RPR (for *Republica Populara Romana* – Romanian People's Republic).

There are two common Romanian marks found on metal parts: 1) "C" in a triangle and 2) an arrowhead in a triangle. This last is nearly identical to the Soviet Izhevsk arsenal marking, but is an arrowhead only in a triangle (see Figure 3-20) while the Izhevsk mark uses a complete arrow with fletching, upright and within a triangle (See Appendix C: Identification and Attribution). As the laurel wreath containing the letters "RPR" is very similar to the Izhevsk arsenal mark, care must be taken to distinguish between the two, especial on worn specimens. Romanian stocks are marked with a "C" within a diamond.

Figure 3-20. Romanian receiver marking on M1944 Carbine.

SPAIN

Although Spain did not produce the Mosin-Nagant, tens of thousands were used there during the Spanish Civil War (1936–39), and ammunition for the rifle was made at munitions factories in Toledo and Seville. For more on Spanish ammunition, see Chapter 7.

The Soviet Union, which backed the "Loyalist" side (i.e., the leftist Spanish government which had been in power since 1931), sold it thousands of M1891 and M1891/30 rifles in varying conditions; the Loyalists also bought Mosins from other suppliers such as Poland. At the beginning of August 1937 there were 209,160 Mosins in the Spanish government's inventory; some 281,670 Mosins were delivered to Spain in 1937–38, including 25,000 of "questionable" quality.

U.S. Mosins from the World War I production were sent to Spain from Mexico. Early in 1937, the Mexican government, which was sympathetic to the far-left Loyalist government, donated some Mosins to it. The rifles were received in very poor condition and were issued to the International Brigades, which consisted of foreign Communists and other leftist sympathizers from a number of countries, including the U.S. Additionally, the Spanish ambassador to Mexico, Félix Gordón Ordás, purchased a number of Mosins in Mexico. The first shipment of 1,000 rifles was dispatched on 19 February 1937 on the ship *Mar Cantábrico,* but was captured at sea by the Nationalist cruiser *Canarias* on 8 March. (The Nationalists were rebel forces led by Gen. Francisco Franco, supported by Italy and Germany. They won.) Ordás sent another 500 Mosins in October-December 1937, and 500 more after that.

One shipment to the "Abraham Lincoln Brigade" (an International Brigade unit consisting mainly of American leftists), which reportedly contained both tsarist- and Soviet-marked Mosins, was found to be wrapped in Mexican newspapers when the crates were opened. The rifles were dubbed "Mexicanskys"; the name stuck for all Mosins, at least among some of the foreigners fighting in Spain. Spanish government "regular" military forces were not issued Mosins: they were given, as noted above, to the International Brigades, and to local militias called the Ejército Popular ("People's Army").

In the late 1950s and early '60s a number of these Mosins were imported into the U.S. from Spain; they are recognizable by a circle containing the words "Made in USSR" stamped on the buttstock, which had to be done to conform to U.S. import laws.

TURKEY

Like their German and Austrian allies the Turks captured large numbers of Mosin-Nagants from the Russians during World War I, which they reissued to some of their own troops, mostly in eastern Anatolia. The Germans also gave the Turks a number of Mosin-Nagants which had been captured on the Eastern Front; some of these had been altered to fire the standard German military 7.92 mm Mauser cartridge.

In the wake of the Russian collapse in 1917 and subsequent Civil

War, many White army deserters and other anti-Bolshevik Russians crossed the frontier into Turkey, seeking asylum. Some brought their weapons with them and these were confiscated.

Ex-Russian Mosin-Nagants were used by the Turks not only during the First World War but during the Turkish War of Independence, and the war against the Greeks in the early 1920s. These weapons were retained as a reserve until at least the late 1940s. Some rifles reportedly had their sight graduations overstamped with Arabic numerals. A Turkish crescent moon can be found stamped on various parts of captured rifles, including the stock.

UNITED STATES OF AMERICA

In November 1914 the Russian government, plagued by a severe shortage of small arms early in World War I, contracted with the Winchester Repeating Arms Co. to supply 293,816 Winchester Model 95 rifles (in Russian nomenclature *Vintovka Vinchestera obrazets 1915-ago goda*, i.e., Winchester Rifle M1915) but utilizing the standard Russian 7.62 x 54 mm R round; Winchester also furnished the bayonets for these arms and tens of millions of rounds of ammunition.

The following year the Tsarist government ordered 1.5 million M1891 infantry rifles, 100,000,000 rounds of ammunition and socket bayonets from Remington Arms-Union Metallic Cartridge Co. This order encountered problems even before production began, when Remington's engineers discovered that the sample rifles and the production diagrams submitted by the Russians were substantially different from each other. Remington had to redraft the working drawings and make other changes to the design before production could commence.

New England Westinghouse received an order for 1.8 million rifles and socket bayonets. Although they were produced between 1915–1918, all New England Westinghouse Mosin-Nagants are dated 1915.

These American-made rifles are instantly identified by the company names, "Remington Armory" or "New England Westinghouse" stamped on the breech above the chamber.

There are two styles of Westinghouse inscription, both used during 1915. On the earlier rifles, the words, "New England" are arched above the Imperial Eagle; on the later rifles, the entire inscription is stamped below the eagle in straight lines.

(Tsarist Imperial Eagle)
П
Remington
Armory
1917
№
53487

(Tsarist Imperial Eagle)
New England
Westinghouse
Company
1915 Г
902163
АНГЛЙСКИ ЗАКАЗЪ
A

The Westinghouse order is the more interesting one: the machinery at New England Westinghouse's Chicopee Falls, Massachusetts, plant was owned by the British government, and the government of Great Britain was the guarantor of payment for rifles made under the contract; to all intents and purposes, the United Kingdom was acting as Nicholas II's co-signer, which is the reason for the words (АНГЛЙСКИ ЗАКАЗЪ "Angliskii Zakaz" — "English Contract") in Cyrillic letters within a circle stamped on the left buttstock of New England Westinghouse rifles.

Westinghouse executives had been quietly soliciting the American government for a contract for these rifles almost from the day they began making them for the Russians in 1915. On February 10, 1916, Westinghouse's vice-president Osborne advised Brigadier General William Crozier, Chief of the Ordnance Corps, that they were manufacturing "the Russian Military rifle, the so-called Moissen[sic]-Nagant 3 line rifle" and that "this arm, with some very slight modifications, can be adapted to use the United States Government standard ammunition", in case "an emergency should arise" and the U.S. government might need another small arm. The War Dept. responded four (!) days later, and expressed its interest in the matter.

In the period 1915–1917, 840,310 rifles were manufactured by Remington-UMC and 770,000 by Westinghouse, of which 131,400 and 225,260, respectively, were delivered to Russia by January 1917. In fact, Remington manufactured 5,000 rifles per day at peak production and Westinghouse approached 160,000 rifles per month according to a letter from the company's Director of Tests to the Chief of Ordnance, dated August 9, 1915.

Both Remington and New England Westinghouse took longer to tool-up and produce the rifles than had been anticipated, and in October 1916 NEW had produced only 9% of their contract and Remington 12.5%. Annoyed by the delays the head of the Russian contract commission, General A. K. Zalyubovski, recommended transferring the Remington weapons machinery to Yekaterinoslav, Russia, where preparations were underway to construct a new arms factory. The matter was overtaken by events when the imperial government fell and the Tsar abdicated in February 1917.

The Russian government, however, defaulted on these contracts after the revolution of February 1917, claiming that the weapons failed to meet Russian quality standards. The Russians' objections to the U.S.-produced rifles were largely that some had a "weak mainspring," the ejector/extractor did not fit properly into the slot in the receiver, and the edges of the magazine box were too sharp and might cut hands. Russian dissatisfaction was evidently limited, as the American-Russian production commission was considering an additional order of 2.7 million rifle barrels as late as 1917.

The American-made rifles were in fact of better quality than those produced in Russia; the Russian rejection of these arms was the result of political and military chaos at home and a simple unwillingness to spend the money. Indisputable proof that these rifles were perfectly acceptable to the Russian government is found in the large volume of correspondence still extant in which the Russians negotiated — and obtained — the option to purchase the weapons even after the U.S. government agreed to take over the contracts in January 1918.

For reasons that remain obscure, in March 1917, the Russian Main Artillery Administration — which controlled small-arms production—sent an unreported number of American-made Mosin-Nagants to military workshops "for inspection." Lacking the resources for whatever tasks were required, the workshops sent the rifles to the Moscow Artillery Depot; evidently the staff there also did not know what to do with them as they were then sent to the arsenal at Kiev where some, or all, were fitted with Russian-made bolts.

The costs to Remington and Westinghouse for tooling-up and other expenses incidental to the Russian contracts were substantial. In order to save the American manufacturers from serious financial damage caused by the Russian default, the U.S. government eventually purchased the balance of the undelivered weapons and a continuing output as well: 200,000 from Westinghouse, and 600,000 from Remington at $30.00 per rifle. The initial U. S. contract with Remington, in January 1918, was for 78,950 rifles which had already been produced and inspected and were sitting in Remington's Bridgeport, Connecticut, warehouses waiting for someone to pay for them.

Even so, Remington claimed to have lost about $300,000 on the Russian contract. Still, this was better than the original $10 million loss estimated upon default. The Russian government had been responsible for payment for the first 1 million rifles, and it was the U.S. government's assuming the obligation for the 600,000 that kept the company out of serious financial difficulties.

Westinghouse's production for the U.S. government began on January 4, 1918. The Russians did not want to foreclose their options in the matter, and agreed to pay one-half the salary of the ninety-seven Russian inspectors remaining at the Westinghouse plant after January 1918. An agreement was reached with the U.S. government shortly thereafter that if the Russians later decided to purchase the post-January 4th production, they would reimburse the Americans for the other half of the inspectors' salaries and, conversely, if the Americans kept the rifles, the U.S. government would reimburse the Russians. As a further compromise it was agreed that both Russian *and* American markings would be placed on the rifles, and that crates packed for shipment to Russia would have discreet U.S. government ownership markings on them in addition to the prominent Russian government indicia. The Russians — then as now hard-up for hard currency — also sold the U.S. 200,000 rounds of their Westinghouse "proof and target ammunition" still at Chicopee.

According to one prominent source the total U.S. purchase from the two manufacturers was in excess of one million (Walter, *Rifles of the World*), although that does not accord with the documentation. Of these rifles, 208,050 were reportedly kept for training American troops during the war and briefly thereafter. Rifles retained for American military use were officially designated the "Russian 3 Line Rifle" by the U.S. Army Ordnance Corps' Engineering Division in July 1918, and were marked with the Ordnance Corps' 'flaming bomb' and other indicia such as an American eagle.

After enough parts had been manufactured to assemble 200,000 rifles under the American government contract, Westinghouse's Mosin-Nagant machinery was shut down and the production line changed over in order to produce Browning machine guns, according to a letter dated June 14, 1918, from Westinghouse's J.E. McCusker, Chief Inspector, Ordnance Department, to Captain E.E. Chapman, Army inspector of Ordnance (O.O. War Department Document 474.4/449).

The American-made Mosin-Nagants were issued to state militias, home guard units and Army training units. The shortage of training and rear-echelon rifles in America during World War I was so acute that a good many Krag rifles were put back into service as well.

After the Armistice on November 11, 1918 the U.S. Army quickly lost interest in the Mosin-Nagant: Rock Island Arsenal officials advised the Ordnance Corps as early as January 10, 1919, that they already had 15,000 Russian rifles so in need of immediate cleaning and repair that they would "be worthless within a few years".

After World War I many of the American government-purchased rifles were sold to foreign countries such as Mexico, while others were sold as commercial surplus in the United States during the 1920s. A number of U.S.-made Mosin-Nagants were off-loaded by the Director of Civilian Marksmanship for the princely sum of $3.00 each: exactly one-tenth of their cost to the government. Some of the rifles were reworked for the standard American .30-06 round — they are marked as such on the receiver — and can still be found either unaltered or 'sporterized' into hunting or target rifles.

One of the principal conversions to .30-06 was done by Bannerman's — the great New York City military surplus house — and was accomplished in two different configurations. One of the major reworks entailed shortening the chamber noticeably and reaming it out to accept the wider .30-06 cartridge: "[t]he barrels were removed and about an inch cut off the rear. This removed the part of the chamber too large for the .30-'06. The barrels were then rethreaded, rechambered for the new round and reinstalled into the receivers (Malloy, "America's Russian Fascist Rifles"). In the other Bannerman 'improvement' the rifle was chopped into a bent-bolt sporter. In both conversions the bolt face and extractor were modified to accommodate the different cartridge and the magazine was widened for the same reason.

Caution: The conversion to .30-06 was ***not*** done to modern standards regardless of how it was accomplished. The chamber dimensions vary considerably and may produce pressures far in excess of normal. These converted Mosin-Nagant rifle can be ***very*** dangerous and should not be fired; they are best kept as collector's display items. The author and publisher recommend that the firing pin be cut off or removed so that the rifle cannot be fired.

After World War I, a number of short Mosin-Nagants were assembled — evidently by the Stevens Arms Company — from parts made by Remington for the Russian contract. These rifles were cut down to approximately 43 inches to simulate the Model 1903 Springfield, and were sold commercially for training purposes to military schools such as The Citadel; they are sometimes called "cadet rifles" for that reason. As Springfields were still in very short supply due to the war, this was a way of meeting a need and reaping a small windfall from what otherwise would have been scrap metal. These rifles are commonly found with a month-and-year assembly date on the barrel or receiver, under the wood; they do not have regular serial numbers.

Purchasers of a World War I surplus Mosin-Nagant who wanted a more conventional rifle could have it sporterized by the Stoeger Arms Corporation of New York, known — in its own advertising, anyway — as "America's Great Gun House". This service was not cheap: $24.00 sounds like a bargain, but in 1939 it was the equivalent of a little over $348.00 in current dollars; the $7.50 French walnut stock would set you back about $109.00 in today's money, see Figure 3-21.

314 STOEGER ARMS CORPORATION 507 FIFTH AVENUE, NEW YORK, N. Y.

PEERLESS REMODELING OF ENFIELDS

DROP, FROM LINE OF SIGHTS, ABOUT 2 x 2⅝"
LENGTH, ABOUT 13¾"
WEIGHT, ABOUT 9 LB. 2 OZ.

ENFIELD MODEL 1917 WITH PEERLESS REMODELING

1. Cutting barrel to 22 inches or 24 inches, round, refinish and polish muzzle.
2. Fitting hooded matted ramp sight with bead.
3. Milling off ears of military sight, refinishing and polishing.
4. First class rebluing of barrel and receiver.
5. Supplying and fitting Redfield Receiver Sight No. 102R.
6. Supplying and fitting Stoeger's Peerless Stock, as described above, complete with all fittings.

Price $27.50

PEERLESS ENFIELD STOCK

This stock is completely finished, as illustrated, with steel butt plate, black forend tip, pistol grip cap, cheek-piece, and detachable swivels.

Ready to attach to rifle........ $12.50
Extra for checkered forearm..... 3.00
Extra for checkered pistol grip... $2.50
Extra for French Walnut....... 2.50

UNFINISHED PEERLESS ENFIELD STOCK

This stock is rough turned without accessories. (See preceding page.)

Price $5.00
Extra for French Walnut.......... 2.50

LEFT HAND STOCKS

Available *only* for Enfields, check-piece on right side and cast-in stock. Finished or unfinished. Extra ... $1.00

ENFIELD SERVICE RIFLE, MODEL 1917, AS ISSUED

The Enfield Rifle, Model 1917, lends itself particularly well to Stoeger's Peerless Remodelling. In its original form it has very poor lines for anything but military use. Because of its particularly well-constructed action, which is even more rugged than that of the Springfield Model 30-06, and its excellent barrel, chambered for the famous Government 1906 Cartridge, it is fundamentally a distinctly first-rate modern arm and practically identical in construction to the present Remington Model 30 Sporting Rifle.

When remodeled by us, the unsightly military rear sight ears are milled off and the bridge neatly filed, polished, and blued. The original sights are replaced with a handsome matted ramp sight with hood, and a Redfield Peep Sight attached in the rear. The Peerless Stock for this model is recessed to accommodate the regulation bent magazine, thus presenting the pleasing lines illustrated, and yet looking neat when viewed from below.

The Enfield Rifle, Model 1917, can be procured at a cost of $7.50 from the Director of Civilian Marksmanship by any member of the National Rifle Association, Barr Building, Washington, D. C.

DROP FROM LINE OF SIGHTS 2 x 2⅝ INCHES, LENGTH ABOUT 13¾ INCHES, WEIGHT 8½ POUNDS

THE REMODELED RUSSIAN 7.62 RIFLE WITH PEERLESS REMODELING

1. Cutting barrel to 24" round, refinish and polish muzzle.
2. Fit hooded matted ramp with bead sight.
3. Polishing barrel and first class rebluing of barrel and receiver.
4. Supplying and fitting Pacific Model R-1 adjustable windage bolt sight.
5. Supplying and fitting Peerless stock as described on page 21.

Price $24.00

UNFINISHED PEERLESS STOCK FOR RUSSIAN RIFLE CALIBER 7.62 MM.

The stock is rough turned without accessories. See page 21.

Price $5.00
Extra for French walnut.............. 2.50

THE PEERLESS RUSSIAN RIFLE CALIBER 7.62 MM. STOCK

This stock is completely finished as illustrated, with steel butt plate, pistol grip cap, cheek piece and detachable swivels.

Ready to attach to rifle......... $12.50
Extra for checkered forend...... 3.00
Extra for checkered pistol grip.... $2.50
Extra for French walnut........ 2.50

DROP FROM LINE OF SIGHTS ABOUT 1⅞ x 2¾ INCHES, LENGTH ABOUT 13¾ INCHES, WEIGHT 8¼ POUNDS (N.M.)

THE WINCHESTER MODEL 54 WITH PEERLESS STOCK

Supplying and fitting Stoeger's Peerless Stock, as described, complete with *all fittings* to Winchester Model 54 .... $12.50
Unfinished Peerless Stock for Winchester Model 54.......... 5.00
Finished Peerless Stock for Winchester Model 54.......... 12.50
Extra for Finished Walnut.......... 2.50

ALL SHIPMENTS ARE INSURED

Fig. 3-21. A page from a post-World War I Stoeger catalog offering a "sporterized" Mosin-Nagant.

A large number of the U.S. government-purchased M1891 rifles and considerable supplies of ammunition were sent to the Siberian port of Vladivostok during the Russian Civil War to arm the White Russian armies opposing the Bolsheviks. In December 1918 seventy-seven thousand of the Remington M1891 rifles were shipped directly from Remington's Bridgeport, Connecticut, factory to Vancouver, Canada, where they were turned over to representatives of the government of the new nation of Czechoslovakia. These rifles were earmarked for the Czech Legion, a group formed mostly of Austro-Hungarian Czech ex-prisoners of war, who constituted what was technically a unit of the Russian Army but which was actually under French command. The Legion also fought on the Western and Italian fronts. Contrary to "gun show lore" this was not a clandestine operation, and contemporary correspondence and reports on the matter were not even classified. The rifles were sent through Canada because Vancouver was the closest and most convenient port to Vladivostok.

By the time of the Bolshevik revolution in 1918 the Legion was about 100,000 strong, and was co-opted by the Allies to join the White Russian forces against the Bolsheviks. After trying unsuccessfully to fight their way back home to Central Europe along the Trans-Siberian Railway, members of the Legion were evacuated through Vladivostok and eventually reached Czechoslovakia. One of the tasks of the U.S. expeditionary force in Siberia was to help to safeguard the Czechs' evacuation.

At about the same time as the Siberian venture, approximately 5,000 American servicemen were sent to participate in the 1918–1920 Allied intervention in Russia. Although this was primarily a British, French and American operation, Japanese, Serbs, Italians and Czechs also participated.

Then, as now, no one knew exactly why they were involved, what they were supposed to do, and how they were supposed to do it. Nominally, the principal task of the Allied forces was to prevent the Bolshevik government from selling stockpiles of Allied-furnished supplies and weapons to the Germans after the Russians withdrew from World War I in March of 1918. As the Russian transport infrastructure was extremely primitive, the new government weak and disorganized, and a civil war was beginning, this was never a realistic possibility. These facts evidently were never recognized, due in no small part to inferior Allied intelligence collection and reporting. One hundred thirty-nine Americans died in that weird little non-war with nothing whatsoever to show for it.

Many U.S.-made Mosin-Nagants were issued to the bewildered American soldiers who served in the Arctic port city of Archangel (the U.S. troops in Vladivostok had been sent there directly from the Philippines and were armed with M1903 Springfields). The U.S. government hoped that the troops could obtain ammunition locally and thereby reduce the costs and logistical problems of supplying the expedition. Ironically, most of these weapons (thoroughly disliked by the soldiery, who preferred the shorter and more accurate 1903 Springfield) were simply abandoned in Russia when the American forces withdrew in March 1920, thereby ending up where they were contracted to be sent in the first place — but at the expense of American, not Russian, taxpayers.

Most of the rifles sent to Vladivostok remained there in storage depots, where some were destroyed in fires and explosions — accidentally and by sabotage — and others rusted away from simple neglect. The arms dumps were left in Japanese care when the Western Allies withdrew. The Reds seized some of these supplies when they overran the area in 1922; but before then the Japanese, ignoring repeated pleas from the U.S. and British governments to destroy the arms and munitions, gave many of them — or sold them cheaply — to a Manchurian warlord named Chang Tso-lin (and probably to other similar types) in return for political influence.

The Pedersen Device

A very small number of American-made M1891s were reportedly altered as part of the Pedersen Device experiments. The Pedersen Device, named after its inventor, Remington firearms designer John D. Pedersen, was a project undertaken in great secrecy by the United States during World War I to enable the M1903 Springfield service rifle to be quickly converted to semiautomatic fire — and back — by means of a device which replaced the conventional rifle's bolt, see Figure 3-22. So secret was the device that it was designated the "U.S. Automatic Pistol, Caliber .30, Model of 1918" in an attempt to mislead any Central Powers spies.

This rather basic blowback device had a unique slide, chamber and feed system desig to use a short .30 round similar to France's 7.65 mm pistol cartridge. The war e before the device could be fully tested, and in 1931 all but about twenty of the 65,00 vices, and 60,000,000 rounds of the peculia ammunition, were destroyed. An unknow very small number of Pedersen devices esc destruction by various illegal subterfuges.

Fig. 3-22. The Pedersen Device. L-r: web magazine pouch, magazine and cartridges, blowback device, metal belt container. Photo courtesy of Remington Arms Company.

In previous editions,the continued tence of the any of the Mosin-Nagant rifles in the Pedersen Device trials was uncertai

Recently, a private collector has sup a photograph of a Mosin-Nagant modifie the Pedersen device. The rifle, in his collec has been verified by Remington Arms and b Remington company historian, Roy Marcot. left receiver rail was partially cut away in a c that would allow the empty cartridge cas eject (arrow). The rifle shown was manufact by Remington at Bridgeport as a test rifle fo Pedersen device and is not serial numbere

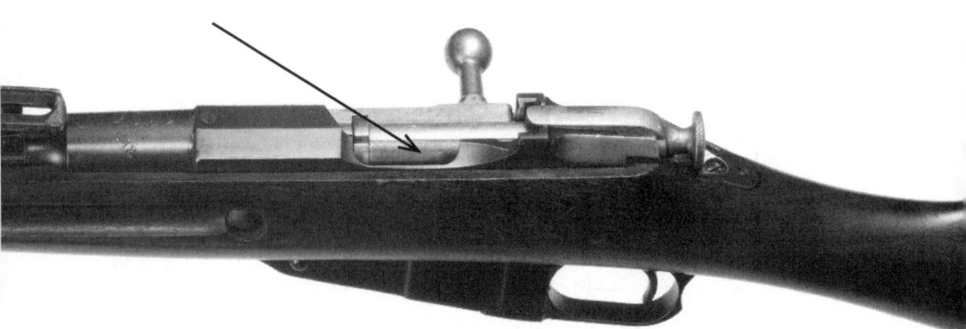

Fig. 3-23. A Mosin-Nagant Rifle modified for the semiautomatic .30 caliber Pedersen Device (U Automatic Pistol, Caliber .30, Model of 1918) by Remington-UMC for trials.

ma Pavlov, from the
ge of Podgrama in the
ov Region, poses for the
era with his dragoon
gunskaya) rifle and saber
March 1, 1915.

Chapter 4
Sniper Rifles

Russian Mosin-Nagant Sniper Rifles

In 1932 it was recommended as part of the military reforms in the Soviets' First Five-Year Plan that the M1891/30 be adapted for snipers. Rifles selected for their accuracy were retrofitted with longer, turned-down bolt handles; this permitted a scope to be mounted without interference from the bolt. Beginning with the 749 units assembled in 1932, some 185,000 sniper's rifles are believed to have been assembled by 1945, with 1942 probably the peak production year with an output of 53,195 units. The final year of production was 1947, although these rifles remained in inventory for decades thereafter, and can usually be found arsenal-refurbished. See Figure 4-1.

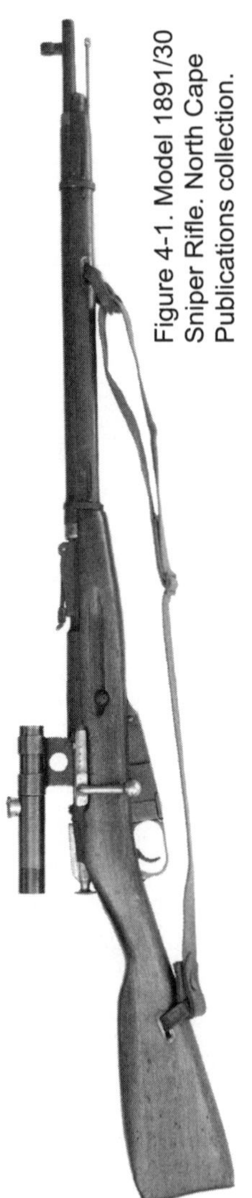

Figure 4-1. Model 1891/30 Sniper Rifle. North Cape Publications collection.

The original scope for this weapon was the 4x Model PT, which was reportedly made for the Soviets by the Carl Zeiss optics company in Jena, Germany. They are dated from 1932 to 1935, see Figure 4-2. The scope is 274 mm (10.78 in) long and weighs 598 gms (1.31 lbs). A Soviet-made variation of this model, called the VP (or PEM), was produced in 1936–1940, see Figure 4-3. Unlike the PT, the VP rear objective cannot be focused.

The PT and VP were replaced in about 1940 (one source says early 1942), by the smaller and lighter 3.5x PU (length: 169 mm [6.65 in], weight: 270 gms [9.52 oz.]), which was origi-

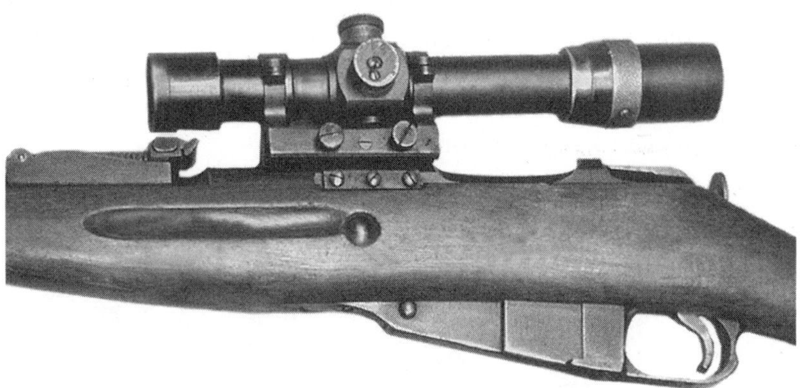

Figure 4-2. Model 1891/30 Sniper Rifle with the PT telescopic sight and first type mount. Ralph Denton collection.

nally developed for sniper use with the semiautomatic Tokarev M1940 rifle (the SVT-40). PT and VP scopes were mounted either over the chamber itself (early style), or on the left side of the receiver (later style), depending on the type of mount used.

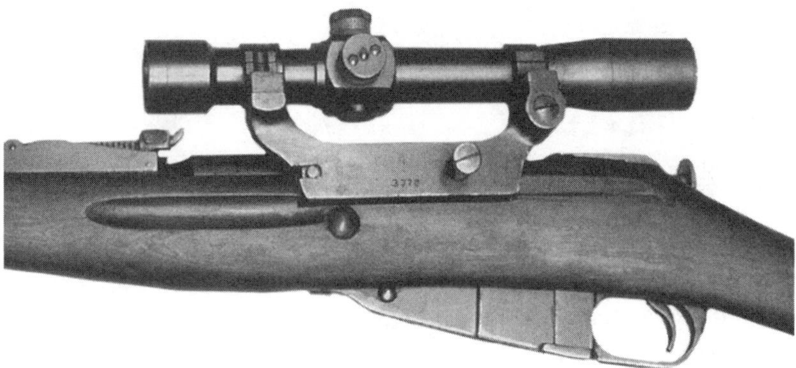

Figure 4-3. Model 1891/30 Sniper Rifle with the VP telescopic sight with the second type mount. Ralph Denton collection.

The PU, with its improved mount, was attached to the left of the receiver, see Figure 4-4. PU scopes made during the Second World War are marked with the Muscova Optical Works' logo, a pentagram containing a star over a moon. Below this is the serial number, the first two digits of which — typically 43 or 44 — indicate the year of manufacture.

The M1891/30 in sniper configuration retained conventional iron sights regardless of the type of scope used.

Figure 4-4. The PU telescopic sight with the long rail mount. North Cape Publications collection.

Note: Scope *mounts* serial-numbered to the individual rifle are reputed to be Polish rather than Russian. On many post–World War II Polish sniper rifles the scope's serial number was stamped on the left side of the receiver just above the stock; this was not done on Soviet rifles.

The designation "PE" is often found in the literature referring to certain Russian sniper scopes. PE is the abbreviation for *pritsel edenii* ("common sight"), and usually means the PU and its various modifications; depending on context, however, PE can also refer to the VP and PT scopes. The U.S. Army manual on the Mosin-Nagant, for example, contains a line drawing of a scope referred to as the PE; this is actually the PT with the early model atop-the-chamber mount. The same manual has an illustration of a scoped M1891/30, part of whose caption reads "model of telescope and mount unknown", which shows the VP on a side-rail mount.

Caution: A huge number of surplus Mosin-Nagants and Mosin-Nagant parts have been imported into Western nations, especially the United States, since the collapse of the Soviet empire in late 1991. Among these items are *a few* genuine, Soviet-fabricated sniper rifles; however, most M1891/30 rifles advertised as sniper models have simply been cobbled together by dealers from common rifles and authentic Soviet-made *snayperskaya* bolt handles, scopes and scope mounts. At this writing, parts or even fully assembled "sniper" rifles can be purchased for comparatively reasonable prices. I mention this in order to warn the prospective *snayperskaya* buyer that his purchase will almost certainly be a postwar reproduction assembled in the United States by the importer or dealer, even if all parts are from the same arsenal and in the same condition of wear. When considering a purchase, remove the scope from the mount and pay particular attention to the screws used to attach the mount to the receiver, see Figure 4-5. The two main screws are held in place by lock screws which were professionally applied. A sloppy job strongly suggests a non-Soviet assembly.

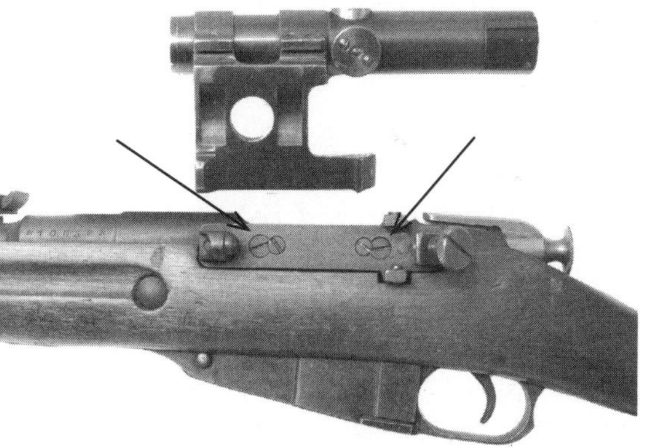

Figure 4-5. The M91/30 Sniper Rifle with the PU telescopic sight and third type mount. Note how the mount is fastened to the receiver.

CZECHOSLOVAKIAN MOSIN-NAGANT SNIPER RIFLES

In the early 1950s Czechoslovakia briefly produced a sniper rifle based on the M1891/30 which was designated the ZG 51/91/30.

Another sniper rifle, the Odstřelovaci puška vz.54 (sniper rifle model [19]54), was manufactured by the Czechs from 1954 to 1957, on original M1891/30 actions, see Figure 4-6. It was lighter and shorter than the Russian M1891/30 at 1,148 mm (45.196 in) long overall, and had a barrel length of 732 mm (28.81 in). It weighed 4.1 kg (9.02 lbs) fully loaded with a box magazine capacity of ten cartridges. The barrel was free-floated and did not have a fore end as the rifle was not configured for a bayonet or cleaning rod. The front sight was open-adjustable, and the rear sight was a 2.5x telescope. It appears that few of these were made, and it was soon replaced in Czech service by the Russian-designed SVD (Dragunov).

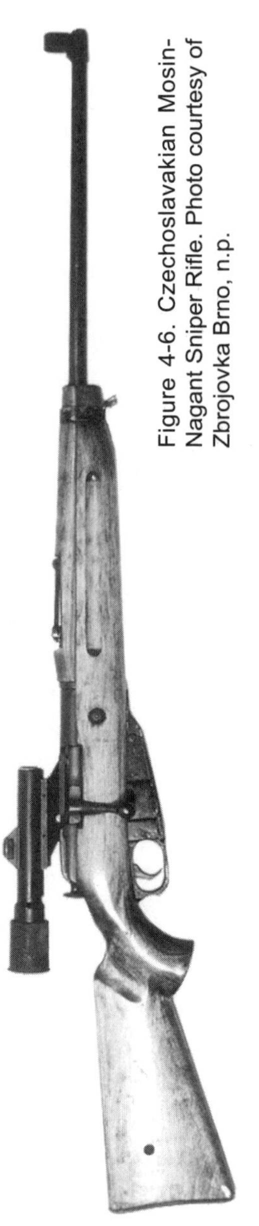

Figure 4-6. Czechoslavakian Mosin-Nagant Sniper Rifle. Photo courtesy of Zbrojovka Brno, n.p.

FINNISH MOSIN-NAGANT SNIPER RIFLES

During the 1930s the Finns began experimenting with the Mosin-Nagant as a sniper rifle. As early as 1925 they had worked with various Mauser and Mauser-type rifles, but ultimately abandoned the concept in favor of a more 'domestic' approach. The Finns began this undertaking with the *Physica* 3x telescope, produced by Physica Oy, an optics company in Helsinki. These scopes were initially mounted on one hundred fifty m/27s, and by 1940 there were about 400 such rifles, which were styled *Tarkka-Ampujakivääri m/37* ("precision" or "sharpshooter" rifle). These weapons were made with Tikkakoski barrels in the serial number range 79,000–87,000.

The *Physica* had been developed for use on mortars and machine guns and was not ideal for other arms. Although the Finns later tried the Physica on the m/39 rifle, the configuration was still awkward and cannot be considered a success.

In 1928 the Finns built prototypes of a sniper version of the m/28. Reportedly only nine were produced in sniper-mode, but the m/28-as-sniper-rifle figures in a bit of Finnish lore from the Winter War: a farmer, Simo Hähya, became a national hero when he shot more than 500 Soviet soldiers with his m/28 during a 15-week period.

The m/28-30 was another Finnish rifle seriously considered for conversion to sniper use. The Civil Guard had scopes mounted on twenty-five m/28-30s in or around 1933. The scopes were produced in Germany by the Zeiss, Hensoldt and Busch companies. They appear to have remained a standard until at least the Winter War of 1939–40, when the Finns began to capture the first of their many Soviet M1891/30 *snayperskaya* rifles.

Another version of the m/39 was known as the *Tarkkuuskivääri JK m/39 Diopterilla*, i.e., Precision Infantry Rifle m/39, with Diopter sights. This model was produced in very limited numbers from 1939 to 1958, and is simply an m/39 fitted with a turned-down, sniper-type bolt handle and diopter sights made for and unique to it, see Figure 4-7.

As noted earlier, the Finns had been experimenting with the concept of a sniper rifle using the somewhat clumsy Physica scope, which had originally been designed for use with mortars and machine guns. In 1941 they mounted the Physica on the m/39 and the result was styled *Tarkka-Ampujakivääri m/39 PH*. This modification was made to an indeterminate number of rifles produced by VKT with serial numbers in the 26,000–65,000 range. See Figure 4-8.

During World War II the m/39 became the standard Finnish sniper rifle — the Finns had a number of Soviet-made M1891/30 *snayperskaya*

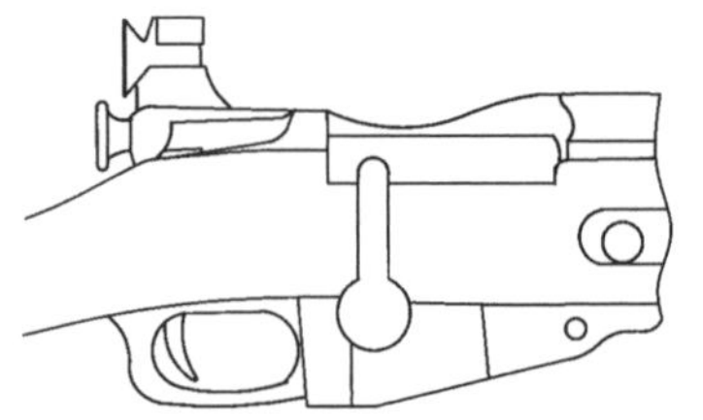

Figure 4-7. *Tarkkuuskivääri JK m/39 Diopterilla*, Precision Infantry Rifle m/39.

rifles as well — and was fitted with German-supplied M43 ("Ajacks") sniper scope. The Finnish designation for this rifle configuration was *Tarkka-Ampujakivääri m/39 AJA*, from the "Ajacks" scope (or *m/39-43*, according to one source). About 500 were made.

At some point during the middle of World War II the *Väisälä* 4x scope — a Finnish copy of the Ajacks developed by Prof. V. Väisälä — was mounted on one hundred m/39s, designated the *Tarkka-Ampujakivääri m/39-44*, see Figure 4-8.

Russian-made PU and VT scopes were also mounted to the m/39, which were then designated *Tarkka-Ampujakivääri m/39 SOV*.

Though possessing an excellent domestic arms industry of their own, when the Finns sought a new sniper rifle in the mid-1980s they turned once more to the Mosin-Nagant. The new rifle, designated *7,62 Kivääri malli 85* (7.62 [mm] Rifle Model [19]85), sometimes referred to as the *TAK 85*, is fabricated with original, tsarist-era (!) actions paired with accurized, heavyweight barrels, nonreflective, plastic pistol-grip stocks with adjustable combs, standard adjustable bipod, silencer and updated optics. In fact, any series of optical, electroptical or non-optical metallic sights can be mounted. The rifle weighs 9.03 pounds and is 46.45 inches long. See Table 4-1 for a compilation of Finnish Sniper Scope Specifications and Table 4-2 for a listing of all Finnish Sniper Rifles built around the Mosin-Nagant action.

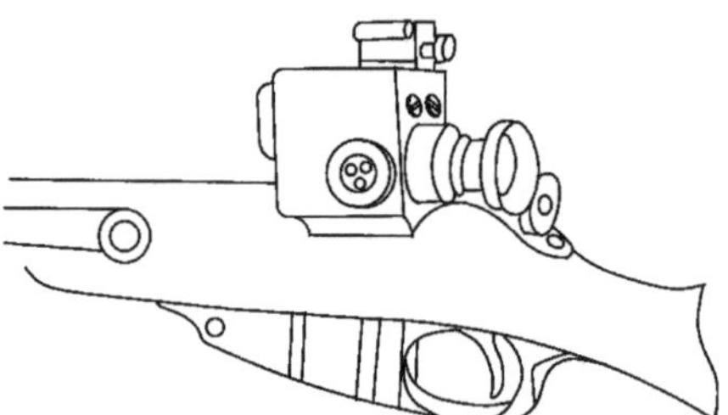

Figure 4-8. *Finnish Tarkka-Ampujakivääri m/39 PH* sniper rifle.

Table 4-1 Finnish Sniper Scope Specifications				
Model	**Magnification**	**Objective**	**Exit Pupil**	**Eye Relief**
Physica	3x	24 mm	4 mm	40 mm
Väisälä	4x	38 mm	9.5 mm	85 mm

HUNGARIAN MOSIN-NAGANT SNIPER RIFLES

During the early 1950s *Fémaru-Fegyver és Gépgyár* (FÉG) of Budapest manufactured a copy of the M1891/30 sniper rifle, using the 48.M which is the Hungarian version of the standard Russian M1891/30 rifle. These rifles saw extensive service with North Vietnamese and Viet Cong forces in the Vietnam War.

Table 4-2 Finnish Sniper and Precision Rifles Based on the Mosin-Nagant				
Model	Scope/Sight	Characteristics	Serial # Range	Number Built
Tarkka-Ampujakivääri m/37	Physica 3x	Tikkakoski Barrel	79,000 to 87,000	400
Jalkaväenkivääri m/28	Physica 3x	Short, boxy optical scope	Unknown	9
Jalkaväenkivääri m/28-30	Zeiss, Hensoldt or Busch	German scopes	Unknown	25
Tarkkuuskivääri JK m/39 Diopterilla	Diopter Sights, front and rear	Non-optical rear, adjustable diopter front	Unknown	Unknown
Tarkka-Ampujakivääri m/39 PH	Physica 3x	Short, boxy optical scope	26,000 to 65,000	Unknown
Tarkka-Ampujakivääri m/39 AJA	Ajacks	German Ajacks Scope	Unknown	500
Tarkka-Ampujakivääri m/39-44	Ajacks - Väisälä	Finnish copy of Ajacks	Unknown	100
Tarkka-Ampujakivääri m/39 SOV	PU or VT Soviet Scopes	Captured M91-30	Unknown	Unknown
7,62 Kivääri malli 85	None	Heavy barrel, pistol grip, adjustable comb, silencer	Unknown	Unknown

Chapter 5
Bayonets

Russian Bayonets

Russians are great believers in the bayonet: the M1891 Infantry and Dragoon rifles (though not the Cossack model) were sighted to be fired with a bayonet fixed. The bayonet for the original M1891 rifle — and which fits all Mosin-Nagant rifles except the M1891/30 — uses a cruciform-blade, socket bayonet design unchanged since the late 18th century. There are at least 23 varieties of Russian Mosin-Nagant bayonet, most of them experimental models which did not enter production; this does not include the many German and Austrian ersatz Mosin bayonets of the First World War.

M1891 Bayonet

At least four variations of the standard M1891 bayonet were produced, differing principally in the degree to which they must be rotated to fix them onto the muzzle. They are all quite similar in appearance. The common Russian Mosin-Nagant bayonet was cruciform in cross section and had a slotted screwdriver tip. The bayonet is 19.875 inches long. The socket is cut to slide over the rifle's front sight and rotate clockwise to seat. A French-style locking ring clamps the bayonet to the rifle. See Figure 5-1.

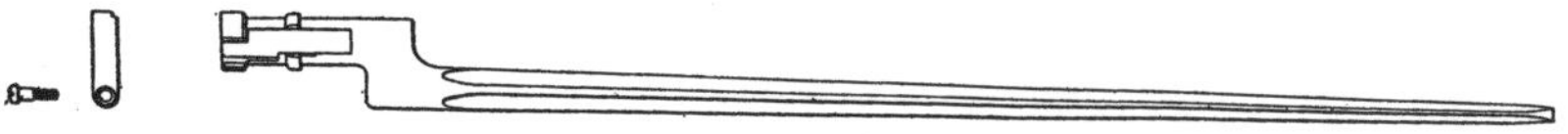

Figure 5-1

At the same time, probably during World War I, the new challenges of trench-warfare resulted in five or more various types of wire cutter attachments being invented and adapted to the bayonet, one of which is shown in Figure 5-2.

M1916 Bayonet

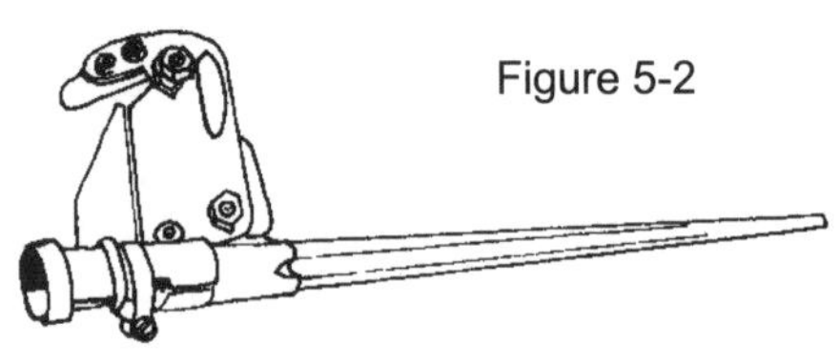
Figure 5-2

The M1916 was a knife-type bayonet possibly designed during the First World War (see Figure 5-3) and according to Zhuk was designated the "bayonet Model 1916" (*shtik obrazets 1916-ago goda*). It appears to have been produced in very limited quantities and is very rare. As was the case with the M1891 bayonet, a wire cutter attachment was also developed for the M1916 bayonet. There is reason to believe that this bayonet was devised as early as 1905, based on the markings found on some examples, but both the exact year or origin and even the official nomenclature are still not definitively established.

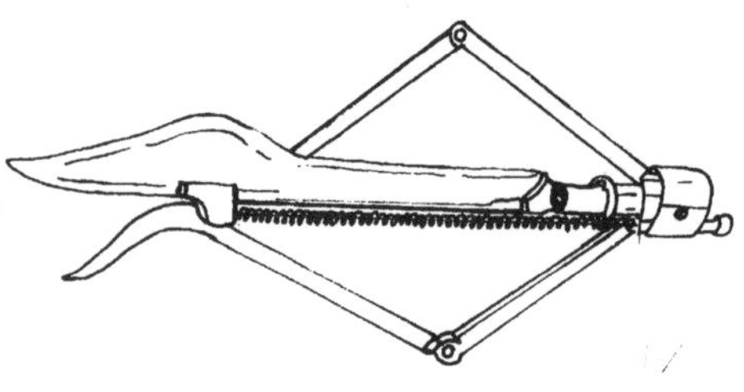
Figure 5-3

M1891/30 Bayonet

Two types of bayonet were developed for the M1891/30 rifle, see Figure 5-4.The **Type 1** bayonet (right) was designed by Kabakov and Komaritskii and was designated the "Bayonet Model 1891/30" (*shtik obrazets 1891/30-ogo goda*). The locking ring of the M1891 bayonet (left) was replaced with a spring-loaded catch. The M1891/30 bayonet fits all M1891 Infantry, Cossack and Dragoon rifles and their variants. The M1891 bayonet, however, will not fit the M1891/30 rifle and its successors as its locking ring will not fit over the sight hood.

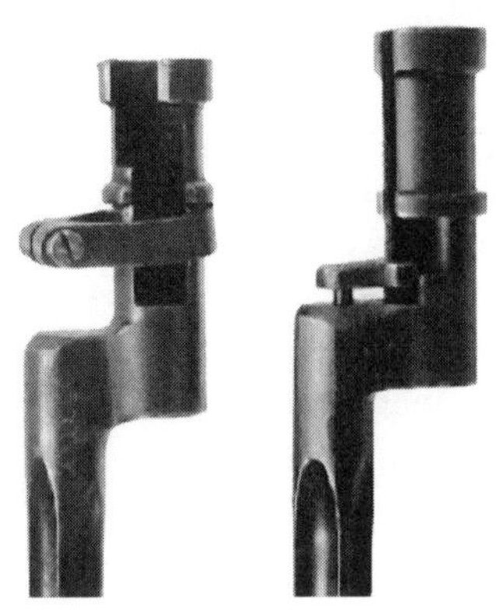
Figure 5-4

The **Type 2** version of this bayonet was designed by P. K. Panshin (see Figure 5-5). It had an extension to cover the unhooded sight found on the M1891 Infantry, Cossack, Dragoon and pre-1930 Soviet rifles. The protective hood was attached to the bayonet socket by two dovetailed mounts integral to the socket. The hood slid onto the mounts and was secured by a small screw. It proved uneconomical to manufacture, was produced only in relatively small numbers, and is rare.

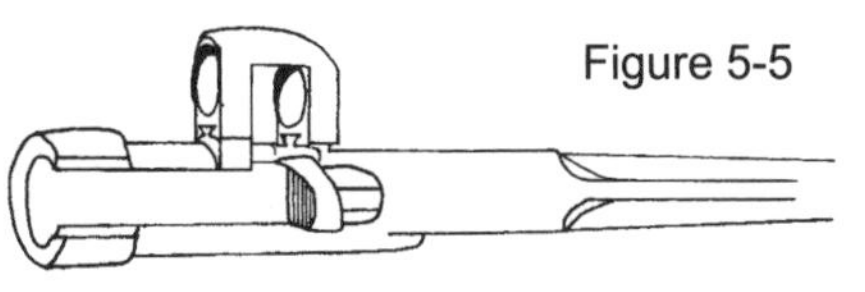

Figure 5-5

M1942 Bayonet

A knife-bladed version of the Kabakov-Komaritskii socket bayonet, the *obrazets 1942-ogo goda* (Model 1942), was also made, though in small quantity and, possibly, only as an experimental or ersatz model. This bayonet is 355 mm long overall; its blade is 258 mm long and 26 mm wide.

Similar in appearance, though much more crudely made, are emergency bayonets produced in Leningrad (now St. Petersburg) during the 1941–43 siege, probably at the famous ZIK works (ZIK = Zavod Imeni Kirova = Kirov Memorial Factory). These are Tokarev rifle bayonet blades welded to the Mosin-Nagant sockets. They are 359 mm long, of which 289 mm is the blade. Some German Mauser bayonets also were thus adapted.

M1944 Bayonet

A folding, permanently attached bayonet was introduced with the M1944 carbine. Two types were developed. Both were heavily blued steel. Both types were cruciform in cross section and had the flathead-screwdriver tip. The blade folded along the right side of the weapon when not in use and rested in a groove routed into the stock. Unlike the M1891 and M1891/30 bayonets, the M1944 was not serial-numbered; some examples have the usual arsenal marks, and others are unmarked altogether,see Figure 5-6.

The **Type 1** M1944 bayonet was 383 mm (15.1 in) long, including the barrel-sleeve and locking bracket, both of which are integral to the bayonet assembly, see Figure 5-7, left. The M1944 bayonet is attached by a single screw to a socketed bracket around the carbine's barrel. The screw secures the bayonet tang between two arms of the bracket and permits the bayonet to pivot forward for attachment by its ring around the muzzle. The inside of the muzzle ring is beveled on the side closest to the sleeve. The front sides of the bracket arms are flat and there are single cams at the rear of each bracket arm.

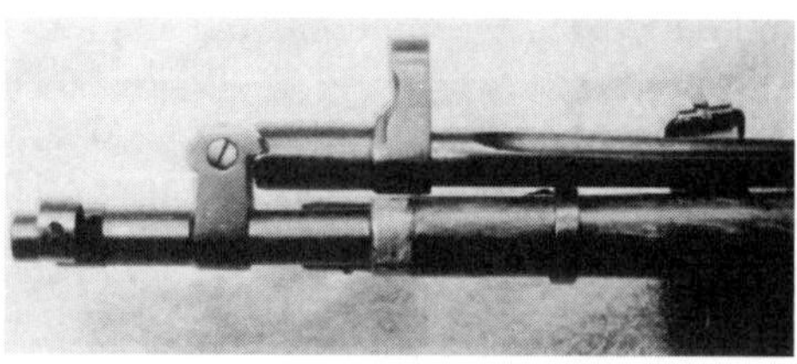

Figure 5-6

Shortly after the end of World War II the Russians produced a **Type 2** modified M1944 bayonet, see Figure 5-7, right. A cam or "ear" was added to the front end of each bracket arm identical to the cam on the rear, resulting in a configuration which was later used on the SKS. The rear of the sleeve was altered by the addition of two cams to replace the notched indentations of the earlier models, and which fitted over the front "ears" when the bayonet was folded back along the stock. Other changes included eliminating the interior of the muzzle ring bevel in favor of a plain socket, and removing metal from the ring on the side farthest from the sleeve, making a cutout nominally 15 mm (0.59 in) wide by 5 mm (0.196 in) deep. All of these modifications are found on Chinese, Hungarian, Polish, and Romanian M1944s as well as on the postwar Russian production.

Figure 5-7. Type 2 M1944 bayonet (right) compared to Type 1 M1944 bayonet (left).

SCABBARDS

Scabbards were very rarely made or issued by the Russians, either Tsarist or Soviet, for use with the Mosin-Nagant bayonets. The authorized methods of carrying the bayonet were: (a) affixing it to the barrel (either in the customary way, or with the blade reversed during non-combat periods); or (b) secured by metal bands attached to the retaining bands of the cavalry saber scabbard, the bayonet point resting in a metal cap. See Figure 5-8.

While leather Mosin-Nagant bayonet scabbards are sometimes found they are — if genuine — Finnish, and are quite rare. Some leather scabbards have appeared on the market recently, but they are newly made products from Pakistan or India. Genuine Russian scabbards are of canvas in the usual varying shades of Russian military khaki (Shalito, et al. Page 54). Finnish leather scabbards for the M1891 bayonet are usually brown with a brass tip; those for the m/39 Sk. Y. bayonet are gray-green and have metal rivets around the edge. See below for a more detailed description of Finnish bayonets and their scabbards.

Figure 5-8

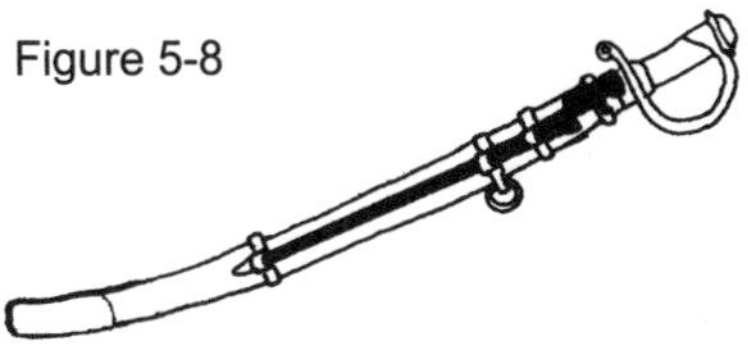

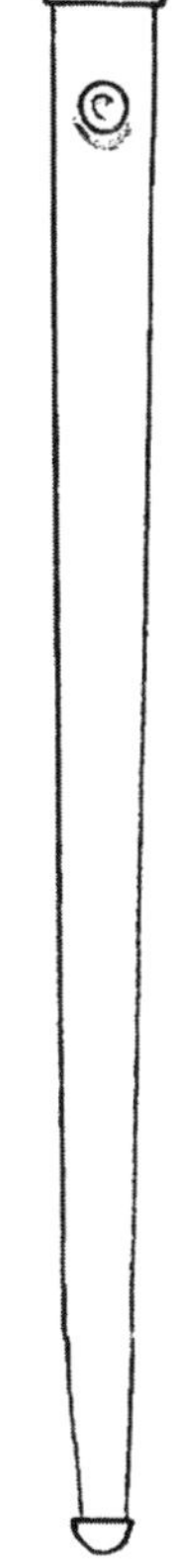

Figure 5-9

GERMAN MOSIN-NAGANT BAYONETS

During World War I the Germans manufactured a tubular metal scabbard, 486 mm (19.13 inches) long, for use with the many M1891 bayonets they captured from the Russians and reissued to their own forces. See Figure 5-9.

AUSTRIAN MOSIN-NAGANT BAYONETS

The Austrians also produced a version of the M1891 bayonet during World War I to fit the thousands of captured Mosin-Nagants. These weapons can be identified by the Austro-Hungarian crest stamped on them and by the straight slot that slides over the front sight base to attach the bayonet. Like the Germans, the Austrians made tubular metal scabbards for these bayonets.

FINNISH BAYONETS

m/91 Finnish Bayonet

The Finns acquired large numbers of M1891 socket bayonets along with their Russian Mosin-Nagants in 1918. They adapted some of the M1891 bayonets for cavalry use by shortening the blade 12.5 cm (about 5 in) which were then designated the *m/91Rv* (the Finnish word for "cavalry" is *ratsuvaki*). Some 3,000 bayonets were so altered between 1925 and 1935.

While the M1891 bayonet was not shortened for use with the m/91-24, the locking ring was altered to accommodate the new, taller front sight blade. Because the new barrels were somewhat larger in diameter than the original Russian barrels, the bayonet sockets were widened correspondingly. In what became a fairly common practice for 'domesticating' captured rifles and bayonets, the Finns ground off the Russian markings and substituted their own — in this case, "S" for the *Suojeluskunta* (Civil Guard), followed by a new serial number to match the rifle with which it was then reissued; SAKO made about 26,000 of these modifications in 1928. Most of these Finnish socket bayonets were destroyed in 1946, and are now sought-after collectors' items.

Russian (Tsarist and Soviet) socket bayonets were almost never issued with scabbards. The Finns, however, produced scabbards for their Mosin-Nagant bayonets of brown leather with a protective brass tip; they have a belt loop, and a retaining strap for the socket to secure it to the scabbard.

m/27 Bayonet

With the development of the m/27 rifle, the Finns began to modernize their bayonet inventory and produced the first of a series of knife-blade bayonets, the m/27, see Figure 5-10.

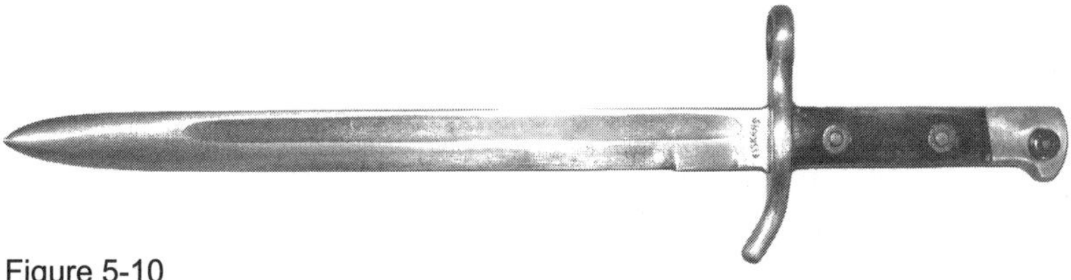

Figure 5-10

Although the m/27 was produced for use on the m/27 rifle, it will fit all the Mosin-Nagant patterns subsequently developed and manufactured by the Finns (except the m/1891 and m/1891-30, put into production in 1940 and 1943, respectively) which use the original socket bayonet.

The m/27 bayonet is 413 mm (16.26 in) long overall. The blade is 300 mm (11.8 in) long. At the ricasso it is 22.3 mm (0.88 in) wide, and 5 mm (0.196 in) thick at the thickest point. The diameter of the muzzle ring is 16.7 mm (0.66 in). Blades were either blued or finished in-the-white. The grips are walnut. The bayonets were manufactured by Fiskars Oy. and Hackman & Co.-Sorsakoski.

The m/27 bayonet uses the m/28 scabbard, which is 320 mm (12.59 in) long, and is made of steel and is found either blued or painted a dark olive-drab, see Figure 5-11.

Figure 5-11

Some m/27 bayonets are serial-numbered, and some also have a Civil Guard number, which is identifiable by the prefix “S”. Occasionally one will see a bayonet with an additional one- to three-digit number on the pommel, which is the rack number within an individual Civil Guard unit.

m/28 Bayonet

This is essentially the same as the m/27, but the walnut grips are secured with hollow rivets. The bayonet will be marked with a *Suojeluskunta* (Civil Guard) logo in the form of a barred **S** on the blade or ricasso, and can have an **S**-prefixed serial number and/or a rack number as well, see Figure 5-12. This model takes the m/28 scabbard.

Figure 5-12

The m/28 rifle was, reportedly, issued originally without a bayonet as the Civil Guard lacked the funds to purchase any at the time; the bayonets were supplied to the troops somewhat later, see Figure 5-13.

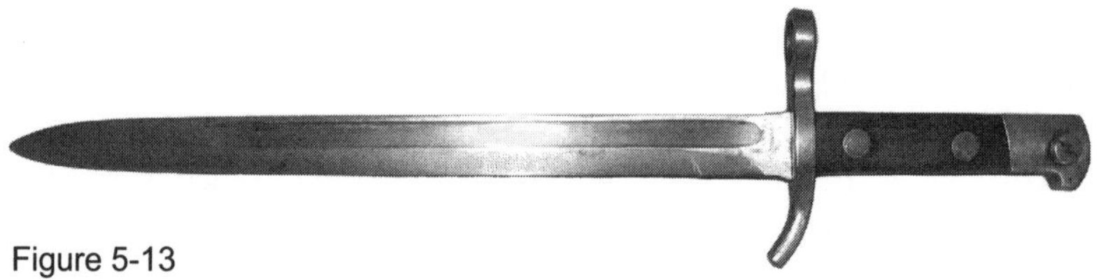

Figure 5-13

m/28-30 Bayonet

This model was used by the Civil Guard and thus has serial numbers beginning with that organization's characteristic "**S**", see Figure 5-14.

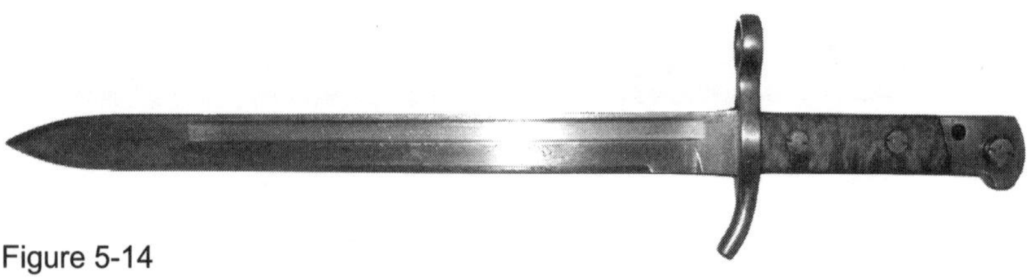

Figure 5-14

These bayonets have grips made of curly-grained birch with a clear lacquer finish. The smooth-sided m/35 scabbard is correct for this model. Approximately 28,500 were made in 1934–1939 by the firm Fiskars Oy. and Hackman & Co. Marked Sk. Y. on the ricasso.

m/28-30/39 Bayonet

This is an extensively modified m/27, whose principal changes consist of a shortened cross guard and a shortened blade; the latter is cut upward into a Bowie-type point similar to that of the m/39 Sk. Y. bayonet. This was an experiment undertaken in 1942 to test the practicality of shortenting existing bayonets. It was not a success, and altered bayonets were withdrawn from service the following year. See Figure 5-15.

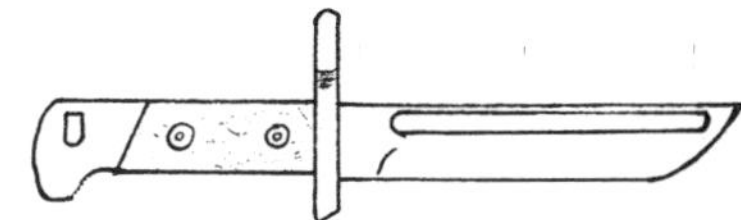
Figure 5-15

m/35 Sk. Y. Bayonet

Two types of this bayonet were produced. The **Type 1** is similar to the m/27, differing in these respects: a) it is 1 mm longer than the m/27 and b) wider at the ricasso (23.4 mm [0.92 in] as opposed to 22.3 mm [0.88 in]), and c) the diameter of the muzzle ring is 16.3 mm [0.64 in] rather than 16.7 mm [0.66 in]. The edge is also slightly different from the m/27 and the rivets securing the grips also differ somewhat. Unlike the m/27, there is no oil hole in the pommel. The bayonet is identifiable by the marking **Sk. Y.** on the ricasso together with the maker's name. This model takes the m/28 scabbard.

The **Type 2** m/35 Sk. Y. bayonet differs from the Type 1 as follows: a) there is an oil hole in the pommel; b) the muzzle ring diameter is 16.2 mm (0.637 in); c) the grips are burled (possibly applewood) rather than plain; d) the maximum blade width is 24 mm (0.945 in). The Type 2 also uses the m/28 scabbard.

m/35 Bayonet

This bayonet was used by the Finnish Army rather than the Civil

Guard and is almost identical to the m/27, differing only in that the channel for the bayonet lug is slightly wider, making for a somewhat better fit; the blade is different (although the sources do not describe the difference) and the scabbard was changed to eliminate the external ribs and grooves of the m/28 scabbard. A button-like protuberance (see Figure 5-16) was added which fits into a slit on the redesigned bayonet frog. The frogs were brown or greenish-gray leather; the early model had a buckled strap (a brass-snap strap on some examples) which was eliminated in later production.

Figure 5-16

m/39 Sk. Y. Bayonet

This model somewhat resembles a Bowie knife, see Figure 5-17. It was manufactured by *Oy Veljekset Kulmala AB* (Kulmalan Brothers, Inc.), and is so marked. It also bears the Sk. Y. mark. This type was first delivered to the Civil Guard in 1942. The bayonet is 295 mm (11.61 in) overall, of which 182 mm (7.16 in) is the blade. The maximum blade width is 25 mm (0.98 in), which is 5 mm (0.196 in) thick at the crossguard. The muzzle ring diameter is 16.3 mm (0.64 in). The scabbard (see Figure 5-17) is made of green-dyed leather, reinforced around

Figure 5-17

Table 5-1 Finnish Mosin-Nagant Bayonet Production (1,2)			
Model	**Manufacturer**	**Years**	**Total**
m/27	Fiskars Oy. and Hackman, Inc.	1928–1938	57,500
m/28	Hackman, Inc.	1928–1934	38,200
	F. Niskala	1928–1934	12,100
	Friitala Oy.	1928–1934	3,300
	Oy Veljekset Kulmala AB	1928–1934	3,000
m/28-30	Fiskars Oy. and Hackman, Inc.	1934–1939	28,500
m/35	Fiskars Oy. and Hackman & Co.	unknown	18,500
m/39 Sk. Y.	Oy Veljekset Kulmala AB	1942 (?)	unknown

1) Because of the comparatively small numbers produced, extensive wartime use, and deliberate destruction, all Finnish bayonets and their accessories are rare, some extremely so.
2) Data derived from Bowser and Dunaway, and other sources.

the perimeter with metal rivets and at the tip by a metal protector. This is a particularly rare item: comparatively few were made, and most surviving examples were scrapped in the 1970s. Table 5-1 presents a summary of Finnish bayonet production for the Mosin-Nagant rifles.

Note: In late 1998, Great Southern Arsenal International, 2138 Patsy Hill Rd., Tylerstown, MS 39667 (601 684-7323) began offering a newly made reproduction of the m/39 Sk.Y. Bayonet and Scabbard for collectors of Finnish Mosin-Nagants. To distinguish them from originals, they are marked "GSA" with a serial number. The originals did not have a serial number. The collector should also be aware that other reproductions of this bayonet have been made that attempt to duplicate the original markings. Notably, they have non-original markings and the scabbards are incorrectly made.

RUSSIAN ERSATZ AND EXPERIMENTAL BAYONETS

During World War I, Germany and Austria-Hungary produced ersatz "literally substitute" bayonets for the Mosin-Nagant rifles they captured from the Russians, both by adapting to the Mosin-Nagant attachment system almost any type of foreign bayonet they acquired and by altering Mosins to accommodate other rifles' bayonets. The Russians also produced *erzats-shtyki* ("substitute bayonets") for their own Mosins, as well as for Arisakas, Mannlichers and Mausers in their inventories.

In the early years of the 20th century, and throughout the 1920s, '30s, and '40s, the Russians experimented with a number of new designs for Mosin bayonets, but they were never quite able to end their attachment to the screwdriver-tipped, cruciform-bladed bayonet they had been using for almost a century. The Russians had a brief flirtation with a dagger-like knife bayonet in the late 1920s, and again approximately fifteen years later when a much different knife-bladed design was proposed for an M1938 carbine bayonet, but neither was accepted or placed into general production. (See below.)

One departure from Russian tradition which appears with some of the experimental bayonets of these decades is the pommel with a spring-loaded press stud; although common on most of the world's bayonets by this time, the Russians had not used it before because Mosin-Nagant rifles and carbines did not have bayonet lugs. In the inter-war years, the Russians experimented with various nosecaps with integral bayonet lugs but the idea never caught on with the Mosin-Nagant series; however, conventional knife bayonets with the lug-and-catch system did go into production as standard issue for the ill-fated Simonov and Tokarev rifles.

Experimental Model (early 1900s)

Overall length: 500 mm; Blade length: 430 mm; Blade width: 17 mm; Interior diameter of the socket: 15 mm; Socket length: 70.5 mm.

This pattern is identical to the standard M1891 Mosin bayonet except for the locking ring, which is located at the rear, rather than the middle, of the socket; moreover, the locking ring can be set in only two positions, rather than turned around the whole socket. At the back end of the ring is a more-or-less triangular cam by which the locking ring is rotated using the thumb. See Figure 5-18.

Gulkevitch Experimental Model (c. 1912)

Figure 5-18

Overall length: 510 mm; Blade length: 425 mm; Blade width: 17 mm; Interior diameter of the socket: 15 mm; Socket length (in battle position): 81.8 mm.

Designed by a tsarist army officer, N. A. Gulkevitch, in the early years of the 20th century, this model is equipped with the usual grooved cruciform blade, but has a novel mounting system. The socket is formed of two tubular pieces connected by a hinge. The muzzle ring is a comparatively long bushing and secures the bayonet in "battle", i.e., fixed, position; in "march" position the bayonet is folded back along the fore end.

The Gulkevitch model received much favorable comment in Russian military circles before the First World War, and unlike most experimental bayonets it actually went into production, albeit limited. This folding bayonet was issued to some Cossack units during World War I, but was not made in great quantities and did not become a standard item, possibly because of the demands of the World War, subsequent revolution, and civil war. See Figure 5-19.

Kholodovskii Experimental Model (1912)

Figure 5-19

Overall length: 515 mm; Blade length: 445 mm; Blade width: 18.4 mm; Socket length: 68.6 mm; Interior diameter of the socket: 14.7 mm.

A quite innovative design, this pattern piece was made from a lightweight alloy that was partly aluminum. The blade is cruciform and is strengthened at the rear of each of the four ribs. The locking ring is highly unusual in that it must be manually pressed down around the muzzle in order to secure it to the barrel. See Figure 5-20.

Ersatz Model (World War I)

Figure 5-20

Overall length: 575 mm; Blade length: 495 mm; Blade width: 19 mm; Socket length: 75 mm; Interior diameter of the socket: 15 mm.

This example was recycled from an M1870 Berdan dragoon rifle bayonet. It has a bushing inserted into the socket to accommodate the smaller diameter of the Mosin barrel, and the locking ring has been enlarged to fit over the front sight. Note that the mortise slot on this model is offset to the left, rather than to the right as on standard Mosin bayonets. See Figure 5-21.

Ersatz Model (World War I)

Figure 5-21

Overall length: 500 mm; Blade length: 420 mm; Blade width: 17 mm; Interior diameter of the muzzle ring: 15 mm.

This example was made using the blade of a Russian M1870 bayonet; it has no socket. The bayonet is fixed to the rifle by a muzzle ring, a supporting lug, and a bushing at the rear. The bayonet slides over the muzzle, and when turned 180° places the bushing behind the front sight to secure the bayonet. See Figure 5-22.

Ersatz Model (World War I)

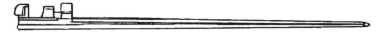

Figure 5-22

Overall length: 480 mm; Blade length: 430 mm; Blade width: 17 mm; Socket length: 55 mm; Interior diameter of the socket: 15 mm.

This is the sort of ersatz bayonet made by Russian army blacksmiths at divisional or even regimental level. Its blade is square in cross section and has no grooves; the socket is much shorter than the standard type. See Figure 5-23.

Experimental Model (1920s)

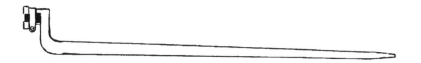

Figure 5-23

Overall length: 490 mm; Blade length: 420 mm; Blade width: 16.2 mm; Bushing length: 35 mm.

This piece has the usual grooved, cruciform blade with a screwdriver tip, but there is no socket, see Figure 5-24. The blade is hinged to an oval-shaped bushing which is slid onto the barrel all the way back to the nosecap at the front of the fore end. In the oval bushing

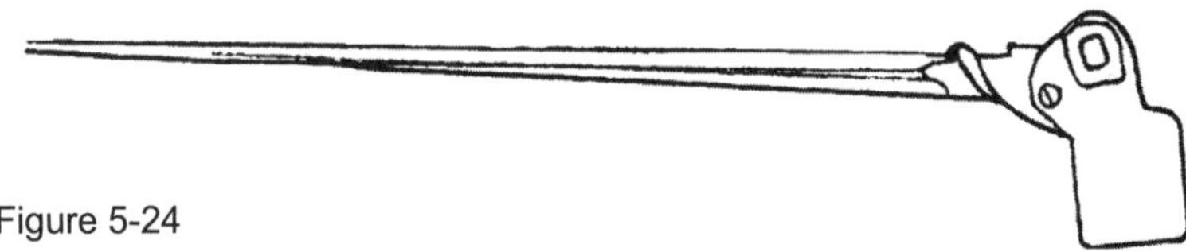

Figure 5-24

is a square hole, also with a bushing; at the front of this bushing is a spring-loaded catch to lock the bayonet in "battle" position, and which is also used to hold it folded back in "march" position.

Experimental Model (1920s)

Overall length: 515 mm; Blade length: 420 mm; Blade width: 15 mm; Socket length: 25 mm; Bushing length: 90 mm; Interior diameter of the socket: 14.8 mm.

This pattern has a typical grooved cruciform blade; at the rear of the blade is a flattened tail by which it is hinged to a long bushing having a trough on one side and, at the front end, a short socket for attaching the bayonet to the muzzle. When the blade is folded back along the stock it is locked by a small, spring-loaded press stud, which is also used to lock the bayonet in "battle" position. See Figure 5-25.

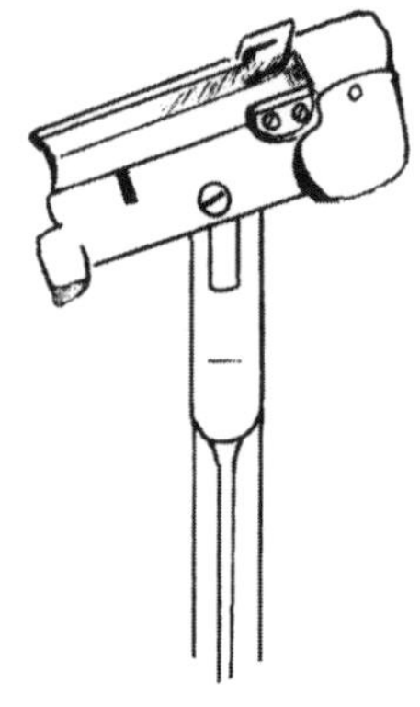

Figure 5-25

Experimental Model (1920s)

Overall length: 570 mm; Blade length: 430 mm; Blade width: 16.5 mm; Interior diameter of the socket: 15 mm.

At some point during the 1920s, the Russians developed an experimental bayonet which looks very much like an ersatz model, but is not, see Figure 5-26. It has the familiar grooved cruciform blade and screwdriver tip, but a shortened socket and straight foresight slot for attaching it to the rifle. The rear part of the blade is cylindrical with longitudinal grooves; at the rear of the (very basic) pommel is a

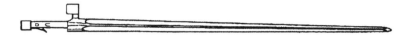

Figure 5-26

T-shaped mortise slot with a spring-loaded press-stud. The bayonet is attached to a rifle by the socket around the muzzle and the mortise slot, which slides onto a bracket on the barrel and is secured by the press-stud.

Markevitch Experimental Model (1920s)
Overall length: 500 mm; Blade length: 420 mm; Blade width: 16.3 mm; Interior diameter of the socket: 15 mm.

Although it is fixed to the rifle much as are some First World War ersatz bayonets, and resembles them at first glance, this model was not made as such. It has the usual cruciform blade, a shortened socket, and a long tang at the rear on which is a single groove; the groove was meant to slide over a lug on the barrel, and was then secured by a single screw in the middle of the tang. See Figure 5-27.

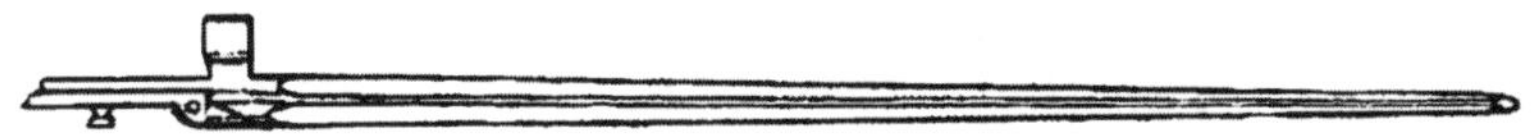

Figure 5-27

Experimental Model (1926–27)
Overall length: 500 mm; Blade length: 430 mm; Blade width: 17 mm; Socket length: 70.5 mm; Interior diameter of the socket: 15 mm.

Another attempt to improve the standard bayonet, this pattern piece differs from the existing M1891 model only by the addition of a sight protector, attached to the socket by a small screw. The measurements are identical to those of the standard bayonet. See Figure 5-28.

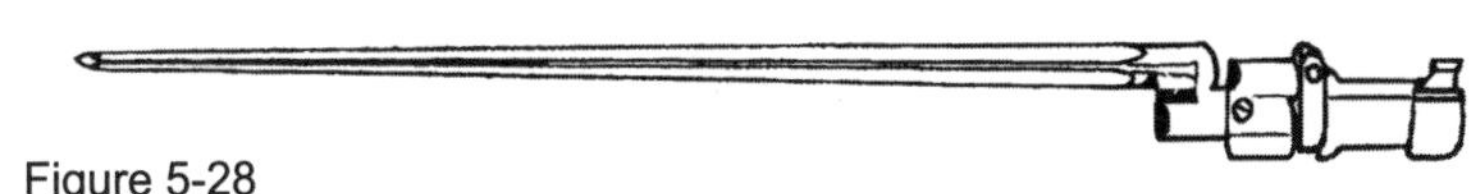

Figure 5-28

Experimental Model (1926–27)
Overall length: 485 mm; Blade length: 425 mm; Blade width: 16.7 mm; Socket length: 60.7 mm; Interior diameter of the socket: 15 mm.

This pattern has the typical Mosin cruciform blade, and a sight protector vaguely similar to the Panshin design (q.v.). Unlike the typical Mosin bayonet, the mortise slot orientation of this one required the bayonet to be turned to the left, rather than to the right, to mount it to the barrel. At the rear of the socket is a spring-loaded catch with a small lug to fix the bayonet to the muzzle behind the front sight. See Figure 5-29.

Figure 5-29

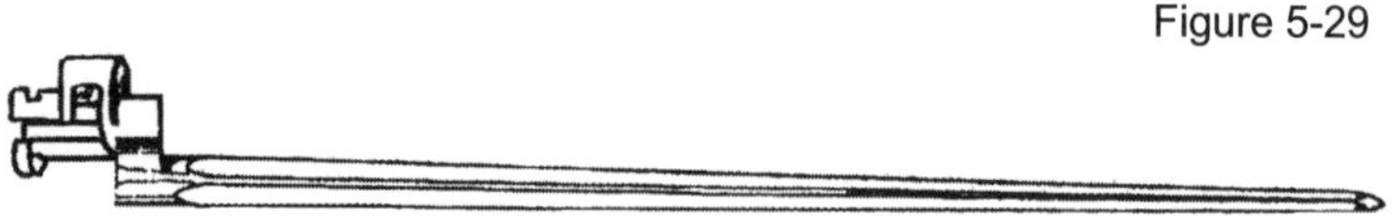

Experimental Model of 1927
Overall length: 575 mm; Blade length: 450 mm; Blade width: 16.4 mm; Interior diameter of the socket: 15.8 mm.

The Experimental Model of 1927 represented a major break from earlier designs as it had a much more conventional hilt, and wooden grips secured to the tang by two screws. The easily held hilt enabled this model, unlike its predecessors, to be used as a dagger. The bayonet was attached to a rifle by a short socket around the muzzle, and a T-shaped mortise slot at the rear of the pommel which slid over a bayonet lug (mounted on an experimental nosecap) and was secured with a spring-loaded press-stud. See Figure 5-30.

Figure 5-30

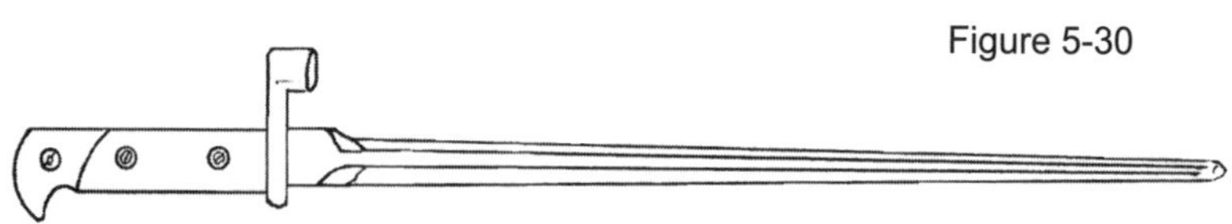

Experimental "Kinzhal" Bayonet
Overall length: 460 mm; Blade length: 340 mm; Blade width: 32 mm; Interior diameter of muzzle ring: 15.8 mm.

During the late 1920s the Russians toyed with the idea of a bayonet based on the kinzhál, the traditional dagger found in the Caucasus region. This bayonet has a double-edged blade with an off-center fuller, and wooden grips secured to the tang by a rivet, see Figure 5-31. The bayonet has a muzzle ring and a T-shaped mortise slot at the rear of the pommel, which slides over a lug on a metal nosecap and is secured with a spring-loaded press-stud. Of additional interest is the hole in the pommel for attaching a sword-knot (*temlyák*). The scabbard is made of wood covered with brown-dyed leather; it has a locket with frog stud, and ends in a ball-tipped chape, all of which are made of blackened metal. This pattern is attractive but overly complex, and probably was rejected because of the time and expense involved in producing it.

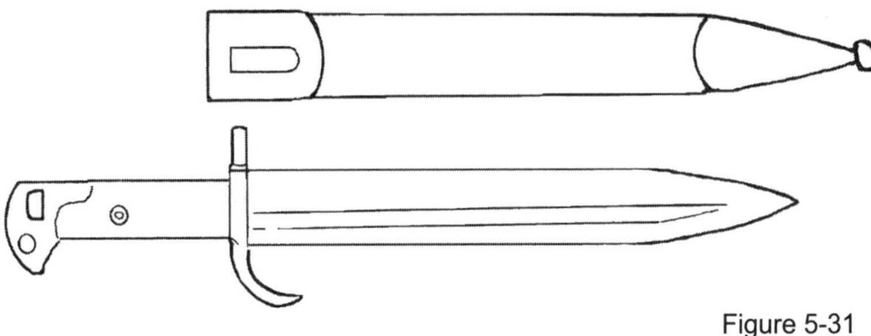

Figure 5-31

Experimental Model of 1936

Note: I have been unable to ascertain the exact dimensions for this model. It appears to have been c. 460 mm long and c. 25 mm wide. See Figure 5-32.

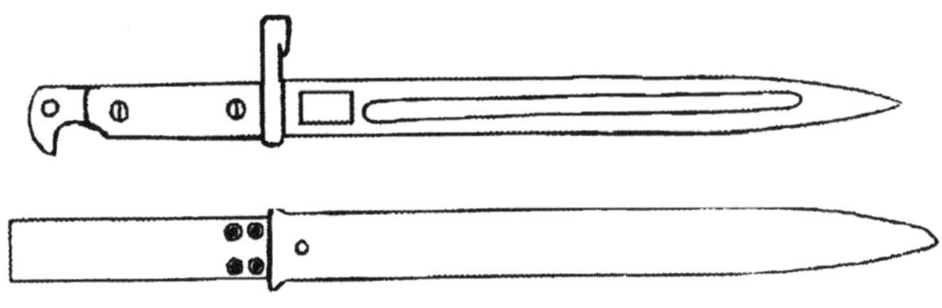

Figure 5-32

This bayonet was designed to fit an experimental Mosin rifle of the period that had a metal nosecap with a bayonet lug, and a front sight protector with which the Russians had been experimenting for several years (resembling that of a Japanese Type 38 Arisaka, already very familiar to them). The bayonet is attached to the rifle by a muzzle ring, and a T-shaped mortise slot at the rear of the pommel which slides over the bayonet lug and is secured with a spring-loaded press-stud. The rectangular area behind the fuller is a lightening cut. The scabbard is metal, attached by four rivets to a webbing loop for sliding over a belt.

World War II Variant of the M1891/30

This is identical to the standard M1891/30 bayonet except for its overall length and blade length (360 mm and 285 mm, respectively, rather than the standard 505 mm and 430 mm), and the blade itself, which has a single edge and only one groove.

Experimental Model of 1943

Overall length: 360 mm; Blade length: 245 mm; Blade width: 25 mm; Interior diameter of muzzle ring: 14 mm.

The Experimental Model of 1943 was quite similar — but not identical — to the Tokarev M1940 bayonet. It was a conventional design, secured to the carbine by a muzzle ring and a T-shaped mortise slot with a spring-loaded press-stud which fitted onto a metal nosecap. Attached to the metal scabbard is a webbing strap with a loop for sliding onto a belt. See Figure 5-33.

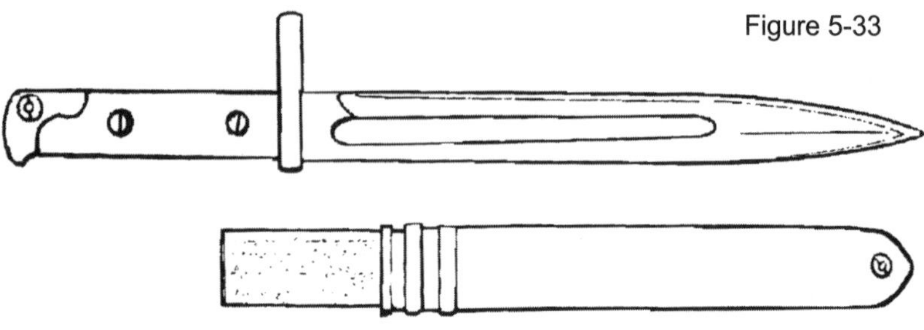
Figure 5-33

Experimental Cruciform Model of 1942
Blade length: 400 mm; Blade width: 15 mm.

This trial piece had the usual grooved, cruciform blade. It was mounted on a bracket attached to the barrel, and secured by a spring-loaded catch which fixed the bayonet in "battle" position, and helped to lock it when it was in "march" position, folded back along the right side of the barrel in a groove in the fore end. See Figure 5-34.

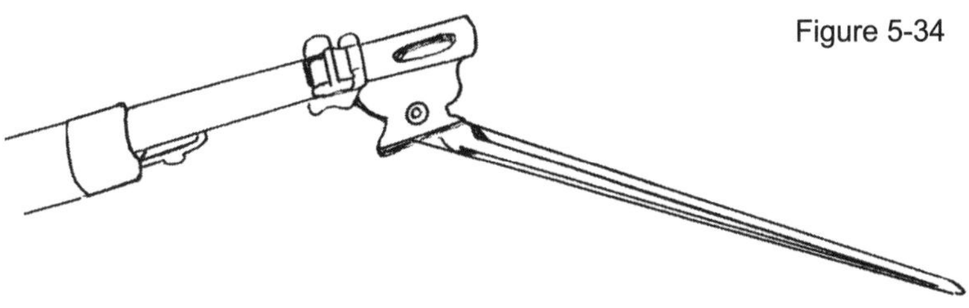

Figure 5-34

Experimental Cruciform Model of 1943
Blade length: 400 mm; Blade width: 16 mm.

Their research into a knife bayonet for Mosins notwithstanding, the Russians continued their efforts to produce a better traditionally shaped cruciform bayonet. The 1943 trial version for the M91/30 rifle differed significantly from other models in that it folded under, rather than along the right side of the barrel, see Figure 5-35. When folded back in "march position" the bayonet was held by a screw in the rear

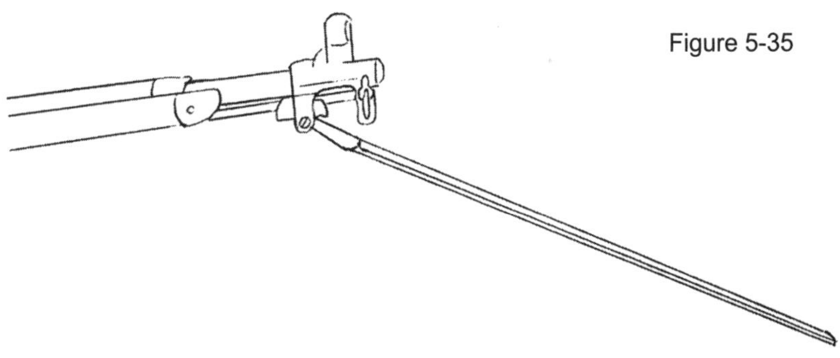

Figure 5-35

of two lugs of a bracket attached to the muzzle; when extended in "battle" position the bayonet was secured by the front lug as well.

Experimental Cruciform Model of 1943

Blade length: 400 mm; Blade width: 16 mm.

This model retains the usual grooved cruciform blade. A spring-loaded catch is located at the back of the tang to lock the blade in march or battle position; the blade rotates through 180° on a hinge attached to a bushing on the right side of the mount. The front of the mounting bracket has two multifaceted segments, requiring additional time and labor. This pattern is another example of over-engineering a simple weapon. See Figure 5-36.

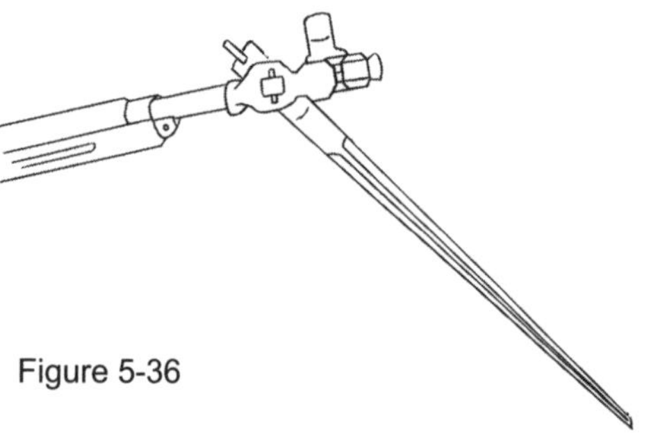

Figure 5-36

Experimental Cruciform Model of 1943

Blade length: 400 mm; Blade width: 16.5 mm.

Another bayonet with the typical grooved cruciform blade, this unusual design had a spring-loaded catch in the form of a round plate which, together with a hinge and bushing, secured the bayonet in march or battle position, see Figure 5-37. As was the case with the foregoing 1943 experimental model, the overly complicated attachment mechanism all but ensured that the pattern would not be mass-produced.

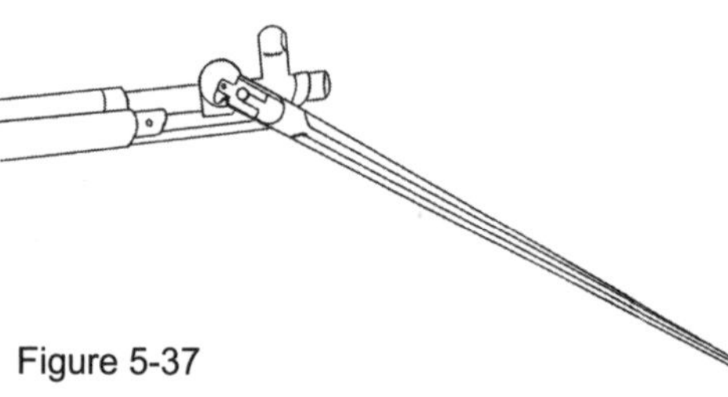

Figure 5-37

Experimental Cruciform Model of 1946
Blade length: 310 mm; Blade width: 15 mm.

This pattern is very similar to the bayonet previously adopted as standard for the M44 Mosin carbine, but differs from it in, among other features, blade dimensions (the M44 bayonet is 383 mm long and 16.5 mm wide). The design has been simplified considerably from earlier experimental models and relies for attachment on a fairly simple tubular bracket with a rivet at the rear and a ring at the end of a spring-loaded tube to secure the bayonet at the muzzle. Note also the unusual fore end, and the ring-type sling swivel, both of which the Russians were toying with at the time. See Figure 5-38.

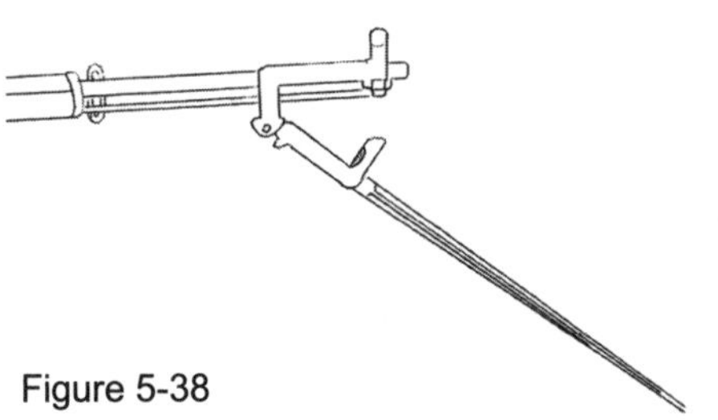
Figure 5-38

Experimental Cruciform Model of 1946, variant
Blade length: 290 mm; Blade width: 14.5 mm.

This trial piece differed from others in that its blade was triangular rather than cruciform; it was also unusual — but not unique — in that it folded under the barrel, rather than to the right side. See Figure 5-39.

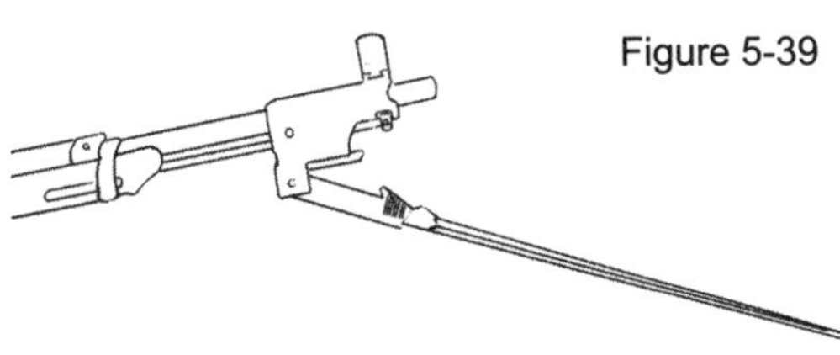
Figure 5-39

Experimental Cruciform Model of 1947
Blade length: 285 mm; Blade width: 14 mm.

This trial piece had the usual grooved, cruciform blade, and is unremarkably different from others of its type aside from the fact that it folds under, rather than parallel to, the barrel and fore end when in "march" position. The bayonet was mounted on a bracket attached to the barrel, and secured by a spring-loaded catch which fixed the bayonet in "battle" position and helped to lock it when in "march" position. See Figure 5-40.

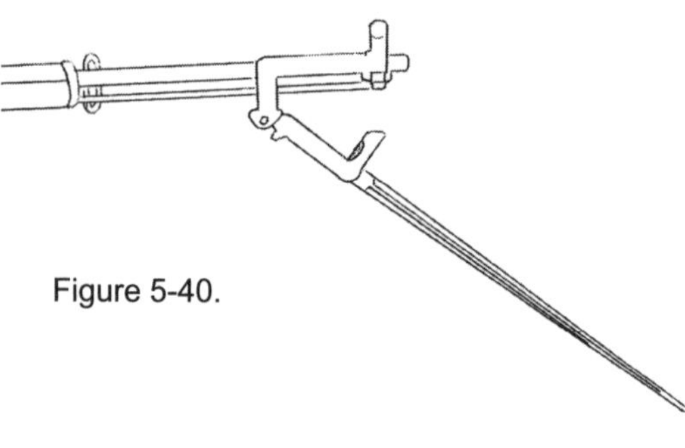

Figure 5-40.

Experimental Cruciform Model of 1948
Blade length: 290 mm; Blade width: 16 mm.

This model, the last one the Russians considered for the Mosin-Nagant series before adopting the M1945 Simonov carbine (SKS-45), is very similar to the bayonet previously adopted for the M44 carbine. The blade is the traditional grooved cruciform type and is attached by a spring-loaded catch and a single screw to a bracket mounted on the barrel; in "march" position it folds back along the right side of the barrel. The major difference from the standard 1944 model is the second bracket, mounted under the front sight protector just behind the muzzle, which provides a locking platform for an additional lug on the bayonet shaft below the muzzle ring. See Figure 5-41.

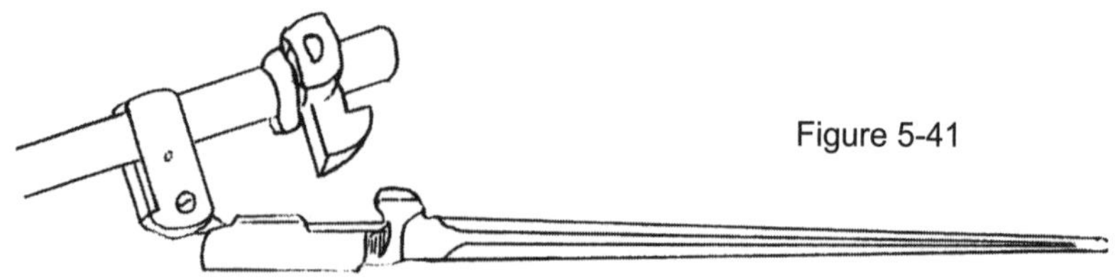

Figure 5-41

Chapter 6
Accessories

The most common Mosin-Nagant accessories issued to the individual soldier are bayonets, slings, ammunition pouches, oil/solvent bottles and cleaning kits. Bayonets were described in Chapter 5. Slings have also been described in other chapters but are summarized here for convenience.

Russian Slings

The original M1891 sling was a common late-19th-century type made of a single strap of brown-dyed leather which passed through the sling swivels and was secured by a brass stud or button. The sling could be adjusted for length by a brass buckle. A rare early variant is reported to have had a swivel integral with the front end of the sling.

In or around 1909 the configuration changed. The swivels were replaced by two slots drilled through the stock and lined with metal washers, and a new sling was designed. It was a leather or web strap with one end sewn into a loop and the other sewn to a metal buckle. The sling was secured to the stock by two small leather straps that were 230 mm–330 mm (9 in–13 in) long and 15 mm (0.590 in) wide, rather like a dog collar, see Figures 6-1 and 6-2 A and B.

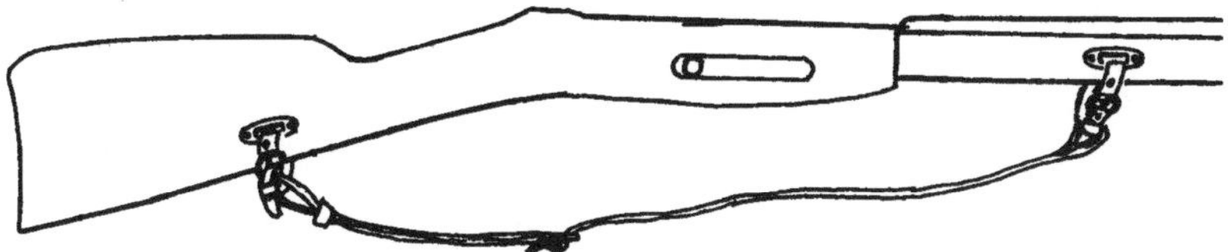

Figure 6-1. Model 1891 Mosin-Nagant sling.

Some of these 'dog collars' had a leather keeper or retainer loop, some had two and some had none. One 'dog collar' was passed through each end of the sling; the 'dog collar' was then buckled through the sling slots. The sling could be adjusted for length by means of the buckle,

Figure 6-2A. Model 1891 Mosin-Nagant leather sling.

see Figures 6-2A and 6-2B. This style remained the Russian standard for the duration of Mosin-Nagant production, and was copied by the other nations producing and using Mosin-Nagants.

A leather sling was manufactured for the carbine version with the 'dog collar' configuration, but which had no buckle and therefore was not adjustable for length. It was usually about 28 in long and 1 1/8 in wide, and was dyed brown.

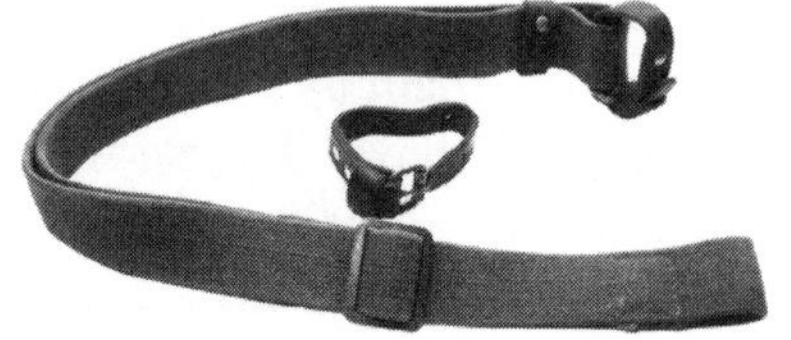
Figure 6-2B. Model 1891 Mosin-Nagant canvas sling.

During the latter part of World War II the Russians developed a shorter version of the web sling for the M1944 carbine. It was 3 feet long, non-adjustable and had leather strengthening tabs behind the front and rear 'dog collar' loops.

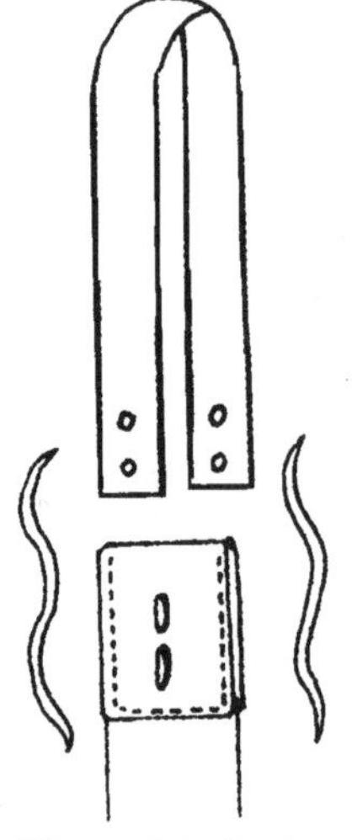
Figure 6-3. Soviet WWII wartime-expedient.

Another type of sling, rather primitive-looking but of World War II vintage, is seldom seen. It was a khaki web strap approximately 1.0 in wide and 28.0 in long, see Figure 6-3. The web strap had a leather tab approximately 2.25 inches on each side of the strap when folded over the end. It was sewn to the strap. The tab had two oval holes, each about 0.25 in long, one above the other so that the upper is about 0.5 in from the end of the sling. Through each hole runs a leather cord. Each of the two cords is fed through two holes in a leather strap approximately

15.0 in long and 0.5 in wide, which runs through the sling slot in the stock.

In an even cruder variation of this sling, the web strap was replaced by a leather strap 700 mm (27.5 in) long and 25 mm (0.98 in) wide, see Figure 6-4. One connecting strap was approximately 250 mm (9.8 in) long, and the other was 430 mm (16.9 in) long; both are 18 mm (0.70 in) wide. The straps (which resemble the usual 'dog-collar' variety, but without integral buckles) have 5 and 9 holes, respectively, for length adjustment, and each has an additional two holes for securing with a cord to the two holes of the sling itself. Each small strap has a leather keeper, resembling a buckle, 35 mm x 30 mm (1.38 in x 1.18 in) in size.

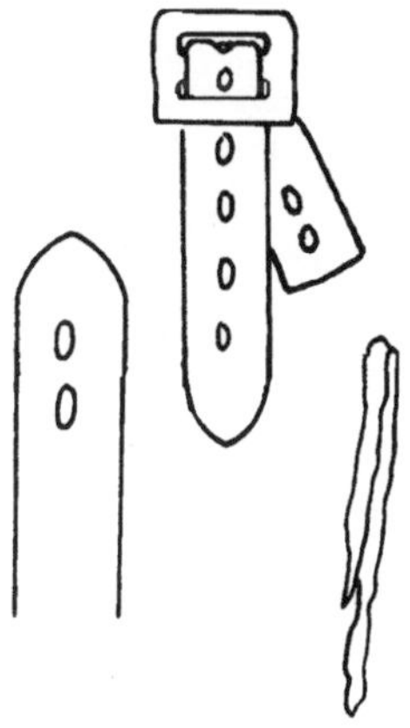

Figure 6-4. Soviet WWII wartime-expedient, another variety.

The sling commonly used on the PPsh and PPS submachine guns was also used on Mosin-Nagant carbines, see Figure 6-5. This type was made in the usual cotton webbing material until the 1950s when it was changed to a synthetic material similar to nylon. It had two permanently attached leather straps and sewn-on leather keepers. This type of sling is approximately 1.375 m (54.13 in) long, of which about 660 mm (25.98 in) is the canvas web (or synthetic material); one leather strap is about 305 mm (12.0 in) long and one about 470 mm (18.5 in) long. (The difference in accumulated length is due to overlapping of leather and non-leather components.) Each strap is secured by an integral buckle and two keepers. This type was extensively used among Polish units serving with the Red Army during World War II.

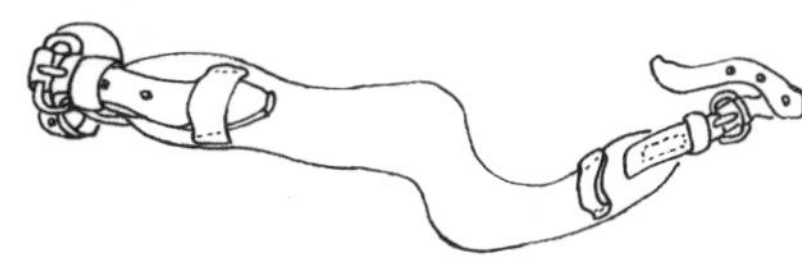

Figure 6-5. The PPsh/PPS submachine gun sling was also used on Mosin-Nagant carbines.

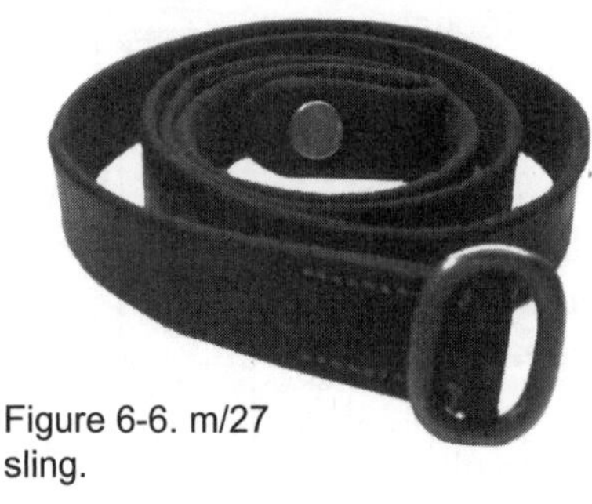
Figure 6-6. m/27 sling.

FINNISH SLINGS

The Finns were well-supplied with captured Russian slings, but developed at least three of their own. Finnish slings were originally dyed brown, though green slings were also made during the 1930s. In 1936, the standard color was set as a grayish-green, though some ersatz slings made during World War II came in various shades of blue-gray.

The sling for the m/27 rifle is a brown leather strap with an oval buckle, see Figure 6-6. This type of buckle proved unsatisfactory as it wore out the leather sling more rapidly than a square or rectangular one would; even so, it was used on the next model Finnish sling, the m/28, which vaguely resembles the U.S. Model 1907 sling used on the Model 1903 Springfield, Model of 1917 Rifle, and the M1 Garand.

Figure 6-7. m/28 sling — both ends are shown.

The m/28 sling consists of two parts: the first is a leather strap 52 inches long which passes through a metal ring attached to the second leather strap, which is about 12 inches long, see Figure 6-7. Each strap is adjusted for length by a buckle. Two types of short straps were used, one with sewn ends and one with a sewn end and a metal stud on the opposite end. The sling was made of brown leather and usually had a maker's marking and, sometimes, a date.

The m/28-30 sling was very similar to the m/28, but the buckles were rectangular rather than oval, the disadvantages of the oval buckle having become apparent by the time of its introduction, see Figure 6-8.

The most common sling used by the Finns was a simple leather strap secured at the front end by a stud through a slit on each side of the sling. The other end passed through a buckle that allowed adjustments for length. The buckle end was held together by a leather keeper. This sling could be used with the sling swivels or the 'dog collar'. It was black, brown, gray, or gray-green and was reportedly used mostly with the m/39 rifle. It is sometimes called the "Model 39" sling, see Figure 6-9.

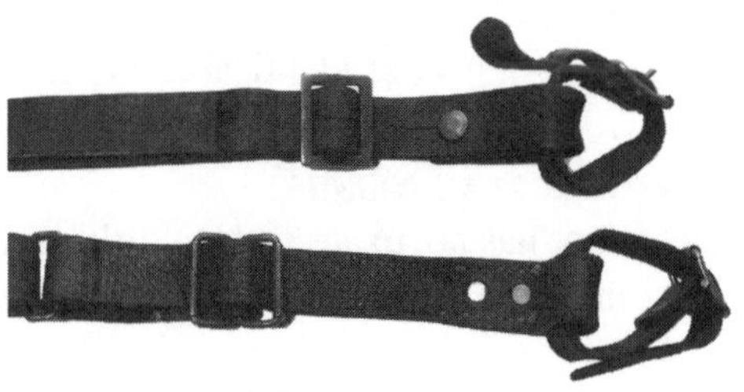

Figure 6-8. m/28-30 sling.

There is an almost identical, but slightly shorter, version in a somewhat lightweight gray-green web, see Figure 6-10. This type sometimes has a leather tab on the rivet end to prevent premature wear from abrasion by the stud.

Figure 6-9. m/39 sling.

The sling can be found with Finnish Army (SA) or Civil Guard (SY or Sk.Y.) markings, or unmarked.

Figure 6-10. m/39 web sling.

CHINESE SLINGS

Chinese slings are very similar to the Russian web variety, but are somewhat narrower and usually appear in a dark olive green or greenish khaki. Some were made with a cloth or thin leather string securing the 'dog collars' rather than the Russian-style buckle. Some are marked with the Chinese characters for "Type 53".

HUNGARIAN SLINGS

Hungarian slings are identical to the Russian web slings.

NORTH KOREAN SLINGS

The author has not examined a North Korean sling due to their extreme rarity in North America and so cannot describe them.

POLISH SLINGS

Polish slings resemble the Russian web type, but in later production were also made of nylon in a medium shade of green. There is also a Polish two-piece web-type of Mosin-Nagant sling based on World War II–era Soviet submachine gun sling. Late 1950s production and after was made of a synthetic material similar to nylon with two permanently attached leather straps and leather keepers sewn on. The sling is approximately 1.375 m (54.13 in) long, of which about 660 mm (25.98 in) is the web or synthetic material; one leather strap is about 305 mm (12.0 in) long and the other about 470 mm (18.5 in) long (difference in accumulated length is due to the overlapping leather and non-leather pieces). Each strap is secured by an integral buckle and two leather keepers. This type of sling is seen very often in World War II–era photographs of Polish units serving with the Red Army and in postwar photographs of Polish soldiers armed with M1944 carbines. Refer to Figure 6-4.

AMMUNITION POUCHES

Russian Ammunition Pouches

The original Russian ammunition pouch for the original M1891 was made of brown leather in the form of a single narrow box-like container with two belt loops sewn to the back, see Figure 6-11. It was used well into the 1930s before being replaced with a two-pocket ammunition pouch, also made of brown leather, some of which were manufactured in Czechoslovakia under contract to the Soviets. Each pocket held three 5-round charger clips. This type and its successors have the two belt loops of the earlier models, as well as a metal C-ring on the back for attachment to suspenders or an assault harness.

This latter type was made in a number of variations, some with their flaps secured by a single leather strap attached to a pointed stud on the underside of the pouch, others with a similar strap which was Y-shaped. Shortages of material during World War II resulted in a cartridge pouch resembling the earlier Soviet pattern, but made of greenish-khaki canvas with leather edging. This model was succeeded, in the late 1940s or early 1950s, by a very similar pattern made of pebble-grained artificial leather with real leather straps and was produced at least as late as the mid-1960s.

Figure 6-11. Note the ammunition pouch on the belt of this Russian soldier in the trenches before Port Arthur, 1904. Contemporary photo by Burton Holmes.

Finnish Ammunition Pouches

The Finns used a variety of ammo pouches from various sources, particularly Russia. German Mauser cartridge pouches from World War I are often found with such Finnish markings as "S.Y." (for the Civil Guard), "SA" (the Finnish Army), etc. All are fairly common.

OIL/SOLVENT BOTTLES

Russian gun oil and bore-cleaner bottles come in several varieties. Some hold only oil and some are dual-compartmented for oil and cleaning solvent. The dual-compartment bottles will often show the Cyrillic letters Щ/Н on the bottle, which stand for *shchalok* ("alkaline solution") and *neft'* ("oil"), see Figure 6-12.

The Tsarist model was a rectangular, dual-compartmented oiler. It was replaced by the round oil bottle in the 1930s. This type was copied by a number of Eastern European countries in succeeding decades. Typical Russian bottles are made of tin-plated steel and have a screw-cap. The caps are all interchangeable with those of all other manufacturers. Occasionally a bottle is found with Tula or Izhevsk arsenal markings — an arrow in a large star or in a triangle, respectively. (See Appendix C: Identification and Attribution.)

Figure 6-12. Two-compartment oil/solvent bottle issued with the Russian Mosin-Nagant.

Bulgarian Oil/Solvent Bottles

Bulgarian oil/solvent bottles are the common East Bloc squarish two-compartment type (see Figure 6-14, overleaf), but are painted a dark olive-drab and have the Cyrillic letters H and Щ on the left and right compartments, respectively, which is the reverse of the Russian configuration.

Chinese Oil/Solvent Bottles

Chinese bottles are identical in size, shape and material to the Soviet types. The dual-container variety has two Chinese characters embossed on one side. The character on the left means 'oil' (pronounced, approximately, "yo"); on the right is the character for cleaning solution: (lit. 'salty') pronounced, approximately, "sheeyan", see Figure 6-13. There is also a Chinese tin-plated steel single-compartment bottle embossed with a large star. The Chinese oil/solvent bottles are otherwise identical to the Russian single-compartment bottles with arsenal marks.

Figure 6-13. Chinese oil/solvent bottle.

East German Oil/Solvent Bottles

These are identical to the round, two-compartment Soviet oil bottles (refer to Figure 6-12) but have the letter "**m**" on the left side and "**H**" on the right side.

Finnish Oil/Solvent Bottles

Finnish oil/solvent bottles are similar to the Russian types, but can be identified by the Finnish Army marking, "SA" or the Civil Guard's "Sk. Y." stamped or embossed on them. The oil and cleaning solvent compartments are marked "F" and "T" respectively. They are often maker-marked. There are also Finnish Civil Guard oilers resembling hi flasks; these come in two sizes and, unlike the round varieties which are "in the white," are painted dark olive drab. The smaller, earlier model is marked "SY" and the later, larger one, "Sk.Y". This change in lettering occurred in 1934.

Hungarian Oil/Solvent Bottles

Hungarian oilers are identical to the Russian types, but the dual-containers have the letters "F" and "T" (for *faggyú*[?] and *tisztítószer*: 'grease' and 'cleanser') embossed on them, making them confusingly similar to the Finnish bottles described above.

Polish Oil/Solvent Bottles

Polish oil/solvent bottles are made of tin-plated steel, in the form of two screw-capped squarish bottles which are soldered together similar to the early Tsarist Russian bottle. The bottles are marked "Pł" (*płyn [do czyszczenia]*) — (cleaning) fluid, pronounced "pwin" ([doh chish-CHAIN-ya]) on the left compartment and Sm (*smar* — lubricant) on the right, see Figure 6-14.

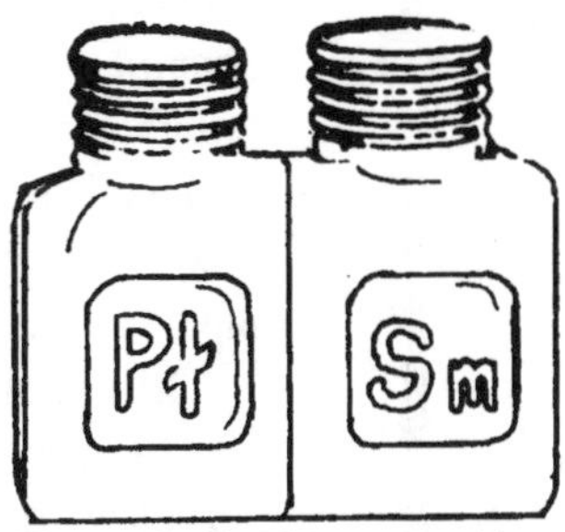

Figure 6-14. This style oil/solvent bottle was in common use in the East Bloc.

Romanian Oil/Solvent Bottles

These are the common two-compartment, squarish East Bloc variety (refer to Figure 6-14) and have the letter "B" (*basâ*, base) on the left and "U" (*ulei*, oil) on the right. There is another type of Romanian-made oiler which also has two compartments; it is larger and more square in shape and has the letter "U" on the left and "S" on the right. Although found with Romanian Mosin-Nagants, it is actually a later model intended for use with the SKS carbine.

CLEANING KITS

Military issue Mosin-Nagant cleaning kits (Figure 6-15) typically consist of a bore brush, cleaning jag, punch, screwdriver, and muzzle crown protector, although there have been some variations in both the number of tools and their configurations over the decades and from country to country. Some tools are found arsenal- or maker-marked, but most are not. Finnish cleaning kits typically come in a pouch secured by a drawstring; in the East Bloc countries the kit was contained in a coarse canvas pouch (in various shades of khaki or, as the Hungarian kit in the illustration, black) which could be tied shut by a piece of cotton tape sewn to the flap.

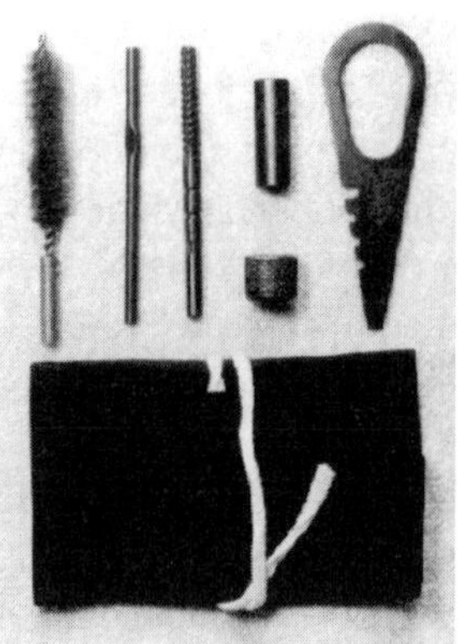

Figure 6-15. (R-L) Screwdriver, cleaning rod head, muzzle crown protector, jag, punch, and bore brush.

Figure 6-16. Assembled cleaning rod.

The bore brush and cleaning jag are threaded on one end for attachment to the cleaning rod. The punch also serves as the handle for the cleaning rod. It is inserted into the round hole in the rod head, see Figure 6-16.

The punch was round in all cleaning kits except that issued for the Finnish m/39 rifle cleaning rod head, see Figure 6-17; this punch was flat. The cleaning rod is threaded through the forward end of the muzzle crown protector, after which the tool — brush or jag — is attached to the rod. The protector is placed to

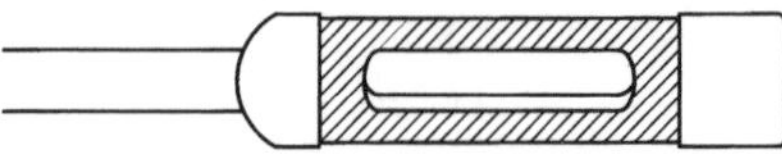

Figure 6-17. Finnish flat-head punch.

prevent wear on the bore during cleaning — which will happen when a steel rod is used frequently, especially by a novice. The muzzle crown protector was usually made of metal with a knurled surface but could also be made of wood (some Finnish examples), or wood with a metal liner (the early Russian type, also made by Remington and, probably, Westinghouse) and even of synthetic materials.

Russian soldiers traditionally used pieces of hemp as cleaning patches. In addition to being a cheap and effective medium for removing propellant residue and other debris, hemp has chemical properties which act as natural cleansing agents.

One of the few small-arms technical tasks an ex-East Bloc soldier was allowed to do was to check firing pin protrusion. This was accomplished with the two middle grooves of the cleaning kit screwdriver, which are actually firing pin gauges. They were marked in *arshini* during the Tsarist era and in millimeters thereafter. The varieties commonly found today are marked "75" and "95".

To use the gauges, remove the bolt and turn the cocking piece to the 'closed' position by grasping the bolt handle in the left hand with the bolt facing skyward. Pull the cocking piece back and turn it to the left. This allows the firing pin to protrude through the bolt face. Place the screwdriver on the bolt face, perpendicular to it, so the groove marked "95" is over the firing pin, see Figure 6-18. If the pin touches the bottom of the groove, it is protruding too far and should be adjusted. The pin should also be checked against the groove marked "75": the pin should touch the bottom of the groove; if it does not, the firing pin is not protruding far enough.

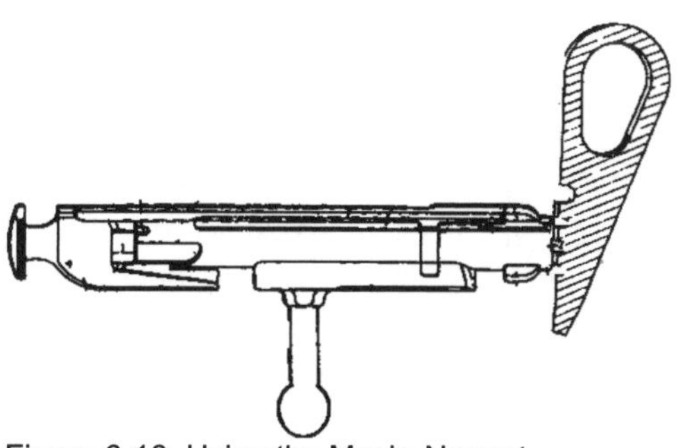

Figure 6-18. Using the Mosin-Nagant screwdriver to check firing pin protrusion.

To adjust the firing pin, turn the slot in the pin's end so that it is in line with the adjustment marks slashed on the back of the cocking piece. If there are no such marks (rarely the case), simply turn the pin, then check the amount of protrusion until it is correct.

Note: Turn the cocking piece to the 'open' position before replacing in the rifle. To do so, pull the cocking piece back and turn to the right.

FINNISH MUZZLE CAPS

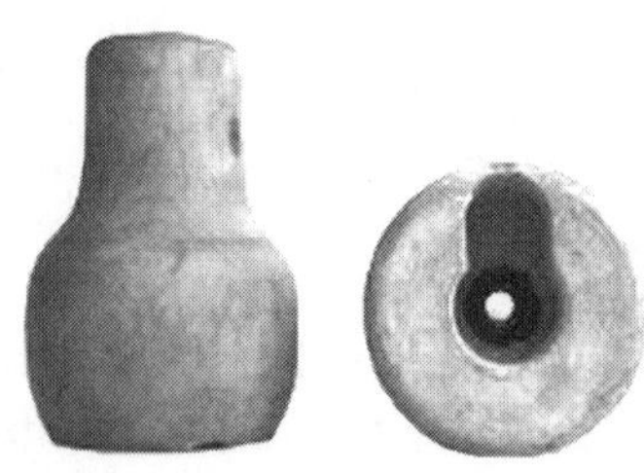

Figure 6-19. m/91 Muzzle Cap.

The main purpose of the cap is to guide the cleaning rod so that it does not wear out the bore, degrading the rifle's accuracy; for this reason, they are sometimes referred to as "bore guides" or, more logically, "cleaning rod guides." Muzzle caps made for the m/91-24 and m/28 are themselves "capped" with screw-on covers, helping to prevent rain, snow, sand, etc., from entering the bore, while others—except the plastic m/39 type—have a hole in the center for the cleaning rod to pass through.

The Finns have produced a variety of muzzle caps for their Mosin-Nagant. The first Finnish muzzle caps (for the m/91) were existing Tsarist-era caps made of wood with a brass sleeve in the upper (narrow) section and an elongated hole through the bottom to enable the cap to be slid over the front sight; these caps can found with and without makers' markings on them. Figure 6-19 shows the m/91 cap from the side and bottom.

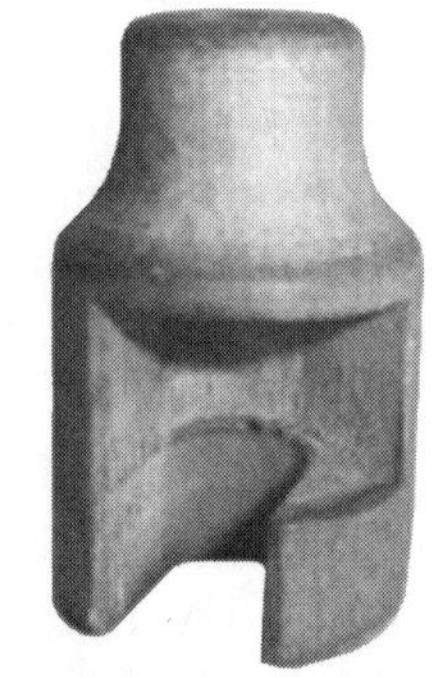

Figure 6-20. m/27 Muzzle Cap.

Wooden caps (Figure 6-20) were also standard issue for the m/27, but with a much different configuration in order to accommodate that model's front sight protector 'ears.' Like the m/91 cap, the m/27 has a metal sleeve in the upper portion.

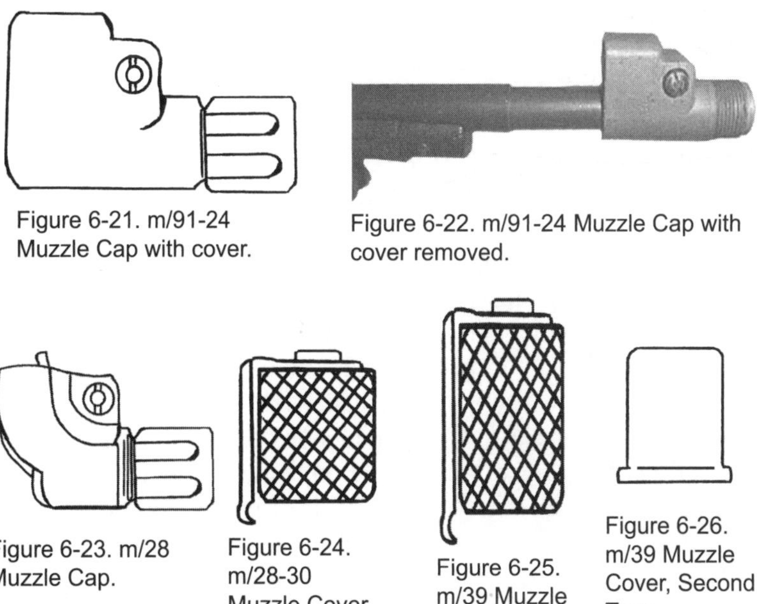

Figure 6-21. m/91-24 Muzzle Cap with cover.

Figure 6-22. m/91-24 Muzzle Cap with cover removed.

Figure 6-23. m/28 Muzzle Cap.

Figure 6-24. m/28-30 Muzzle Cover.

Figure 6-25. m/39 Muzzle Cover, First Type.

Figure 6-26. m/39 Muzzle Cover, Second Type.

Metal muzzle caps were produced for the m/91-24, m/28, m/28-30, and m/39. The caps for the m/91-24 (Figures 6-21 and -22) and m/28 (Figure 6-23) were made of a light-gray metal alloy and, as noted above, had a fluted cover which screwed onto the unit's body; Figure 6-22 shows the muzzle cap with the cover removed, mounted on the barrel of an m/91-24. The m/91-24 cap is about 35 mm by 50 mm, and the m/28 is somewhat smaller. They are heavy and overly complex for the simple tasks for which they were intended and were replaced by lighter, simpler models as the years went by.

The m/28-30 cap (Figure 6-24) and the m/39 cap (Figure 6-25) were made of sheet steel with a heavily knurled exterior surface; they are almost identical except as to size: both are about 18 mm in diameter, but the m/39 is 30 mm tall and the m/28-30 approximately half that height. A smooth-surfaced brass cap was also made for the m/39; it is otherwise identical to the steel model. On the top and side of the cylindrical caps is a flexible steel clip with a hook at its end which snaps onto the front of the sight base to secure the cap to the rifle.

After World War II, plain, smooth-sided plastic caps were produced for the m/39. They were 25 mm tall and 22 mm wide at the base, including the bottom flange (Figure 6-26).

FINNISH OIL BOTTLES

There are two principal types of Finnish Mosin-Nagant oil bottles: the round type (a design inherited from Tsarist days), and a rectangular bottle in the shape of a can of more limited production.

Figure 6-27. Finnish Oil Bottles, left, early Civil Guard type; right, Finnish Army type.

The round type is found in two sizes: the smaller one is 65 mm in diameter; the larger is 75 mm in diameter. The smaller oil bottle can be found both with the Finnish Army SA mark in a flattened circular area in the center of the bottle and with a plain, unmarked center. The larger bottle has the Civil Guard's **SY** marking. The round bottles are of unpainted metal "in-the-white"; unlike later Soviet Bloc models, the Finnish types have a single spout, rather than having separate compartments for oil and cleaning solution, see Figure 6-27.

Figure 6-28. Finnish "Civil Guard" Oil Bottles, Second Type.

The rectangular bottles are also found in two sizes and are painted a dark olive drab; they are marked with either of the Civil Guard's designations: **SY** until 1934, and **Sk. Y.** thereafter; this change in lettering occurred two years after the same marking change for slings. The larger bottle is 95 mm tall (excluding spout and cap; 110 mm including them) by 60 mm wide; the small bottle is 65 mm tall (excluding spout and cap; 75 mm including them) by 50 mm wide, see Figure 6-28.

Chapter 7
Ammunition

Introduction

Measurements in this book are almost always given in both metric and English units. The weights of bullets and propellants are given in both grains (gr) and grams (gm); 1 gr = 64.79 mg and 480 gr = 1.097 oz. For the reader's convenience, other common metric and English weights and measures equivalents are given in Table 7-1.

Table 7-1
Metric Equivalent Weights and Measures

1 meter = 1,000 millimeters = 100 centimeters = 39.37 inches	1 kilogram - 1,000 grams = 2.2 lbs
1 inch = 25.4 millimeters	1 oz = 28.3495 grams
1 foot = 12 inches = 304.8 millimeters	1 lb = 16 ounces = 453.59 grams

All models and derivatives of the Mosin-Nagant, both rifles and carbines, use the standard Russian 7.62 x 54 mm R (rimmed) cartridge. The only exceptions are those rifles altered by the Austrians and Germans during World War I, Poland's 7.92 mm wz.91/98/25, and the post–World War I American conversions to .30-06, all of which are described in Chapter 3.

Bullets

The bullet used in the original M1891 was round-nosed and weighed 13.636 gm (210.4 gr) — typical of late-19th-century military cartridges, see Figure 7-1. When first employed in actual combat, during the Russo-Japanese War of 1904–05, the bullet proved wanting in accuracy and power at realistic battle ranges. Fortunately for the Russians, the Germans saved them the time, effort and costs associated with research and development of a new bullet when they invented the *spitzer* (i.e., pointed) bullet, which was easily adaptable to Russian needs.

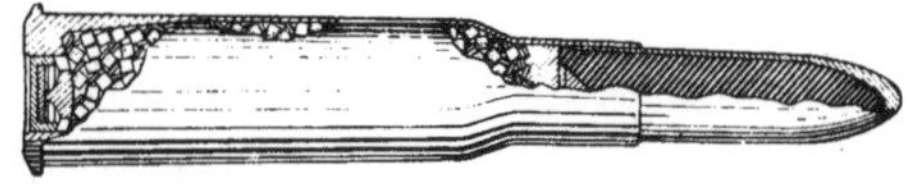

Figure 7-1

Russian ballistics experts began work on a new rifle round in the spring of 1906. By 1908, using smokeless powder and the new *spitzer* bullet, they had developed an effective cartridge which weighed only 22.45 gm (just over 0.792 oz.), thus enabling a soldier to carry 137 new rounds for the same weight as 120 old cartridges (the standard field issue) — an increase of about 14%, see Figure 7-2. The 1908 bullet had a lead core in a tombak (an alloy of 90% copper and 10% zinc) jacket, and was designated *lyokhkaya pulya obrazets 1908 g* (M1908 light[weight] bullet), usually referred to simply as the L bullet. During World War I the Russians used the L round as standard ball ammunition, and employed tracers, incendiary, armor-piercing and exploding bullets as well.

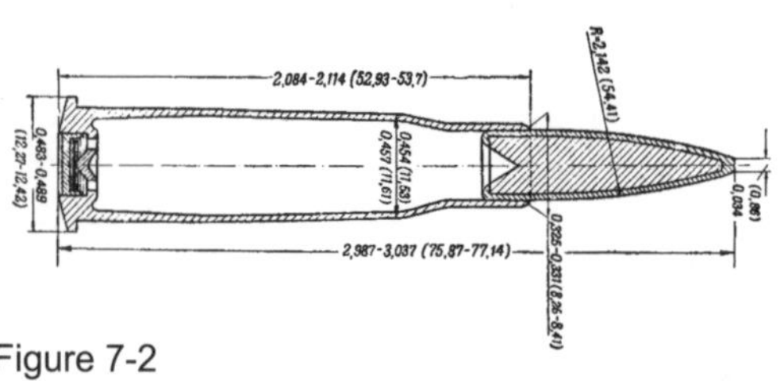

Figure 7-2

In 1930 the Russians introduced a new L round which differed slightly from the M1908 in the shape of the bullet and cartridge case. The new L bullet had a brass-plated iron jacket, was ogival in shape and had a small cannelure into which the case neck was rolled. See Figure 7-3. The L bullet was meant for short- and medium-range use against 'live targets' as, at long ranges, the bullet's small cross-section resulted in decreased velocity and penetrating power.

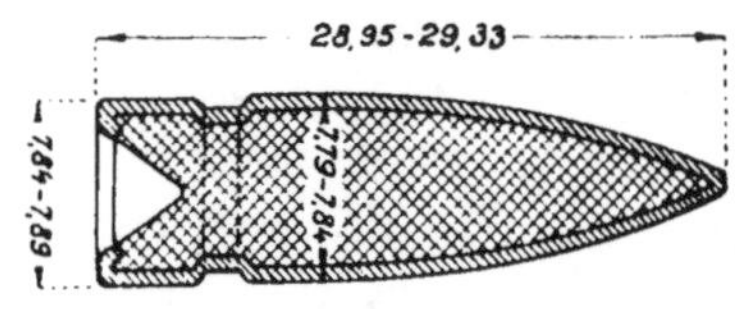

Figure 7-3

A heavier round, weighing about 11.82 gm (182 gr) and having a boat-tailed bullet to increase flight stability, was also introduced in 1930, see Figure 7-4. Rather than being called "T" for *tyazhelaya* ("heavy"), as one would expect, it was styled "D", for *dal'noboinaya* (long-range); the reason for this inconsistency of nomenclature goes unremarked and unexplained in the sources (Shipp, "Red Army Infantry Weapons, Tanks and Armored Cars" — Based on "Jäläväe Relvad, Tankid ja Soomusautod", Intelligence Study prepared for the Estonian General Staff and presented in March 1933).

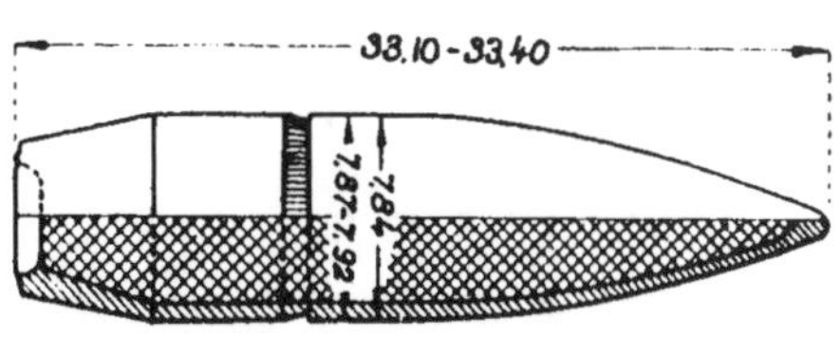

Figure 7-4

Virtually all Finnish Mosin-Nagants will have a capital "D" stamped on their chambers (generally on the buttstock as well) to indicate that they have been chambered for the Finnish D166 cartridge, which was developed to take advantage of the huge amount of captured Soviet "D" ammunition.

As the Estonian intelligence study which was the primary source noted, the "D" round was preferable for use at ranges greater than 1,000 meters because, even though it had a lesser muzzle velocity, due to its shape and greater cross-section load it maintained its velocity longer and "produces casualties even at the maximum range (1500 meters) when its final velocity is 140 meter/second (the bullet can still penetrate a man at a velocity of 116 meter/second".)

CARTRIDGE SPECIFICATIONS

Specifications for the two M1930 rounds are given in Tables 7-2 and 7-3. For shooters and collectors, a variety of ammunition is now obtainable for the Mosin-Nagant, ranging from high-quality American, Swedish and Finnish hunting rounds to corrosive military surplus from Russia, Egypt, Eastern Europe and China. Bullet weights vary, with 147-grain and 174-grain being the most common though a number of others are available. The typical cartridge weighs 21–23 grams (copper-coated steel or tombak case) or 22–24 grams (brass case); of this the propellant accounts for 3.25 grams. Total length of the cartridge is 77.16 mm (3.03 in); the bullet's length is 32.3 mm (1.3 in) and the cartridge case is 53.72 mm (2.11 in).

Table 7-2 The "L" Round	
Bullet Length	28.95 to 29.33 mm
Bullet Weight	9.5 to 9.7 gm
Bullet Cross-Section Load	21.2 gm/sq cm
Muzzle Velocity	825 to 855 m/sec
Maximum (powder) Pressure	2,750 - 2,800 kg/sq cm

Table 7-3 The "D" Round	
Bullet Length	33.10 to 33.40 mm
Bullet Weight	11.82 gm
Bullet Cross-Section Load	25.5 gm/sq cm
Muzzle Velocity	770 - 785 m/sec
Maximum (powder) Pressure	2,800 to 2,850 kg/sq cm

With military equipment of every sort from long underwear to weapons-grade plutonium hemorrhaging from the former East Bloc, we should not be surprised to find ammunition for the 7.62 mm ShKAS (*sistemy Shpitalnogo-Komaritskogo aviatsionniy skorostrelniy pulemet* (Shpitalniy-Komaritskii Rapid-fire Aviation Machine-gun) surfacing now and then. While it *can* be fired in Mosin-Nagant rifles and carbines, it is not wise to do so as it can cause damage, principally to the interrupter-ejector. These rounds are easily identified by the red-enameled foil covering the primer on the bottom of the cartridge case and the Cyrillic letter Ш (*sh*, for Shpitalniy) next to it.

Cartridge Codes

In keeping with common military practice, the Russians mark special-purpose cartridges for easy identification. The bullet tips are colored as shown in Table 7-4.

Tracers

Tracers from the prewar Soviet period derived their illuminating quality from a mixture of barium salts, highly pulverized magnesium,

Table 7-4
Soviet Rifle Ammunition Codes

Color Code	Bullet Type	Bullet Weight (grains)
Bullet – none	Ball	148
Bullet – Yellow	Heavy Ball (D round)	182
Bullet – Silver	Light Ball (L round)	(?)
Bullet – Green	Tracer	148
Bullet Tip/Primer – Green	Practice Ball (post-1941)	60
Green Bullet, Case-head & Case-mouth	Subsonic Silencer (pre-1941)	142 (?)
Bullet – Black	Armor-Piercing (B-30)*	170
Black/Red Band	Armor-Piercing Incendiary (B-32)*	155
Bullet – Black/Green	Subsonic Silencer (post-1941)	142 (?)

Table 7-4, cont.
Soviet Rifle Ammunition Codes

Color Code	Bullet Type	Bullet Weight (grains)
Bullet – Red	Ranging Incendiary (PZ) **	142
Red Bullet & Case-mouth, Black Case-head and Bullet Tip	Armor-Piercing Incendiary/ Tracer (BS-40)	187
Bullet – Violet/Red	Armor-Piercing Incendiary/ Tracer (BZT) ***	142
Bullet – Copper Cap	Armor-Piercing Incendiary (pre-1930)	167

* B – *Broneboinaya*, Armor [piercing]
** PZ – *Pristrelnochno-zazhigatel'naya,* Ranging incendiary (Erroneously rerferred to as the ZP on occasion)
*** BZT – *Broneboino-zazhitgatel'naya trassiruyushchaya,* Armor [piercing] incendiary tracer

aluminum, etc. The compound was pressed into the bullet's jacket and weighed 1.0 to 1.1 gr; duration of combustion was up to five seconds. See Figure 7-5.

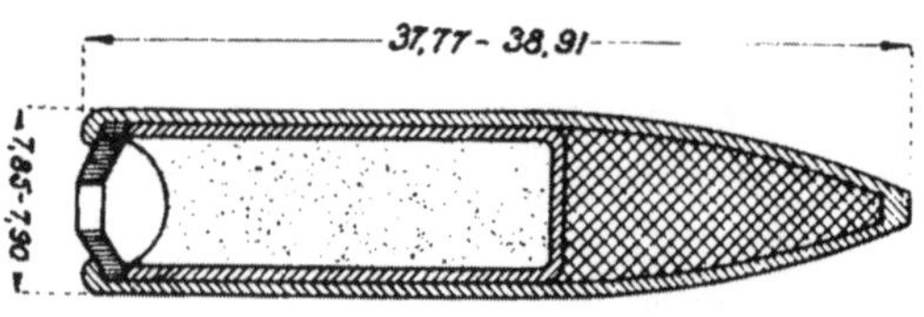

Figure 7-5

Although the Soviets' technical requirement for a tracer's range was 1,500 meters, the actual range was only about 1,200 meters. This should have been acceptable under normal battlefield conditions as the tracers were able to penetrate 54–55

Table 7-5 Pre–World War II Soviet Tracer (M1930 Type T) Specifications	
Weight	9.5 gm
Weight of Combustible Compound	3.2 gm
Length	38.34 mm
Muzzle Velocity	825 m/sec
Range	1,200 m

pine boards 2.5 mm thick at 150 meters, and could penetrate 3–4 mm thick aircraft armor at close range. Because it was designed primarily as an antiaircraft round the early Soviet tracers had two colors of illumination to aid in range-finding: red for ascent (up to 750–800 meters) and light green for the descent. The specifications for this round, designated M1930 Type T, are listed in Table 7-5, above.

At least two types of 7.62 mm tracer rounds were in service with the Soviets from the end of World War II, and both apparently were designated "T-46"; however, they differ from each other in some respects. Both rounds have the green tip characteristic of Russian tracers, but the earlier model was 38 mm long and had a flat base, while the later model was somewhat boat-tailed and only 35 mm long. The tracer cannister with the cartridge was open at the back in the first model, but open at both ends in the second.

Armor-Piercing Incendiary Cartridges

Pre–World War II Soviet armor-piercing incendiary rounds were quite similar to the tracer round described above. They differed only in that the core was steel rather than lead, and the tracer compound was contained in a cavity at the rear of the core, see Figure 7-6.

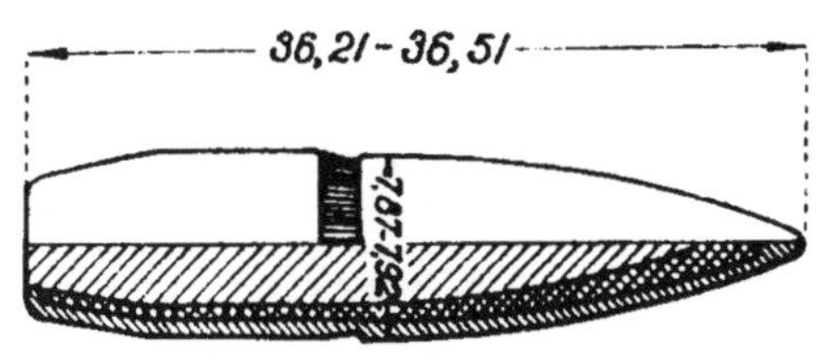

Figure 7-6

There were also two types of B-32 armor-piercing incendiary rounds, also not differentiated by nomenclature. Both varieties were boat-tailed and steel-cored. The first type weighed 9.99 g (154 gr) and was 36.8 mm long; the second type was slightly longer. They differed also in that the second model had the incendiary mixture in both ends of the cartridge, rather than only in the forward end as was the case with the first pattern. The first type of incendiary agent was a phosphorus/aluminum compound. Later, thermite was used.

Warning: The PZ round was designed for use in machine guns: attempting to fire it from rifles or carbines is exceedingly dangerous and should be strictly avoided. This round is unstable, having a striker device and an explosive vial or capsule in the bullet's center; it has been known to explode at highly inconvenient times for the shooter.

Armor-Piercing Cartridges

Pre–World War II non-incendiary armor-piercing rounds were based on a 1930 design by Boino-Rodzevich. The bullet was a steel core made into a double jacket: the outer core of nickel and brass alloy, and the inner core of copper or lead. The theory of the round is that upon striking armor the jacket was destroyed and the steel penetrated the target, the lead acting as a lubricant. Specifications for this round are listed in Table 7-6.

Table 7-6 **Pre–World War II Soviet Armor-Piercing Bullet**	
Length	33.25 mm
Weight	10.7 gm
Cross-Section Load	25.6 gm/sq cm
Weight of Charge	3.05 gm
Armor-Piercing Capacity	7.0 mm at 400 m

Sniper Cartridges

The Russian sniper bullet, still current and used in the USSR's successor states, is designated **7N1**; there is no color code.

Other Mosin-Nagant Ammunition

Other ex-East Bloc 7.62 mm R ammunition which may be encountered are Bulgarian-, Czech-, Hungarian-, Polish-, and Romanian-manufactured versions of the "D" round, which are marked, as the Russian ones are, with a yellow tip. There is also a Czech heavy ball round weighing 181 gr, boat-tailed, and 38.5 mm long. This type was made in the early 1950s. There is a Czech tracer round (designated TzSz), also boat-tailed, which weighs 182 gr and whose length is 37.7 mm; it, too, was produced in the early '50s, and is green-tipped like its Russian counterparts.

Chinese 7.62 mm ammunition is still fairly plentiful and cheap, despite the ban on its importation into the U.S. dating from the mid-1990s. Like all Mosin-Nagant ammunition produced in communist countries, it is corrosive.

Excellent non-corrosive ammunition is available from Finnish commercial manufacturers such as Lapua. Finnish military ammunition dating from the Second World War and earlier is also still available, but is corrosive and usually past its prime.

Charger Clips

Mosin-Nagants can be loaded with standard ball rounds either individually or in 5-round charger clips. See Figure 7-7. The first type of charger was a cumbersome two-piece frame, needlessly expensive to produce and awkward to use. The design was abandoned after a few years. Modern chargers are made of brass or steel, and are found in two basic types. In addition to the charger shown in Figure 7-7 there is a flatter variety similar to that used in Mauser-type rifles. Charger clips have been made — and are

Figure 7-7

still being made — by many producers in many countries and can be found either unmarked or with any one of a profusion of arsenal as well as manufacturer's logos.

Ammunition Identification

Almost all Mosin-Nagant ammunition can be identified by markings ("headstamps") on the bottom of the cartridge case. There are many variations, of which the following may be only the proverbial tip of the iceberg. Not all countries that produce — or produced — 7.62 x 54R ammunition used Mosin-Nagants: this ammunition is made for other weapons, such as the Soviet SVT-38 and SVT-40 semiautomatic rifles, Russia's *Dragunov* sniper rifle, its Chinese and Romanian copies, the very similar Iraqi *al-Kadisiyah*, as well as several different light or heavy machine guns, and so on.

Russia/USSR. On Russian ammunition the two-digit factory code number is found at the 12 o'clock position. On Tsarist and early Soviet production the code can also be three-digit. The year of manufacture is found at 6 o'clock; on Tsarist and early Soviet production the date can be three-digit, but usually is only two-digit. There are also Cyrillic letter factory codes, which are customarily located at 9 o'clock. On some ammunition there are three code numbers located at 12, 3, 6 and 9 o'clock (with one spot blank; the factory code, however, is always at 12 o'clock, even on these multiple-marked cases).

Russian ammunition made during the Tsarist period can be identified by the following headstamps: П. ТУЛЬСКІЙ 3.99 = *Tulskii Patronii Zavod* (Tula Cartridge Factory), 3rd production run of 1899 (there appear to have been three runs that year). After 1899 the date was given in three numerals, e.g., 901 for 1901. There was another munitions factory at Tula, the *Tulskii Gubernii Zavod* (Tula Provincial Factory), which used "Т" and "ЛТ" plus a two-digit year date. The *Luganskii* factory headstamp was "Л" and a two-digit date. The *Petrogradskii* factory markings were "П" (on the left side of the cartridge base at 9 o'clock), a two-digit date at 12 o'clock, "K" or "B" or "P" at 3 o'clock, and "I" or "II" or "III" (the production run) at 6 o'clock.

To complicate matters, a letter was used as code for the manufacture date on some ammunition produced, probably, in the later 1940s. Following are some of these codes: 3, 10, 17, 30, 38, 46, 50, 58, 60, 179, 188, 270, 304, 529, 540, 541, 543, 545, 547, 611, 710, 711, К, Т, ЗОУ, ЗВ, Л. Some known date codes are г (1952), А (1953), Е (1954), И (1955), and К (1956).

Albania uses the number 3 as a letter code.

Austria produced Mosin-Nagant ammunition at the Hirtenberger (Hirtenberg) and Keller & Co. (Vienna) factories.

Bulgaria followed the Russian stamping system, the typical marking being Bulgaria's East Bloc country code, 10 (which is also a Soviet factory mark), although the Cyrillic letters БВФ (i.e., BVF) and ВДФ (i.e., VDF) were also used, as was a star at 12 o'clock. In the 1970s a new headstamp "10" appeared, evidently neither Russian nor Bulgarian, but its origin is unknown.

China used several marking patterns. In 1951, the factory code was D followed by two numerals, all located at 6 o'clock. From 1952 to 1955 the code was shifted to 12 o'clock, and consisted of several digits for the factory code followed by the year and month of manufacture, although the older 6 o'clock position for the factory code — though not the date — was sometimes used. Beginning in 1955 the Chinese adopted the Soviet pattern placing the factory code at 12 o'clock and the two-digit date at 6 o'clock. There are exceptions to all the foregoing, with codes and dates located at other points around the base. The following are factory codes for China: D22, D25, D53, 31, 41, 61, 71, 81, 121, 321, 451, 671, 791, 21215. Patterns formed of circles and interlocked circles were used as well.

Cuba may or may not have produced Mosin-Nagant ammunition; in any event, its small arms ammunition codes are 13 and PMV.

Czechoslovakia adopted the Soviet 12 o'clock/6 o'clock pattern in 1952, using a three-letter factory code system: aym, bxn, and uxa; 0 was also used, as was ZV.

East Germany used the Soviet system, though apparently not until the later 1950s. The DDR also sometimes put the factory code at 6 o'clock. East German code numbers are 04, 05, 06, 5, and 22.

Finland, not being part of the East Bloc, used and uses its own code system. Ammunition marked SAT, SMT and VPT is Finnish.

France manufactured 7.62 x 54R ammunition at the Société Française de Munitions factory. As was the case for Great Britain, the U.S. and several other countries, this was principally a World War I undertaking with little or no post-war production.

Germany, not surprisingly, given the number of Mosin-Nagants it captured during both World Wars, produced ammunition for them, both at the Polte Company in Magdeburg and at the DWM (Berlin) works.

Great Britain produced ammunition for its Russian ally during the First World War. These cartridges are marked C.17.F1 or KYNOCH (the latter was, reportedly, sometimes stamped in Cyrillic letters). Mosin-Nagant ammunition was also made at the National Arms & Ammunition Company in Birmingham.

Hungary used the common Soviet marking system; Hungarian factory code numbers are 21 and 23.

North Korea uses Korean letters on some, but not all, of its domestically made ammunition instead of numbers to indicate the manufacture date; "93" is a North Korean marking.

Poland also used the Soviet marking system, although the factory number is sometimes found stamped in an oval. The Polish code numbers are 21 — distinguished from the Hungarian 21 by being upside down, at 12 o'clock — and 343 and 361.

Romania followed East Bloc procedure in their markings, and used the codes 22, CMC, RPR 21, RPR 22, 23, 312, 314, 315, 317, 319, 321, 322, 324, 325, and 325.

Spain began making 7.62 x 54R ammunition for the Mosin-Nagant in 1937, at *Fabrica No. 3 de la Subsecretaría de Armamento* (Subsecretariat for Armament Factory No. 3) at Toledo. The headstamp for this factory was *38-38. The factory was renamed *Fábrica Nacional de Toledo* (Toledo National Arms Factory) after the Civil War and is now the *Empresa Nacional Santa Bárbara de Industrias Militares, SA* (Santa Bárbara National Military Industries Enterprise, Ltd.). Beginning, probably, in 1944, the cartridge headstamp for this factory was F.N., but was later changed to F.N.T. Mosin-Nagant cartridges were also made in Seville at the *Pirotécnica de Sevilla*, whose headstamp is PS plus the year of manufacture. In 1973 a batch of blank cartridges was made in a factory in Palencina, using cases salvaged from the Civil War era and which still had the original Russian headstamps.

Spain stopped making 7.62 x 54R military ammunition in 1986.

The United States produced ammunition as well as rifles and bayonets for the Russians during World War I, and the ammunition is easily identified by the maker's name, REMINGTON, followed by the year of production: 16, 17 or 18.

Yugoslavia used both letters and numbers for factory codes at the 12 o'clock location. On some ammunition the date is marked at 4 o'clock, and the caliber at 8 o'clock. Commercial (as opposed to military) ammunition has the factory code at 12 o'clock and the caliber at 6 o'clock. Although lettering is usually in Yugoslav Cyrillic it is often found in

Latin letters on ammunition made for export. Codes for Yugoslavia are 11, 12, 14, PP, ppy, BT3, ГП, ППУ, nny, ИК, and IK.

Several Arab states with well-developed weapons industries (Egypt, Iraq and Syria) also produced 7.62 x 54R ammunition. These products can be identified by Arabic letters on the base, as well as the caliber marking for 7,62 — ٧,٦٢. Ammunition marked with the caliber and ٥٣ (i.e., 53 in Arabic) is Iraqi.

APPENDICES

Appendix A
Production Totals

The following table is, by necessity, incomplete: production figures for many Mosin-Nagant varieties are simply unavailable and the reasons are not difficult to understand. Since the beginning of Mosin-Nagant production Russia has undergone three revolutions, a civil war, two world wars, and the internal collapse of the Soviet Union. And the Russians are obsessively-secretive by nature, particularly in matters of national security and armaments production.

China and North Korea are also notoriously paranoid about releasing any information about anything. Thus, the matter of production figures must remain vague, and that of serial numbers almost wholly enigmatic.

In many instances more than one total can be found for a particular model, and I have given the number which most sources agree upon; where no model is listed it is because I found no production statistics for it, and not because it was overlooked. The omission of one or more years in a list means that I found no figure for the same, and it should not be inferred that the model was not made in an omitted year — although that may in fact be the case — unless the main text of this book so specifies.

The totals I discovered for late tsarist/early Soviet production were ambiguous, it being unclear whether they referred to a particular model or to all bolt-action weapons. Not wanting to throw more muck into already muddied waters, I chose to omit them altogether.

The data in Table A-1 are derived principally from Mavrodins' *Iz istorii otechestvennogo oruzhiya* (2nd ed.), and those in Tables A-5 and A-6 from Wrobel's *Drei Linien*. The data in Table I-1 and I-2, Appendix I, originally appeared in an article in the March 1993 issue of the Finnish magazine, *Ase* [Weapons], and are kindly furnished to the author by Mr. Brent Snodgrass, master of the excellent site, www.mosin-nagant.net and its affiliates. For the reader's convenience the

Table A-1, Production Totals, Russia

Arsenal	Rifle Type	Years					Total
		1892	1893	1894	1895	1896	
Tula	Infantry	1,439	79,308	204,000	256,000	272,000	812,747
Sestror-yetsk	Infantry		16,517	50,915	71,000	64,500	202,932
Izhevsk	Infantry		33,513	26,209	14,210	27,038	100,970
	Dragoon		12,470	41,049	57,779	79,412	190,710
	Cossack			30,000	60,906	73,550	164,456
Totals		1,439	141,808	352,173	459,895	516,500	1,471,815

author translated the entry *Sk Päälystökoulu*, found in Tables I-1 and I-2, to its English equivalent, "Civil Guard Officer's School." The author compiled all other production data from a number of sources.

The following figures must therefore be regarded as approximations rather than specifics. In almost every instance there was a disparity — sometimes extreme — among the sources for production totals of the same model. This statistical uncertainty comes as no surprise to anyone who has seen the various production figures quoted for even common American firearms such as the M1 Garand and M1911 Colt .45, whose histories are amazingly well-documented. In any event I have endeavored to provide as much information on the matter as I have been able to find, in the hope that it will be of interest or use to the reader.

Table A-2, Production Totals, M1891 Infantry Rifles	
Russia/USSR	
All Russian Arsenals, 1892–1902	2,964,484
All Russian Arsenals, 1892–1922	9,350,000+
France	
Châtellerault, 1892–1896	503,540
United States	
New England Westinghouse 1915–1917	769,520
Remington Arms-UMC, 1915–1918	840,310

Table A-3, M1891/30 Production Totals, Soviet Union			
1930	102,000	1937	560,545
1931	154,000	1938	1,124,664
1932	283,451	1939	1,396,667
1933	239,290	1940	1,375,822
1934	300,590	1941	873,391
1935	136,959	1942	3,026,765
1936	?	1943	3,400,000 (?)
Total 1930–1945: 17,465,000			

Table A-4, M1891/30, Sniper Rifle Totals, Soviet Union			
1932	749	1936	12,752
1933	1,347	1937	13,130
1934	6,637	1938	19,545
1935	?	1942	53,195
Total 1932–1945: 185,000 (?)			

Table A-5, M1938 Production, Soviet Union (Izhevsk)	
1939	34,508
1940	162,162
1941	419,065
1942	687,426
1943	978,297
1944	167,000
1945	(?)

Table A-6, M1944 Production, Soviet Union (Izhevsk)	
1944	3,620,000
1945	3,472,245
1946	189,027
1947	120,061
1948	160,495

Table A-7, Production Totals, Finland	
m/91 (SAT Rebuilds)	Fewer than 200
m/91/24 (SIG Barrels)	8,000
m/91/23 (Böhler-Stahl Barrels)	18,000
m/91 "P" Series	13,000
m/91 Tikkakoski (unstepped barrels)	7,000
m/91 Tikkakoski (stepped barrels)	3,000
m/91 Tikkakoski (1940–1943)	3,300
m/91 VKT (1940–1944)	45,000
m/91 "B" (1942 only)	11,293 (?)
m/27 Tikkakoski	6,000
m/27 VKT	Less than 1,000
m/27 Cavalry Model	2,500
m/28 SY (SIG Barrels)	14,000
m/28 SY (SIG Barrels) double	6,000
m/28 (Tikkakoski Barrels)	13,061
m/28-30 SkY	40,000
m/39 SkY	10,588
m/39 SAKO	59,278
m/39 VKT	48,990
m/39 Tikkakoski (made from m/91 barrels)	5,000
Total	315,210 (?)

Appendix B
Russian Serial Numbering

The original system of serial numbering used by the Russians — and continued into the early Soviet era — was the common European custom of running up to the end of a six-figure series per year, and beginning at 0001 the following year. The Russians followed the usual pattern, and the only distinguishing characteristic during this period is the prefix Каз (Russian Kaz) before the serial number of Cossack rifles.

In late 1937 or early 1938 the Soviets began an alphanumeric serial numbering system, under which the former six-digit annual pattern was retained, but preceded by a Cyrillic letter, in alphabetical order as the series progressed. When production reached huge numbers in World War II a second Cyrillic letter was added, again in alphabetical order, at the end of each five-digit series. This system was first employed on the M1891/30 rifle, and became the Soviet standard.

Some confusion has arisen in the United States recently over the profusion of serial number letters on the same Russian rifle or carbine, obviously made by different tools and in different alphabets. This puzzlement is the result of both federal law which requires that a serial number be stamped on all firearm receivers as well as a Bureau of Alcohol, Tobacco, Firearms and Explosives mandate from the mid-1990s requiring that the importer transliterate the Cyrillic letters and stamp them on the barrel and on the receiver together with the numerals, even though the serial number had never been on the receiver - the U.S. government has decreed that the receiver is the firearm and must bear a serial number.

The reason for this government-imposed vandalism is obtuse: the BATFE feel that, as the Russians repeated their numbering every year, there is a possibility of duplication of original serial numbers in a given series of weapons. As there are more letters in the Cyrillic alphabet than in the Latin, this possibility is even more remote in the Russian series than in one using Western letters. In any event, transliterating the Cyrillic letters would not obviate the problem even if it existed.

Appendix C
Identification and Attribution

The following are some of the most common markings found on Mosin-Nagant receivers, bolt assemblies, etc.; they are a convenient means to establish the origin of a firearm and can tell a knowledgeable observer quite a lot about an individual rifle's history. The list below cannot be all-inclusive as so many markings exist, some of which are not found in the available literature. Occasionally a rifle may cross the reader's path which has odd, sometimes rather whimsical stamps on it; in some instances they are simply importers' logos and have nothing to do with the origin or production of the weapon. This is especially common on surplus firearms in Europe. In other cases the markings may have genuine historic interest but are as yet uncatalogued, and this element of discovery is one of the things which makes older firearms so fascinating.

Some Russian and Finnish words present on rifles but not found in the list below do appear in the Russian and Finnish glossaries later in this book; this is because they are not necessarily pertinent to identifying a weapon, but nonetheless may be of interest or use to the reader.

Note: 'Russia' refers to pre-Soviet-era markings.

Letters & Lettering

Ижевскій Оружейный заводъ	Russia ("Izhevsk Arsenal")
Ижевский Оружейный завод	USSR ("Izhevsk Arsenal")
	Russia ("Sestroryetsk Arsenal")

ИМПЕРАТОРСКIЙ ТУЛЬСКIЙ ОРУЖЕЙНЫЙ ЗАВОДЪ	Russia ("Imperial Tula Arsenal", pre-1913)
ИМПЕРАТОРСКIЙ ПЕТРА ВЕЛИКАГО ТУЛЬСКIЙ ОРУЖЕЙНЫЙ ЗАВОДЪ	Russia ("Imperial Tula Arsenal of Peter the Great", 1913-1917)
ОРУЖЕЙНЫЙ ЗАВОДЪ ШАТЕЛЬРО	France ("Châtellerault Arsenal"; found on first M1891s)
ТУЛЬСКIЙ ОРУЖЕЙНЫЙ ЗАВ	USSR ("Tula Arsenal"; used in 1919)
Первый в Туле Оружейный завод	USSR ("Premier Arsenal, in Tula"; after 1919)
ПЕРВЫЕ ТУЛЬСКЫЕ ОРУЖЕЙНЫ ЗАВОДЫ РСФСР	USSR ("Premier Tula Arsenals [of the] RSFSR"; used in 1920–23)

AV 2 Finland (Arms Depot No. 2 [*Asevarikko-2*], located at Viipuri)

AV 3 Finland (Arms Depot No. 3 [*Asevarikko-3*], located at Kuopio)

AZF Austrian war-booty mark found on World War I–captured rifles (Artillerie-Zeugs-Fabrik)

AZR German World War I capture mark

B [on barrel] Finland (When found without a manufacturer's logo it almost certainly means the barrel is made of Belgian-produced steel)

B [on barrel] Finland (Indicates a bore width)

B Hungary, found on buttstock

BÖHLER - STAHL Finland (Indicates German-made barrels)

© France (Châtellerault parts mark)

C Russia (Sestroryetsk parts mark)

D Finland (Stamped on barrels and/or stocks to indicate that the weapon had been reworked to fire the Finnish D166 cartridge)

DEUTSCHES REICH German World War I capture marking (lit. "German Empire")

DEUTSCHLAND German Empire World War II marking

E Finland (Used in 1928–34; high-pressure proof mark of SAKO inspector Erikson)

F — Finland (Seen on Tikkakoski m/27; indicates barrel made of steel from Swedish firm Fagersta

G — Finland (Found on m/91 receivers; meaning unknown)

Ⓗ — Russia and USSR (Final smokeless "nitro" proof)

HV — Finland (Found on magazine housing; indicates the magazine has been lengthened to accommodate a longer round)

INSTRUCŢIE — Romania (indicates rifle fit only for training)

J.P. — Finland (Jääkäri Pataljoona = "Jaeger Battalion")

JR — Finland (On buttstock I.D. disc: indicates Jaeger regiment)

K — Russia and USSR (Point of aim proof)

KKK — Finland (On buttstock I.D. disc: machine-gun regiment)

KLP — Finland (Indicates issuance to a communications batallion, *kulkulaitos pataljoona*)

←(KE)→ — Finland (Mark of Civil Guard inspector Kosti Eakola; found on Tikkakoski m/28 and m/28-30 rifles)

K.M. K. HUOLT. O. R. — Finland (Pre–World War II marking for supply and maintenance troops)

K ru — Germany (*Karabin, russisch* = "Russian carbine"; World War II capture mark on M1938 and M1944 carbines)

Ⓜ — Finland (indicates rifle sold as surplus; M = *myyty* = sold)

MM — Finland (Before serial number on m/28-30; extremely rare: indicates one of 440 rifles made by SAKO for the World Championship competition)

N — Austria-Hungary (World War I mark on reissued Russian bayonet: identity as Austro-Hungarian is unconfirmed but believed correct)

NSD — Finland (Mark of the Nylands Civil Guard Regiment)

ПК ПК — Russia/USSR (*Probaya Komissiya* [Proof commission] acceptance marks)

(П) — Russia and USSR (Proof Commission)

P-25 — Finland (Indicates m/91 rifle barrel made in 1925; **P-26** and **P-27** markings also exist)

Р.С.Ф.С.Р. — Soviet Union (R.S.F.S.R. = *Russkaya Sovietskaya Federativnaya Sotsialisticheskaya Respublika* = Russian Soviet Federated Socialist Republic; the country's name from July 1918 through December 1922)

PPP — Finland (On buttstock I.D. disc: indicates bicycle battalion)

PUOLUSTUSLAITOS — Finland (lit. "Defense Dept."; marking used for two months in mid-1942 before being replaced by **SA** [see below])

R	Finland (Meaning unknown; found on m/28 barrels)
RUK	Finland (On buttstock I.D. disc: *Reserviupseerikolu* = Reserve Officer's School
®	USA (Remington, World War I contract)
R	USA (New England Westinghouse, inspector's mark)
RPR	Romania (found within a laurel wreath on M1944 carbine chambers) (*Republica Populara Romana* = Romanian People's Republic)
S	Finland (SAKO factory; also can indicate Civil Guard property)
S2	Austria-Hungary (World War I captured rifle reissue mark)
	Finland (Civil Guard acceptance mark)
	Finland (Civil Guard acceptance mark)
	Finland (SAKO factory mark, at Riihimäki)
 **SAKO RIIHIMÄKI**	Finland (Used on civilian production m/28-30 in 1934–41; serial # range 100,000–102,000)

Finland (*Suomen Armeija* = Finnish Army; a property mark)

Finland (*Suomen Ampumatarvetehdas* = Finnish Ammunition Factory)

Schweiz. Industrie-Gesellschaft Neuhausen

Finland (seen on m/91-24 and m28 barrels made by SIG, the Swiss Industry Co. of Neuhausen, Switzerland)

SK.Y.

Finland (*Suojeluskuntain Yleisesikunta*; Civil Guard General Staff)

SY

Finland (Earlier version of above; found on m/28 rifles)

SYT

Finland (Civil Guard acceptance mark for modification to stocks for the m/28)

Finland (*Tikkakoski Oy* factory at Sakara; pre-1936 logo)

Finland (*Tikkakoski Oy*, post-1936 logo)

Russia (Mark of Tula-made parts. This is not a "T", but a T-shaped hammer.)

TR

Finland (Found on buttstock I.D. disc: antiaircraft regiment)

USSR (Black powder proof mark; replaced П, probably during World War II)

Finland (*Valtion Kivääritehdas*; State Rifle Factory, at Jyväskylä)

NUMBERS

1 (in triangle)	East Germany (refurbishment mark); first-quality weapon
2 (in inverted triangle)	East Germany (refurbishment mark); lower-quality weapon
02	Hungary (Budapest arsenal code)
7	Imperial Russia (Tula arsenal inspector's mark)
10 (in double circle)	Bulgaria (Factory No. 10 code)
11 (in oval)	Poland (Radom arsenal code)
26	China (Mark of Factory No. 296; found on Type 53 carbines)
36.00	Finland (High-pressure proof mark as found on m/39 **B** rifle)
36 S **00**	Finland (Post-1934 SAKO high-pressure proof mark. Indicates 3,600 atmospheres, i.e., 52,884 psi; 1 atmosphere = 14.69 psi)
36 VKT 00	Finland (VKT high-pressure mark)
296	China (later-production mark of Factory 296)

SYMBOLS

五三式 China ("Type 53"; literally, "53 Model")

五三年式 China (As above, but with the character for "year")

China (logo of Factory 296 at Chongqing)

1296 China (later-production logo of Factory 296)

Czechoslovakia (refurbishment mark)

East Germany (Factory code of the Ernst Thalmann Werk in Suhl)

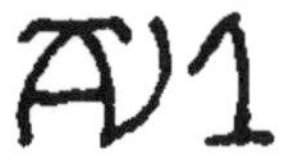

Finland (Arsenal No. 1 [*Asevarikko-1*], at Helsinki)

Finland (Earliest version of Sk. Y. marking) (*Suomalainen Ampumatarvikkeettehdas*, "Finnish Ammunition Factory" at Riihimäki; a very rare mark)

Finland (*Suomalainen Ampumatarvikkeettehdas*, "Finnish Ammunition Factory" at Riihimäki; a very rare mark)

Finland (*Aseseppakoulu*, "Armorer's School")

Finland (Arms depot mark. Letter can be **L**, **Z** or **S**)

Finland (Barrel refurbishment mark[?])

Finland (Finnish Army mark; replaced **SA** c.1970)

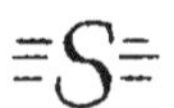

Finland (Civil Guard acceptance mark)

Finland (Civil Guard acceptance mark)

Finland (Civil Guard acceptance mark)

Hungary

Hungary (Stamped on receiver; indicates a weapon deactivated in the 1980s)

North Korea

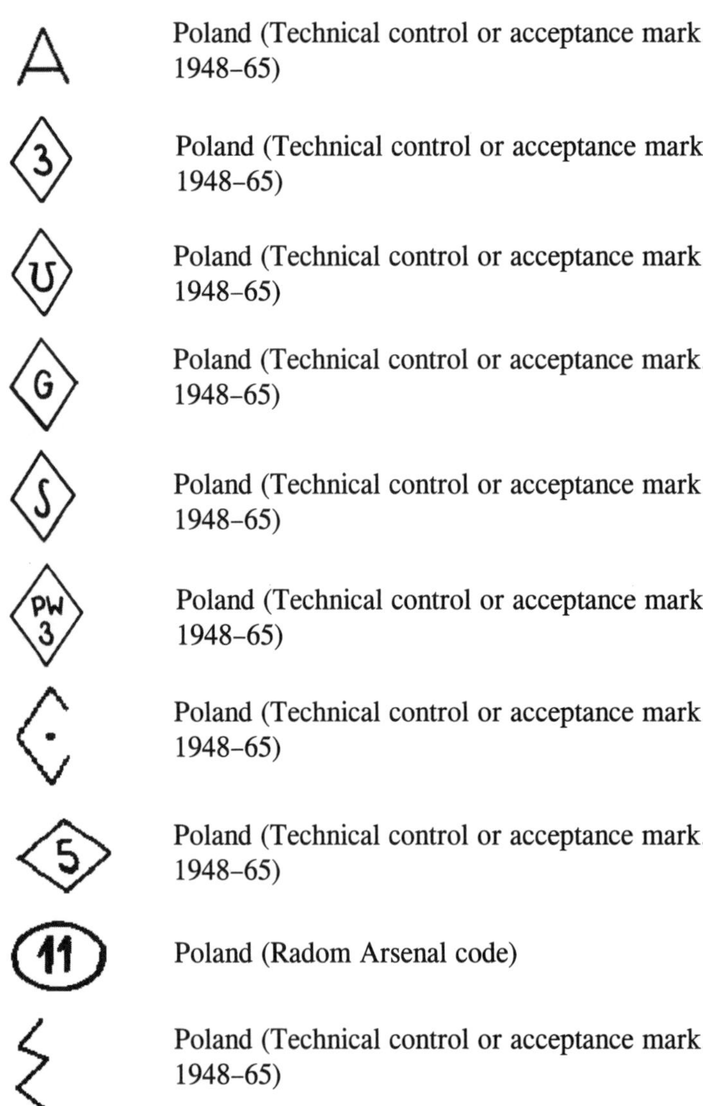

Poland (Technical control or acceptance mark, 1948–65)

Poland (Technical control or acceptance mark, 1948–65)

Poland (Technical control or acceptance mark, 1948–65)

Poland (Technical control or acceptance mark, 1948–65)

Poland (Technical control or acceptance mark, 1948–65)

Poland (Technical control or acceptance mark, 1948–65)

Poland (Technical control or acceptance mark, 1948–65)

Poland (Technical control or acceptance mark, 1948–65)

Poland (Radom Arsenal code)

Poland (Technical control or acceptance mark, 1948–65)

Poland (Technical control or acceptance mark, 1948–65)

Poland (Technical control or acceptance mark, 1948–65)

Poland (Technical control or acceptance mark, 1948–65)

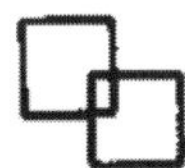

Poland (Technical control or acceptance mark, 1948–65)

Poland (Technical control or acceptance mark, 1948–65)

Romania

Romania

Romania (parts mark on stocks)

Romania (parts mark on metal)

USA (Remington, World War I contract)

USA (Westinghouse, 1st logo; World War I contract)

USA (Westinghouse, 2nd logo; World War I contract)

The seven symbols below are believed to be New England Westinghouse WWI contract inspection marks.

USSR (Izhevsk, pre-1928)

USSR (Izhevsk, 1928-)

USSR (Tula, pre-1928)

USSR (Tula, 1928-)

Russia (Sestroryetsk arsenal)

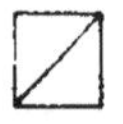

USSR (Post–World War II; indicates arsenal-refurbished wood parts)

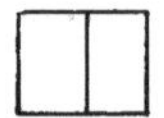

USSR (Post–World War II: indicates arsenal-refurbished metals parts)

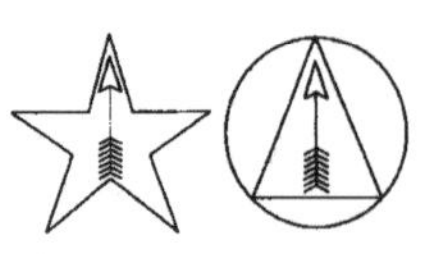

USSR (post-World War II; Tula, left, and Izhevsk, right, arsenal marks)

DATING

Ascertaining the age of most Mosin-Nagants requires examining at least two parts of the weapon: the barrel and the receiver tang. In many instances the two dates will be different, although that does not necessarily indicate that the weapon has been reworked: it is entirely possible that the barrel and the receiver were made at the same arsenal and were assembled there at the time of the later part's manufacture, or even thereafter.

The date of the receiver is especially important in the United States as it is one of the key factors for a weapon's classification as a "firearm" or a "curio or relic" (most of the rest of the world regards the date on the barrel as that of a firearm's manufacture). Under United States law (The National Firearms Act 26 U.S.C. Chapter 44, §5845[g] and The Gun Control Act 18 U.S.C. Chapter 53, §921[a][16], for example) a firearm made prior to January 1, 1899 magically assumes the dignity of an antique. This is significant as it means that the antique is not subject to many of the restrictions imposed by various federal firearms laws, for example, the prohibition on interstate shipment to people who do not hold a Federal Firearms License.

Generally, the date of a barrel's manufacture is found atop the chamber. There are, however, exceptions: for example, Finland's m/91-24 barrels (both the SIG and BÖHLER-STAHL varieties) are undated, and the Finnish m/1891 Tikkakoski-made barrels produced in 1925 and 1926 almost always have the date ("25" or "26", respectively) on the underside of the barrel shank, though those made in 1927 are typically dated in the usual position atop the chamber.

Russian-made receivers are dated on the underside of the tang, behind the screw hole. The date of pre-1900 rifles consists, usually, of the number of the month and the last one or two digits of the year the weapon was made, e.g., "597" indicates a manufacture date of May 1897; often, however, the month is not indicated. Post-1900 rifles may have the year's last three digits, e.g., "915" (= 1915), or the full four-digit year. The date is almost always followed by the Russian letter *geh* Г, which is the abbreviation for the word *god*, meaning "year". (See Appendix H: Russian Alphabet and Pronunciation.)

In some instances it will simply not be possible to date a piece or to attribute it to a specific arsenal; I am referring in particular to Finnish reworks on which the original Russian markings have been deliberately ground off, although even then some small clue, such as a Tula T-hammer or Izhevsk bow-and-arrow, may remain to assist the careful examiner. As most Mosin-Nagant parts are interchangeable among virtually all varieties, it is common to come across rifles comprised of parts from several arsenals and even from different countries; this is, in fact, the natural state for Finnish rifles (see Chapter 3, Foreign Variations, Finland). Stocks, handguards and barrel bands are the principal exceptions due to the obvious difference between rifle and carbine sizes and the less obvious differences among models.

Appendix D
Fieldstripping the Mosin Nagant

Caution: As with all firearms first, foremost and always personally make certain that the weapon is unloaded before proceeding further.

All Mosin-Nagant models are fieldstripped and cleaned in the same way. To remove cartridges from the magazine without having to work the bolt, pull back and hold the floor catch located at the rear of the magazine's underside and swing the floorplate down and forward. Any cartridges in the magazine will then fall out, but this procedure will NOT remove a round still in the chamber: you must make a visual inspection to ensure that the weapon is clear, working the bolt to remove a chambered cartridge. To remove the bolt: lift the bolt handle; draw the bolt rearwards, simultaneously pulling the trigger and holding it while continuing to draw back the bolt until it is free of the rifle. To replace the bolt simply reverse this procedure (do not forget to pull the trigger first and hold it while seating the bolt).

Normally the foregoing is all the fieldstripping necessary before cleaning the rifle, although in the interest of preserving your Mosin-Nagant you will want to disassemble the bolt and clean it. The interrupter/ejector should also be disassembled and cleaned periodically as the accretion of oil and dirt on it is the most frequent cause of ejection problems.

To disassemble the bolt, remove the bolt from the rifle and:

a) Hold the bolt handle in your left hand, cocking piece facing you; pull the cocking piece back and turn it to the left, i.e., counterclockwise, till it stops.

b) Pull the bolt head and firing pin guide forward and off the assembly.

c) Turn the bolt head to the left and pull it off the guide.

d) Gripping the bolt assembly firmly — it is under tension from the mainspring, so care is required: do NOT point it at anyone or anything damageable — push the firing pin down on a piece of soft wood or other firm but slightly yielding and non-marring surface. You must push firmly enough to disengage the cocking piece from the bolt in order to unscrew the cocking piece.

e) Unscrew the cocking piece; remove the firing pin and spring.

Note: There is an alternate method to remove the firing pin and spring: hold the cocking piece securely, and use the slot at the rear of the firing pin guide as a wrench by placing it over the square part of the firing pin body and unscrewing the pin.

To reassemble the bolt, simply reverse the order of disassembly. Be sure that the rear of the firing pin is flush with the cocking piece. Note that the slot on the rear of the firing pin must be aligned with the slash-like mark on the cocking piece; this can be done with a small-bladed flathead screwdriver or similar tool and is necessary to ensure correct protrusion of the firing pin through the bolt face.

Occasionally it will be necessary to perform additional maintenance on the action which entails removing it from the stock. Although the different models require the removal of somewhat different barrel bands and nosecaps in different ways, the following instructions apply to all Mosin-Nagant types.

a) Remove the cleaning rod.

b) Remove the nosecap only on Finnish models m/27 (rifle and carbine), m/28, m/28-30, and m/39.

c) Remove the barrel bands.

d) Remove the handguard.

e) Remove the front and rear trigger guard screws.

f) Carefully lift the barrel and action out of the stock.

To reassemble, follow the above instructions in reverse order.

To remove the extractor — and this should be done only in order to replace it — first disassemble the bolt assembly as described above, then secure the bolt head firmly in a vise or otherwise. Using a punch or similar tool, and a hammer, gently tap the extractor towards the rear of the bolt head and off. Clean the extractor groove of accumulated oil, grease and dirt, then lightly oil it. Install the new extractor by tapping it forward from the rear.

To remove the magazine follower and floorplate, press the floorplate catch and, simultaneously, swing the floorplate assembly forward. Pinch the floorplate and follower together between thumb and forefinger and pull them down and to the rear out of the magazine.

The interrupter-ejector (one piece on the original M1891 and variants, two pieces on the M91/30 and its successors) is removed by unscrewing the retaining screw and sliding the rest of the assembly forward out of the groove in which it is seated.

The two-piece interrupter-ejector can sometimes be a bit difficult to remove, so extra care is necessary. The following method will facilitate disassembly:

a) Remove the retaining screw.

b) Gently drift the ejector forward by tapping the rear with a punch or similar tool while — and this is important — carefully elevating the front of the ejector sufficiently to disengage it from the nipple on the interrupter.

c) Continue to drift the ejector forward until it is completely disengaged. The interrupter can then easily be lifted out of its groove.

d) To reassemble simply reverse the foregoing procedure.

The interrupter-ejector and its groove should be cleaned occasionally after firing to avoid accumulation of oil, grease and dirt — the most common cause of extraction/ejection problems. A toothbrush and lint-free cloth are excellent for this purpose.

One of the few small-arms technical tasks permitted to soldiers of the ex-East Bloc was to check firing pin protrusion. This is done with the two middle grooves of the cleaning kit screwdriver, which are actually firing pin gauges; they are marked "75" and "95" and are used as follows:

Remove the bolt from the weapon. Return the cocking piece to the "closed" position by grasping the bolt handle in the left hand with the bolt facing skyward; pull the cocking piece back and turn it to the left; the firing pin is now protruding through the bolt face. Place the screwdriver on the bolt face, perpendicular to it, so the groove marked "95" is over the firing pin. See Figure D-1. If the pin touches the bottom of the groove, it is protruding too far and should be adjusted. The pin should also be checked against the groove marked "75": the pin should touch the bottom of the groove; if it does not, there is insufficient protrusion and the pin must be adjusted. To adjust the firing pin, turn the slot in the pin's end so it is in line with the adjustment marks slashed on the back of the cocking piece. If there are no such marks — it is rarely the case, but it is possible — you must turn the pin and continue to check the protrusion until it is proper.

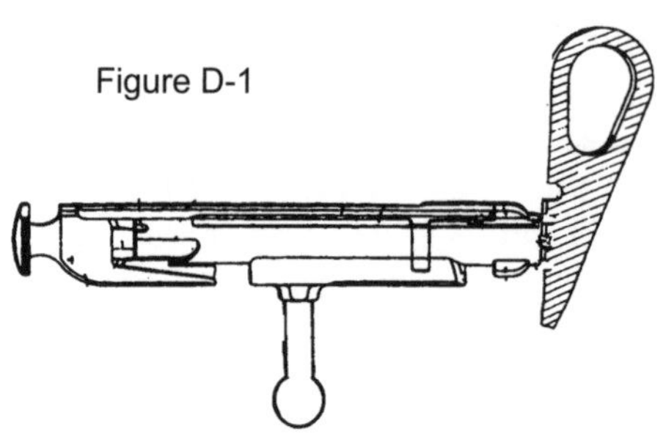
Figure D-1

Note: You must return the cocking piece to the "open" position before reinserting it into the weapon. To do so simply reverse the procedure described above.

Appendix E
Loading, Firing and Cleaning the Mosin-Nagant

CAUTION: Shooting is fun and educational; it is also inherently dangerous. Anyone operating a firearm should be thoroughly versed in basic firearms safety before attempting to load, fire or clean a gun. While this may sound like common sense it is ignored so often by otherwise intelligent people, as well as idiots, that I feel obliged to repeat it here. I will also mention at this point the vital need for the shooter to wear proper eye and ear protection: anyone willing to pay $300 for a firearm but unwilling to spend $30 on a pair of shooting glasses and hearing protectors deserves to be blind and deaf.

The rifle may be loaded either one round at a time or by using a five-round charger clip. To use the charger: draw back the bolt, place either end of the clip into the slots machined in the top of the receiver, align the palm of the hand parallel to the cartridges and, using the thumb, press them firmly and smoothly into the magazine. Remove the charger clip, close the bolt and turn down the bolt handle; some individual weapons will be cooperative enough to allow you to close the bolt without removing the charger, the action of the bolt doing that for you as it was designed to do. The rifle is now ready to fire — release the safety only when ready to fire.

The Mosin-Nagant has a safety mechanism which, though sturdy and reasonably reliable, is also clumsy and difficult to manipulate; anyone who uses it will instantly understand why the design was never imitated. To set this beast, pull the cocking piece to the rear as far as it will go then turn it counterclockwise. If properly set the cocking piece will remain locked in the turned position. To unlock the safety, pull back on the cocking piece, turn it clockwise and let it slide forward. The safety is now off.

The Mosin-Nagant can also be set on "safe" before loading if you first draw the bolt to the rear as far as it will go, then load the cartridge(s) into the magazine in the usual way. At that point, with the bolt all the way to the rear, pull the trigger and hold it fully back while sliding the bolt forward and turning the bolt handle down. The weapon will then be on "safe" although there is a cartridge in the chamber, and the bolt must be fully-worked in order to cock and fire the weapon.

Note: The "safety" method described in the foregoing paragraph is extremely dangerous if not done properly, as the weapon will be loaded and ready to fire. Anyone wishing to use this method should first practice extensively with empty cartridge cases or other inactive rounds. Use of the foregoing method of placing the weapon on "safe" is NOT recommended, and is presented here only for informational purposes and to avoid accidents caused by people attempting to apply misunderstood or garbled accounts of this method.

This safety catch design is so cumbersome that many individuals ignore it and simply lift the bolt handle fully upright to act as a safety; this will work only if there is at least one round in the magazine to exert pressure on the underside of the bolt carrier, otherwise the entire bolt assembly will slide to the rear of the receiver if the butt is even minimally tilted downwards. I do not endorse any slovenly precautions where firearm safety is concerned, and this method strikes me as being, well, half-cocked...

In addition to being employed to set the safety the cocking piece serves the function its name indicates: it can be used to cock the rifle in the event of a misfire without working the bolt. Simply grasp the cocking piece firmly, pull it to the rear as far as possible, then let it run forward. At the risk of stating the obvious, use of the cocking piece to reset the mechanism for shooting (as opposed to dry-firing) assumes the presence of a round in the chamber which, for whatever reason, did not fire when the trigger was pulled after cocking with the bolt in the usual manner.

Because the ammunition you have fired is almost certainly corrosive, a prompt and thorough cleaning of the weapon is essential. The corrosive effects of old-fashioned, Berdan-primed ammunition — which includes all military surplus from China and the ex-East Bloc countries—derives from the mercury salts used in the primers. The salts adhere to the metal parts of the gun and, as is the nature of salts, attract moisture: if the weapon is not cleaned it will soon become a piece of rust and wood suitable to use as a club, but little else.

The traditional means of cleaning a black-powder gun was to pour hot, soapy water through the barrel, then rinse, dry thoroughly, and coat with gun oil. This will work for corrosive-ammo cleanup as well, but is unnecessarily sloppy and primitive. There are many commercial corrosive-ammo cleaners on the market today; they are inexpensive and available at almost any gun or sporting goods store.

Another alternative is U.S. military bore cleaner from the World War II era: this can be found at most gun shows and some surplus stores and costs about $0.50–$1.50 a can. The little green cans themselves make interesting bits of militaria.

The essential parts for post-shooting cleanup are the barrel, the chamber, the bolt, and the magazine housing. The conscientious shooter will want to clean the ejector/interrupter and the trigger guard follower assembly as well.

To begin: Remove the bolt assembly and set it aside. Attach a barrel brush to the cleaning rod, soak it in bore cleaner and run it through the barrel from the breech end. Wipe the brush on a rag and rewet with bore cleaner before pulling it back through the barrel. Repeat.

Next, using a slotted tip attachment or a cleaning jag, run a dry patch through the barrel, again from the breech end. Repeat with a patch soaked in bore cleaner. Continue alternating dry and wet patches until they come out clean. Run a final dry patch through, then a patch moistened — but not soaked — with gun oil.

Caution: Do not saturate the chamber area with oil or pour oil into that area: it can cause unnaturally high pressure to develop while firing and is very dangerous.

To continue with post-shooting cleanup: fieldstrip the bolt assembly and clean each piece with bore cleaner and a clean, lint-free cloth until no residue remains. Then wipe each part dry and coat lightly with gun oil. Reassemble.

Ideally, the magazine housing and trigger guard follower assembly should also be scrubbed with bore cleaner, dried and given a very light coat of gun oil.

On the following day the barrel and the bolt face should be given another cleaning with wet and dry patches, and then followed by a light oiling.

Having said the foregoing about cleaning from the breech end, I will note that the military-issue cleaning kit common to countries which used the Mosin-Nagant implies a preference for cleaning the barrel from the muzzle end: there is a protective muzzle cap specifically designed to ensure that neither the muzzle crown nor the bore is damaged by using the cleaning rod. If you have an issue cleaning kit and wish to use it in the East Bloc way:

a) Slide the muzzle crown cap over the threaded end of the cleaning rod, making sure than the open end of the cap faces the threaded end of the rod. (Figure E-1)

b) Screw the bore brush (or the jag) onto the rod.

c) Place the punch through the hole in the rod head; this forms a cross-shaped handle for the rod.

d) Proceed to clean as in the foregoing instructions.

The main flaw in the East Bloc cleaning technique is that muzzle-end cleaning does not adequately clean the chamber; you will have to do it separately.

There are some who omit cleaning the magazine and bolt assembly; if you wish to treat your piece of history like a cheap screwdriver, so be it.

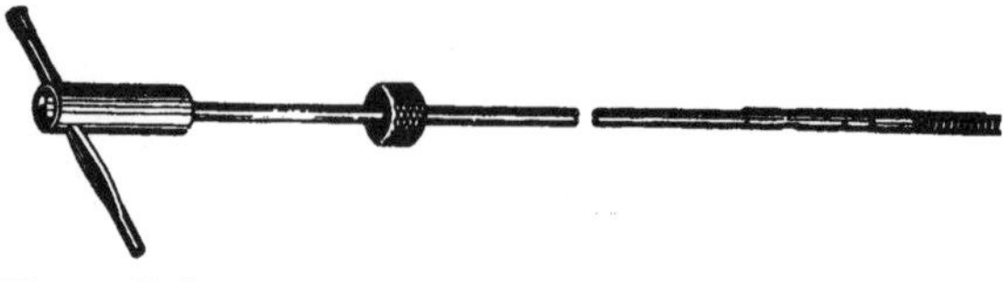

Figure E-1

Appendix F
Troubleshooting

1. Cartridge jams while being chambered	a. Defective inter-rupter/ejector b. Cartridge not properly positioned below interrupter/ ejector	a. Clean and oil inter-rupter/ejector b. Press cartridge down to correct position
2. Cartridge is difficult to chamber	a. Dented cartridge case b. Dirty cartridge	a. Discard cartridge b. Clean cartridge
3. Misfire	a. Defective primer b. Insufficient firing pin protrusion c. Mainspring weak, defective or broken	a. Discard cartridge b. Adjust firing pin c. Replace main-spring
4. Hangfire	a. Dirty trigger mechanism	a. Clean and oil mechanism
5. Cartridge fails to extract	a. Broken or defec-tive mechanism b. Worn or broken bolt-stop	a. Replace extractor b. Replace bolt-stop
6. Cartridge fails to eject	a. Dirty interrupter/ ejector b. Bent or broken interrupter/ejector	a. Clean the slot b. Replace inter-rupter/ejector

7. Magazine floor-plate falls open	a. Loose or broken floorplate catch b. Loose or broken floorplate catch screw	a. Repair or replace b. Tighten or replace screw
8. Bolt comes entirely out of receiver when retracted	a. Loose sear spring-screw b. Worn or broken bolt-stop	a. Tighten screw b. Replace bolt-stop

Appendix G
Cleaning and Refurbishing

The Mosin-Nagant, of whatever model, is an antique: even those made in the 1970s are throwbacks to an earlier era. Antiques in general are best left untampered-with; unnecessary or unskilled "improvements" destroy the historical integrity of a piece. But judicious cleaning of accumulated oil, grease and dirt of decades is desirable and the replacement of worn or broken parts with a part of proper manufacture is allowable. There is a limit beyond which restoration becomes fakery, even if well-intentioned; I leave the determination of that limit to the conscience and discretion of the reader.

The typical Mosin-Nagant comes home from the gun shop or show with an accretion of muck ranging in degree from slightly soiled to toxic waste. The first step, if you are going to clean the piece at all, is to disassemble it. Fortunately, the Mosin-Nagant is a simple weapon designed for simple soldiers with little or no education and, often, with no mechanical skills or training.

Before cleaning, all metal pieces should be removed from the stock **except** the following:

1) The stock bolt. Do not attempt to remove it unless you absolutely must replace it. Trying to do so without the proper tool and expertise will damage the stock. A tool specifically designed for the stock bolt is now available from various suppliers for those who really must remove the piece.

2) The nosecap (except that of the Finnish m/27, m/28, m/28-30, and m/39, which are made to be easily removable with a common flathead screwdriver).

3) The cleaning rod retainer.

4) The barrel-band retaining springs (unless they can be removed without damage to them or to the stock).

For most models — those without detachable nosecap — the easiest disassembly procedure is as follows: 1) remove the cleaning rod and 2) barrel bands. 3) Remove the bolt, 4) then the screws holding the trigger guard/magazine to the receiver. 5) Now separate the barrel and action from the stock. If the metal will not come easily out of the wood, turn the rifle upside down and holding it parallel to the floor, gently tap the muzzle on a padded surface until they separate. 6) Complete the initial disassembly by unscrewing the two butt plate screws and removing the butt plate.

For a stock in reasonably good shape, all that is necessary is a good scrubbing with either naphtha, household ammonia, mineral spirits or kerosene. Really dirty and oily stocks may require cleaning with acetone. All of these products are cheap and readily available at any hardware store — acetone can be purchased by the gallon quite inexpensively at beauty supply outlets catering to manicurists. Non-petroleum-based compounds that are effective in cleaning both wood and metal are clothes-washing detergents like Tide or strong cleaning compounds like Simple Green.

Do not mix any of these compounds together and always use in a well-ventilated space, preferably outdoors. Always wear eye protection and, as many are cancer-causing organic compounds, rubber gloves.

Always follow the manufacturer's instructions.

Note: Never use gasoline, not even outdoors. Gasoline vapors can travel long distances before being ignited by pilot lights, electrical switches and so on.

One of the best cleaning tools for this job is a nylon brush of the kind commonly used for household cleaning. An old toothbrush is perfect for cleaning the slots and inletted areas of the stock. Whenever possible, clean with the grain of the wood.

If the stock and handguards are only slightly oily or greasy they can be cleaned with any of the common lanolin-based hand cleaners. Simply rub the stock with a cloth or paper towel to which a small amount of the hand cleaner has been applied, then polish thoroughly with a clean cloth.

Once the wood has been thoroughly cleaned it is ready for a protective finish. The original treatment of Mosin-Nagant stocks appears to have been a basic military-type oil finish. Linseed oil or tung oil will give a good result, as will a good grade of furniture oil. The Russians gave many of their stocks, especially those of the M1938 and M1944 carbines, a heavy coating of clear varnish as added protection against their harsh climate; you may wish to do so as well if you have a Russian model. Spar varnish is not recommended as it never completely dries. The recent arsenal-refinished imports from Russia appear to have a clear lacquer (rather than a varnish) finish, but this may not prove to be the case.

Anyone wishing to restore a badly dented or otherwise abused stock will have to strip, steam, sand, stain, and refinish the wood. This is an undertaking best left to those willing to expend considerable time and effort. If this is on your agenda please consult any of the numerous and excellent books available on refinishing wooden furniture and similar items before you begin.

Metal parts should be cleaned with gun oil or a similar product. For additional remarks on cleaning, refer to Appendix E and F.

Remove rust by carefully rubbing the rusted areas with fine steel wool soaked with oil. I do not recommend rebluing metal parts (historical integrity again), but if you insist, commercial bluing agents are available at any reasonably well-stocked hobby or gun shop as well as gun shows or you can turn the job over to a professional gunsmith.

Fortunately, most missing or damaged parts are easy to replace: so many parts have been imported in the past decade that few are hard to find and most are inexpensive. The important thing here is to obtain parts which are authentic to the particular model.

At this point I will expand upon an earlier observation: any Finnish, French, Russian, or American Mosin-Nagant bolt component, wood screw, butt plate, cleaning rod nut, trigger, sear spring, trigger guard, magazine follower, or hexagonal receiver will be authentic to any Finnish Mosin-Nagant. Unfortunately, the same cannot be said of all front or rear sights, nosecaps, stocks, barrels, sling swivels or barrel bands.

Mosin-Nagants from other countries (China, Hungary, etc.) generally require parts made in those countries for authentic restoration.

Appendix H
The Mosin-Nagant and the Russian and Finnish Languages

Russian Alphabet and Pronunciation

The following sections are meant to help the reader decipher markings found on Russian-made Mosin-Nagants. This book is not a language primer, and there is no reason to address the finer points of Russian grammar. I would, however, like to mention one grammatical item which may be confusing to those who have taken a close look at the Russian names and words appearing here and there in the text: I refer to the *a* and *ogo* (pronounced "avo") at the end of designers' names (e.g., *Mosina*, *Sudayeva*; *Komaritskogo, Shpitalnogo*) and certain words (e.g., *goda, sistema*). This *a* or *ovo* (spelled oro [*ogo*] — *avo*, spelled aro [*ago*], in pre-Revolution Russian) merely indicates the genitive (i.e., possessive) case for singular masculine nouns and names: *goda* means "of the year" (*god* = year)*;* *Mosina* and *Sudayeva* mean "Mosin's" and "Sudayev's", respectively, and *Vinchestera* is "Winchester's"; *Komaritskovo* is "Komaritskii's", and so forth. Russian, by the way, has six cases, nominative, genitive, dative, accusative, prepositional and instrumental. Sometimes the locative case sneaks in as well.

The Russian language is written in the Cyrillic alphabet, the letters of which are given below with their English equivalents; these are mostly approximations as the sounds in spoken Russian represented by these letters differ considerably depending on stress, position in a word, etc. The following list is, however, adequate for our purposes. Two of the letters are orthographic signs which are important to Russian spelling and grammar but which do not represent sounds of their own; these are indicated by the words "no sound."

After seizing power late in 1917 the Communists — compulsive meddlers in all aspects of life — decided to reform Russian spelling; in the process several letters were liquidated by a decree of the Council of People's Commissars, dated October 10, 1918. Though not found in post-Revolution Russian one of these abolished letters does appear on weapons made during tsarist times and has therefore been included at the end of the following alphabetical list for your convenience.

Russian	English
А	A
Б	B
В	V
Г	G in 'go' (sometimes 'v'; see *Russian Alphabet and Pronunciation*, above)
Д	D
Е	'ye' in 'yet'
Ё	'yaw' in 'yawn' (the dots are usually absent)
Ж	's' in 'measure'
З	Z
И	'ee' in 'seen'
Й	'ee' (only used after another vowel)
К	K
Л	L
М	M
Н	N
О	O
П	P
Р	R
С	S
Т	T
У	'oo' in 'moon'
Ф	F
Х	'ch' in 'Bach'
Ц	'ts' in 'cats'
Ч	'ch' in 'church'
Ш	'sh' in 'ship'

Ы	rather like 'wi' in 'willow'
Ь	no sound
Э	'e' in 'let'
Ю	'u' in 'universe'
Я	'ya' in 'yacht'
I	'ee' in 'seen'; abolished in 1918 and replaced by Й
Ѣ	'ye' as in 'yes'; abolished in 1918 and replaced by 'E'

RUSSIAN-ENGLISH GLOSSARY

The following are the more important Russian words and abbreviations found in the foregoing text, and those which commonly appear on Mosin-Nagants manufactured in Russia. They are placed in English alphabetical order, followed by a transliteration and phonetic approximation of their pronunciation. Where pre- and post-Revolution spellings differ, and are pertinent, the latter is given in parentheses.

банник	bannik (BAN-neek) = cleaning rod
дальнобойная	dal'naboinaya (dal-nah-BOY-nah-yah) = long range
драгунская	dragunskaya (drah-GOON-ska-ya) = dragoon
г.	g. — abbreviation for *god* (GAWT) = year. In Russian a date expressed in years is an adjective: e.g., 1891 is "[the] one thousand eight hundred and ninety-first" and requires (in the written language) the word "year" after it; this is almost always indicated by a "g".
года	goda (GOD-ah)= of the year
императорскій	imperatorskii (eem-per-AH-tor-skee) = imperial
Императора	imperatora (eem-per-AH-tor-a) = Emperor's

The Mosin-Nagant Rifle

Ижевскій (Ижєвкий)	Izhevskii (ee-ZHEV-skee) = (adj.) Izhevsk
карабин	karabin (ka-ra-BEEN) = carbine
казачья	kazach'ya (ka-ZACH-ya) = (adj.) Cossack
лёгкая	lyogkaya (LYOKH-ka-ya) = light[weight]
намушник	namushnik (na-MOOSH-neek) = front sight protector
образец	obrazets (ah-brah-Zyetz) = model/pattern
оружейный	oruzheinii (ah-roo-ZHEY-nee) = (adj.) firearm
патрон	patron (pah-TRON) = cartridge
пехотная	pekhotnaya (pee-KHOT-na-ya) = (adj.) infantry
первый	pervii (PYEHR-vee) = first
Петра Великаго	Petra Velikovo (pee-TRA vee-LEE-ka-va) = (adj.) Peter I
пулемёт	pulemyot (poo-leem-YAWT) = machine gun
пуля	pulya (pool-YAH) = bullet
Сестроретскій	Sestroyetskii (sees-tror-YET-skee) = (adj.) Sestroryetsk
штык	shtik (shtihk) = bayonet
Тульскій (Тульский)	Tulskii (TOOL-skee) = (adj.) Tula
винтовка	vintobka (veen-TOF-ka) = rifle
заводъ (завод)	zavod (za-VAWT) = Factory

NOTES ON THE FINNISH LANGUAGE

Finnish is a pleasant-sounding, highly inflected, complex language of northern Central Asian origin; it is not related to any Western languages but it is quite similar to Estonian and very distantly akin to Hungarian. If you thought Russian was difficult with its six noun cases you will want to avoid Finnish, which has fifteen.

All Finnish words are stressed on the first syllable; in compound words the first syllable of each of the component words is stressed, e.g., *kivääritehdas* (rifle factory) is pronounced KIH-vaar-ih-TEHH-duhss. Compound words are a characteristic of Finnish; some are composed of a considerable number of elements and are quite long. Consonants are pronounced much like their English counterparts, with a few exceptions: **h** is always pronounced, even after a vowel; **j** is like the"y" in "yes"; and **s** is always as in "sin", never as in "rose".

Finnish vowels are pronounced more or less as follows: **a** like *u* in "but"; **e** as in "bed"; **i** as in "kin"; **o** as in "hop"; and **u** as in "bull"; **ä** is like *a* in "hat"; **ö** is like the German *ö* or French *eu*; **y** is like the French *u* or German *ü*; **aa** is like a long version of the *a* in "father"; **ää** is something like the *a* in "piano", but drawn out; **ii** is like *ee* in "seen"; **uu** is rather like *oo* in "look", but drawn out.

Finnish Glossary

ampumatarvikkeet	ammunition
ase	weapon
aseseppa	armorer
aseseppakoulu	armorer's school
asevarikko	arsenal
kivääri	rifle
konepaja	machine-shop
malli	model, or pattern
osakeyhtiö	corporation
Oy	inc., ltd., corp. (abbreviation of *osakeyhtiö*)
Puolustuslaitos	Defense Dept.
putki	[rifle] bore

ratsuvaki	cavalry
SAKO	Acronym of *Suojeluskuntain Ase- ja Konepaja Osakeyhtiö* = Civil Guard Arms Machine-shop Co. Ltd.
Suojeluskunta	Civil Guard
Suomen	Finnish
Suomessa	in Finland
tehdas	factory
Valtio	State (i.e., government)
Valtion	of the State
Yleisesikunta	General Staff

Appendix I
Finnish Civil Guard Serial Numbers

Table I-1 Finnish Civil Guard Serial Numbers, Pre-1939 to 1943			
Civil Guard District	**Serial Numbers**		
Helsinki	1-6000	153001-154000	
Nylands-Sodra	6001-13000		
Pohjois-Uusimaa	13001-17000		
Turunmaa	24641-24660	126002-126300	
Varsinais-Suomi	17001-26000	25541-25590	148001-150000
Satakunta	26001-33000		
Etelä-Häme	33001-41000		
Pohjois-Häme	41001-48000	150001-151000	
Kyme	48001 -55000	140501 -142000	
Viipuri	55001-69000	132501-137500	
Sortavala	69001-73000	142001-143500	143501-144000
Mikkeli	73001-78000	150001-151000	
Pohjois-Savo	78001-84000	131501-132500	144001-145000
Pohjois-Karjala	84001-89000	146001-147000	
Vaasa	89001 -96000	145001-146000	
Etela-Pohjanmaa	96001-102000	125001-126000	147001-148000
Keski- Pohjanmaa	102001-105000		
Jyväskylä	105001-111000	151001-153000	
Raahe	111001-115000		
Kainuu	115001-117000	127001-127500	130501-131500
Oulu	117001-121000	139501-140500	
Pohjola	121001-1125000	127501-128500	137501-139500
Civil Guard Officer's School	130001-130500		

Table I-2a Finnish Civil Guard Rifle Serial Numbers (1943–1944)			
Serial Numbers	**Civil Guard District**	**Serial Numbers**	**Civil Guard District**
1-6000	Helsinki	13863-14282	Pohjois-Uusimaa
6001-7025	Raasepori	14283-14475	Salo
7026-7150	Helsinki	14476-14670	Pohjois-Uusimaa
7151-7625	Raasepori	14671-14802	Salo
7626-8100	Etalä-Uusimaa	14803-15023	Pohjois-Uusimaa
8101-8200	Helsinki	15024-15085	Salo
8201-8425	Etalä-Uusimaa	15086-15302	Pohjois-Uusimaa
8426-8515	Helsinki	15303-15307	Salo
8516-11300	Etalä-Uusimaa	15308-15387	Pohjois-Uusimaa
11301-11500	Helsinki	15388-15412	Salo
11501-11600	Etalä-Uusimaa	15413-15450	Pohjois-Uusimaa
11601-11800	Raasepori	15451-15484	Etalä-Kymenlaakso
11801-12350	Etalä-Uusimaa	15485-16000	Pohjois-Uusimaa
12351-12600	Raasepori	16001-16050	Salo
12601-12750	Helsinki	16051-16099	Pohjois-Uusimaa
12751-12850	Etalä-Uusimaa	16001-16050	Salo
12851-13000	Helsinki	16051-16099	Pohjois-Uusimaa
13001-13729	Pohjois-Uusimaa	16100-16200	Salo
13730-13811	Pohjois-Kymenlaakso	16201-16250	Etalä-Kymenlaakso
13812-13862	Etalä-Kymenlaakso	16251-17000	Pohjois-Uusimaa

Table I-2b Finnish Civil Guard Rifle Serial Numbers (1943–44)			
Serial Numbers	**Civil Guard District**	**Serial Numbers**	**Civil Guard District**
17001-17130	Varsinais-Suomi	19841-20270	Varsinais-Suomi
17131-17340	Salo	20271-20350	Vakka-Suomi
17341-17440	Varsinais-Suomi	20351-20410	Salo
17441-17520	Raasepori	20411-20530	Vakka-Suomi
17521-17690	Varsinais-Suomi	20531-20650	Varsinais-Suomi
17691-17790	Raasepori	20651-20800	Turunmaa
17791-18100	Turunmaa	20801-21260	Varsinais-Suomi
18101-18180	Varsinais-Suomi	21261-21510	Turunmaa
18181-18240	Vakka-Suomi	21511-21780	Salo
18241-18310	Varsinais-Suomi	21781-22060	Varsinais-Suomi
18311-18450	Salo	22061-22170	Vakka-Suomi
18451-18650	Raasepori	22171-22390	Varsinais-Suomi
18651-18830	Salo	22391-22780	Salo
18831-18930	Varsinais-Suomi	22781-22850	Vakka-Suomi
18931-19050	Turunmaa	22851-22960	Varsinais-Suomi
19051-19110	Salo	22961-24660	Turunmaa
19111-19160	Varsinais-Suomi	24661-25080	Vakka-Suomi
19161-19460	Vakka-Suomi	25081-25160	Varsinais-Suomi
19461-19780	Varsinais-Suomi	25161-25310	Vakka-Suomi
19781-19840	Vakka-Suomi	25311-25350	Varsinais-Suomi

Table I-2c Finnish Civil Guard Rifle Serial Numbers (1943–44) Serial Numbers			
Serial Numbers	**Civil Guard District**	**Serial Numbers**	**Civil Guard District**
25351-25440	Raasepori	29041-29230	Etalä-Satakunta
25441-25540	Vakka-Suomi	29231-29560	Pori
25541-26000	Varsinais-Suomi	29561-29640	Vakka-Suomi
26001-26115	Pori	29641-29790	Pohjois-Satakunta
26116-26390	Vakka-Suomi	29791-30710	Pori
26391-26520	Pori	30711-30880	Etalä-Satakunta
26521-26685	Vakka-Suomi	30881-31331	Vakka-Suomi
26686-26775	Pohjois-Satakunta	31332-31530	Pori
26776-27000	Etalä-Satakunta	31531-31725	Etalä-Satakunta
27001-27230	Pohjois-Satakunta	31726-31850	Vakka-Suomi
27231-27325	Etalä-Satakunta	31851-32150	Etalä-Satakunta
27326-27455	Pohjois-Satakunta	32151-32375	Pori
27456-27685	Etalä-Satakunta	32376-32485	Varsinais-Suomi
27686-27815	Pohjois-Satakunta	32486-32600	Pori
27816-28065	Etalä-Satakunta	32601-32730	Vakka-Suomi
28066-28155	Vakka-Suomi	32731-32885	Pohjois-Satakunta
28156-28348	Etalä-Satakunta	32886-32910	Pori
28349-28430	Pori	32911-32965	Etalä-Satakunta
28431-28630	Vakka-Suomi	32966-33000	Pori
28631-28780	Etalä-Satakunta	33001-33300	Lahti
28781-29040	Pori	33301-33320	Kanta-Häme

Table I-2d
Finnish Civil Guard Rifle Serial Numbers (1943–44)

Serial Numbers	Civil Guard District	Serial Numbers	Civil Guard District
33321-33640	Lahti	42400-42500	Pohjois-Satakunta
33641-34150	Kanta-Häme	42501-42718	Pirkka-Häme
34151-34800	Lahti	42719-42781	Pohjois-Satakunta
34801-34990	Kanta-Häme	42782-42909	Etalä-Satakunta
34991-35260	Pohjois-Uusimaa	42910-43059	Pirkka-Häme
35261-35470	Kanta-Häme	43060-43260	Kanta-Häme
35471-35570	Lounais-Häme	43261-43550	Pirkka-Häme
35571-36290	Pohjois-Uusimaa	43551-43799	Lounais-Häme
36291-36660	Kanta-Häme	43800-43851	Pirkka-Häme
36661-36760	Pohjois-Uusimaa	43852-43919	Pohjois-Satakunta
36761-37500	Kanta-Häme	43920-44100	Pirkka-Häme
37501-37670	Lounais-Häme	44101-44404	Lounais-Häme
37671-38330	Kanta-Häme	44405-44799	Pirkka-Häme
38331-38460	Lounais-Häme	44800-44999	Lounais-Häme
38461-38920	Kanta-Häme	45000-45100	Pirkka-Häme
38921-39300	Lounais-Häme	45101-45499	Pohjois-Satakunta
39301-39330	Lahti	45500-45660	Pirkka-Häme
39331-40950	Lounais-Häme	45661-45738	Etalä-Satakunta
40951-41000	Kanta-Häme	45739-45799	Pohjois-Satakunta
41001-42399	Pirkka-Häme	45800-46099	Pirkka-Häme

Table I-2e Finnish Civil Guard Rifle Serial Numbers (1943–44)			
Serial Numbers	**Civil Guard District**	**Serial Numbers**	**Civil Guard District**
46100-46250	Etalä-Satakunta	50901-51300	Etalä-Kymenlaakso
46251-46300	Pirkka-Häme	51301-51900	Pohjois-Kymenlaakso
46301-46470	Lounais-Häme	51901-52100	Etalä-Kymenlaakso
46471-46500	Pirkka-Häme	52101-52500	Pohjois-Kymenlaakso
46501-46560	Lounais-Häme	52501-54000	Etalä-Kymenlaakso
46561-47100	Pirkka-Häme	54001-54400	Pohjois-Kymenlaakso
47101-47250	Pohjois-Satakunta	54401-55000	Etalä-Kymenlaakso
47251-47699	Pirkka-Häme	55001-57700	Viipuri
47700-47999	Lounais-Häme	57701-58020	Etalä-Kymenlaakso
48000	Pirkka-Häme	58021-58566	Pohjois-Kymenlaakso
48001-48850	Pohjois-Kymenlaakso	58567-58600	Viipuri
48851-49100	Etalä-Kymenlaakso	58601-59110	Suur-Saimaa
49101-49300	Pohjois-Kymenlaakso	59111-59441	Savolinna
49301-49700	Etalä-Kymenlaakso	59442-59600	Suur-Saimaa
49701-50100	Pohjois-Kymenlaakso	59601-59620	Viipuri
50101-50500	Etalä-Kymenlaakso	59621-60400	Suur-Saimaa
50501-50900	Pohjois-Kymenlaakso	60401-60811	Saimaa

Table I-2f Finnish Civil Guard Rifle Serial Numbers (1943–44)			
Serial Numbers	**Civil Guard District**	**Serial Numbers**	**Civil Guard District**
60812-60820	Viipuri	73541-73660	Saimaa
60821-61130	Saimaa	73661-74290	Suur-Saimaa
61131-61280	Viipuri	74291-74410	Saimaa
61281-61420	Saimaa	74411-74800	Suur-Saimaa
61421-67450	Viipuri	74801-74821	Saimaa
67451-67550	Saimaa	74822-74941	Savonlinna
67551-68249	Viipuri	74942-75270	Saimaa
68250-68300	Saimaa	75271-75350	Savonlinna
68301-68450	Viipuri	75351-75440	Saimaa
68451-68600	Saimaa	75441-75700	Savonlinna
68601-68800	Viipuri	75701-76120	Saimaa
68801-68900	Suur-Saimaa	76121-77060	Savonlinna
68901-69000	Saimaa	77061-77150	Suur-Saimaa
69001-70479	Sortavala	77151-77250	Lahti
70480-70859	Savonlinna	77251-77360	Savonlinna
70860-71100	Sortavala	77361-77400	Saima
70101-71138 [sic]	Savonlinna	77401-77430	Suur-Saimaa
71139-71435	Sortavala	77431-77680	Saimaa
71436-71510	Savonlinna	77681-77750	Savonlinna
71511-73000	Sortavala	77751-77799	Lahti
73001-73540	Lahti	77800-77820	Suur-Saimaa

Table I-2g Finnish Civil Guard Rifle Serial Numbers (1943–44)			
Serial Numbers	**Civil Guard District**	**Serial Numbers**	**Civil Guard District**
77821-77825	Lahti	85092-85238	Pohjois-Karjala
77826-77870	Savonlinna	85239-85416	Savonlinna
77871-77934	Saima	85417-85606	Pohjois-Karjala
77935-77966	Pohjois-Karjala	85607-85626	Savonlinna
77967-77800	Savonlinna	85627-86239	Pohjois-Karjala
77801-79000	Pohjois-Savo	86240-87103	Kainuu
79001-80450	Iisamii	87104-87495	Pohjois-Karjala
80451-80650	Pohjois-Savo	87496-87551	Kainuu
80651-81100	Iisamii	87552-87963	Pohjois-Karjala
81101-81300	Sisä-Suomi	87964-88053	Kainuu
81301-81600	Pohjois-Savo	88054-88410	Pohjois-Karjala
81601-81800	Sisä-Suomi	88411-88442	Savonlinna
81801-82000	Savonlinna	88443-88730	Pohjois-Karjala
82001-82250	Pohjois-Savo	88731-88930	Kainuu
82251-82500	Pohjois-Karjala	88931-89000	Pohjois-Karjala
82501-83200	Pohjois-Savo	89001-96000	Vaasa
83201-83275	Iisamii	96001-102000	Etalä-Pohjanmaa itäi
83276-84000	Pohjois-Savo	102001-104700	Kokemä
84001-84821	Pohjois-Karjala	104701-104850	Sisä-Suomi
84822-85019	Kainuu	104851-105000	Kokkola
85020-85091	Savonlinna	105001-106100	Jyväskylä

Table I-2h Finnish Civil Guard Rifle Serial Numbers (1943–44)			
Serial Numbers	**Civil Guard District**	**Serial Numbers**	**Civil Guard District**
106101-106200	Sisä-Suomi	111841-112140	Kokkola
106201-106550	Jyväskylä	112141-112650	Raahe
106551-106800	Sisä-Suomi	112651-112700	Kokkola
106801-107000	Jyväskylä	112701-113200	Raahe
107001-107500	Sisä-Suomi	113201-113450	Iisalmi
107501-108120	Jyväskylä	113451-113950	Raahe
108121-108250	Lahti	113951-114100	Kokkola
108251-108700	Jyväskylä	114101-114550	Raahe
108701-108800	Lahti	114551-114800	Kokkola
108801-108920	Jyväskylä	114801-115000	Raahe
108921-109500	Sisä-Suomi	115001-116050	Kainuu
109501-109800	Jyväskylä	116051-116400	Oulu
109801-110100	Sisä-Suomi	116401-116750	Kainuu
110101-110350	Pohjois-Satakunta	116751-118800	Oulu
110351-110650	Etalä-Pohjanmaa itäi	118801-118900	Pohjola
110651-110750	Sisä-Suomi	118901-119450	Oulu
110751-110875	Jyväskylä	119451-119800	Raahe
110876-110950	Sisä-Suomi	119801-120550	Oulu
110951-111000	Jyväskylä	120551-120900	Raahe
111001-111270	Kokkola	120901-121000	Oulu
111271-111840	Raahe	121001-122340	Länsi-Pohja

Table I-2i Finnish Civil Guard Rifle Serial Numbers (1943–44)			
Serial Numbers	**Civil Guard District**	**Serial Numbers**	**Civil Guard District**
122351-122400	Pohjola	128401-128500	Länsi-Pohja
122401-122700	Länsi-Pohja	130001-130500	Civil Guard Officers' School
112701-122900	Pohjola	130501-130900	Oulu
122901-123230	Länsi-Pohja	130901-131000	Kainuu
123231-124450	Pohjola	131001-131100	Oulu
124451-124700	Länsi-Pohja	131101-131500	Kainuu
124701-125000	Pohjola	131501-132100	Pohjois-Savon
125001-126000	Etalä-Pohjanmaa itäi	132101-132150	Iisalmi
126001-126300	Turunmaa	132151-132180	Pohjois-Savon
127001-127050	Oulu	132181-132351	Savonlinna
127351-127200	Kainuu	132352-132500	Pohjois-Savon
127201-127350	Oulu	132501-132650	Viipuri
127351-127500	Kainuu	132651-133100	Suur-Saimaa
127501-128400	Pohjola		

Bibliography

Black, Douglas. "The Guns of the German Navy 1914–1918", *Gun Collector's Digest, 5th Edition.* Northbrook, IL: DBI Books, 1989.

Bolotin, D. N. *Sovietskoye Strelkovoye Oruzhie. [Soviet Firearms].* Moscow: Voennoe Izdatel'stvo, 1990.

Bolotin, D. N. *Soviet Small-Arms and Ammunition*. Hyvinkaa, Finland: Suomen Asemuseosaatio/Finnish Arms Museum Foundation, 1995.

Bowser, Doug and Powers Dunaway. *Rifles of the Snow; A Collector's Guide to Finnish Military Rifles 1918–1944, 2nd Ed*. McComb, MS: Camelia City Military Publications, 1996.

Datig, Fred A. "Russian Military Firearms: A Rapidly Growing Collector's Field/ The Imperial Era", *Gun Collector's Digest, 5th Edition*. Northbrook, IL: DBI Books, 1989.

Datig, Fred A. "Russian Military Firearms: Another Rapidly Growing Collector's Field/ The Soviet Era", *Gun Collector's Digest, 5th Edition*. Northbrook, IL: DBI Books, 1989.

Dzenishkevich, A. R. *Voennaya pyatiletka rabochikh Leningrada 1941–1945, [The Leningrad Workers' Military Five-Year Plan, 1941–1945]*. Leningrad: Leninzadt, 1972.

Ezell, Edward Clinton. *The AK-47 Story*. Harrisburg, PA: Stackpole Books, 1986.

Ezell, Edward Clinton. *Handguns of the World.* Harrisburg, PA: Stackpole Books, 1981.

Fedoseev, Semyon. *Mosinskie vintovki: Made in USA*, wisiwyg://50/ http://history.library/bookshelf/online/misc6_r.html.vif.2.ry

Gibson, Shawn and Tomasz Pietrazak. "1942 Russian Emergency St. Petersburg [sic] Bayonet". Feature 14 on the *Bayonet Connection* Website, www.bayonets.com, 1997.

Gilbert, Adrian. *Sniper: The Skills, the Weapons, and the Experiences*. New York: St. Martin's Press, 1995.

Grzelak, Czeslaw and Henryk Stanczyk and Stefan Zwolinski. *W Czterdziestolecie Zwyciestwa [In Forty Years of Victory*]. Warsaw: Krajowa Agencja Wydawnicza, 1985.

Gwóźdź, Zbigniew and Piotr Zarycki. *Polskie konstrukcje broni strzeleckiej. [Polish Firearms Design]*. Warsaw: SIGMA NOT, 1993.

Hogg, Ian and John Weeks. *Military Small Arms of the 20th Century*. Northfield, Il: Digest Books, Inc., 1973.

http://home.wanadoo.nl/coatl/Mosin.html

Hyytinen, Timo (tr. Tony and Erja Melville). *Arma Fennica — Suomalaiset Aseet [Finnish Firearms]*. Jyväskylä, Finland, 1985.

Janzen, Jerry. *Bayonets from Janzen's Notebook*. Tulsa, 1987.

Karwan, Charles W. "Type 38 Arisaka", *Guns & Ammo: Surplus Firearms, Vol. III*, January 1984.

Kiesling, Paul. *Bayonets of the World, Vol. I.* Kedichem, Holland: Military Collectors Service, N.D.

Kirkland, K. D. *Remington, America's Premier Gunmaker*. New York: Exeter Books, 1988.

Kolychev, V.G., et al. *Vooruzhennye sily Velikovo Oktyabrya, [Armed Forces of the Great October]*, Moscow: Izdatel'stvo "Nauk", 1977.

Komarov, I. A., et al. *Istoriya vintovki ot pischchali do avtomata, Vypusk 2. [History of Rifles, from Arquebus to Automatic, Vol. 2].* Moscow:Tekhnika-Molodezhi, 1993.

Krimov, L. *Voroshilovskii strelok vtoroi stupeni. [Voroshilovskii Marksman, Second Stage].* Moscow: Izdanie Ts.S. Soyuza Osaviakhim SSSR, 1935.

Kulinskii, Alexander. "Shtyki k trekhlineike," [Bayonets of the Three Liners], *Ruzhye, Oruzie i Amunitsiya, [Rifles, Weapons and Ammunition]*, No. 3, 1999.

Kulinskii, Alexander. *Shtyki mira [Bayonets of the World]*, 2 vol. St. Petersburg: Atlant, 2002.

Lapin, Terence W. *The Soviet Mosin-Nagant Manual.* Arlington, VA: Hyrax Publishers, LLC. 1999.

Lombard, Claude. *La Manufacture National d'Armes de Chatellerault* (1819–1968). Poiters: Brissaud, 1987.

Author Unknown. "Los Mexicanskis, Fusiles rusos en la Guerra de España", Asturias Liberal, 4 February 2004.

Malloy, John. "America's Russian Fascist Rifles", *The American Rifleman*, July 1992.

Markham, George. *Guns of the Empire, 1837–1987.* London: Arms & Armour Press, 1990.

Mavrodin, V. V., and Val. V. Mavrodin. *Iz Istorii Otechestvennogo Oruzhiya; Russkaya Vintovka.* [*From the History of the Motherland's Weaponry; the Russian Rifle.*] Leningrad: Izdatel'stvo Leningradskogo Universiteta, 1984.

Moyer, Frank A. *Special Forces Foreign Weapons Handbook*. Secaucas, NJ: Citadel Press, 1983.

Ommundsen, G. M., and Ernest H. Robinson. *Rifles and Ammunition and Rifle Shooting*. New York and London: Funk & Wagnalls Co., 1915.

Ordnance Department. *Description and Rules for the Management of the Russian Three-line Rifle, Caliber 7.62 mm (.3 Inch)*. Washington, D.C.: War Department, August 1918.

Pérez, Artemio Mortera. "Artillería para la República", Revista de Historia Militar, No. 18, December 2001.

Puolustusministeriö [Finnish Defense Ministry]. *Kivääri 91: Rakenne, Hoito ja Käsittely, [The 91 Rifle: Construction, Care and Handling]* (No place indicated): 1940.

Shalito, Anton, Ilya Svachenkov and Andrew Mollo. *Red Army Uniforms in World War II*. London: Windrow & Greene, 1993.

Shipp, Major W.E., U.S. Army, "Red Army Infantry Weapons, Tanks and Armored Cars", U.S. Army G-2 Report, December 29, 1933. Based on *"Jäläväe Relvad, Tankid ja Soomusautod"*, Intelligence Study prepared for the Estonian General Staff and presented in March 1933.

Stoeger Gun Catalog and Handbook, No. 31, NY: Stoeger Arms Corp., 1939.

Underhill, Garrett. "Under the Red Star", *The American Rifleman*, August 1941.

U.S. Army Ordnance Corps. *Manual for Soviet Mosin-Nagant Models of 1891 - 1910 - 1891/30 - 1938 - 1944, Rifles, Carbines & Sniper Rifles; Ordi 7-101*. Ordnance Corps, May 1954.

Walter, John. *Rifles of the World*. Northbrook, IL: DBI Books, 1993.

Wojciechowski, Ireneusz J. *Karabin Mosin Wz 1891*. Warsaw: Wydawnictwo Ministerwa Obrony Narodowej, 1982.

Wrobel, Karl-Heinz. *Drei Linien: Die Gewehre Mosin-Nagant, [Three Lines: The Mosin-Nagant Rifles]*. Schwabisch Hall: Journal Verlag Schwent Gmbh, 1999.

www.municion.org

www.sbhac.net/Republica/Fuerzas/Armas/Polemica/Polemica.html

Zhuk, A.B. *Strelkovoe oruzhie, [Firearms]*. Moscow: Voennoe Izdatel'stvo, 1992.

About the Author

Terence W. Lapin was educated in the United States, Europe, and the Middle East as a linguist, national security analyst, and attorney. He is a member of the Bar of the U.S. Supreme Court, U.S. Court of Appeals for the Armed Forces, and a number of other federal and state bars. Mr. Lapin has written numerous articles on a variety of subjects, and his work has appeared in the *Economist*, the *Washington Times*, and other publications; he contributed research and translations for a book on U.S. policy, *The Carter Years*. In addition to *The Mosin-Nagant Rifle*, he had also translated and annotated *The Soviet Mosin-Nagant Manual*; *The Mannlicher Model 95 Rifle and Carbine; The Royal Italian Infantry Manual*; and written *Mauser Military Rifle Markings*.

The author is a member of the National Rifle Association and the Virginia Shooting Sports Association, and has a longstanding interest in and knowledge of firearms, dating from the time when, as a small child, he found a German machine gun in the family garage.

Books from North Cape Publications®, Inc.

The books in the "For Collectors Only®" and "A Shooter's and Collector's Guide" series are designed to provide the firearms collector with an accurate record of the markings, dimensions and finish found on an original firearm as it was shipped from the factory.

For Collectors Only® Series

Collecting the American Sniper Rifle, 1900 to 1945, by Joe Poyer ($22.95). How do you tell if the telescopic sight on that Model 1903A4 Sniper Rifle you are thinking of buying is a real military telescopic sight for that rifle, or a fake? Weaver made many variations of the 330-C telescopic sight which became the M73B1 when used by the U.S. military. But Weaver made other variations of the 330-C— Model 330-S and M8—which were never installed on the Model 1903A4. But Weaver did not mark its Model 330 as "C" or "S." To make matters worse, the M73B1 telescopic sight has been reproduced. Which Winchester and Lyman telescopic sight models were used on the Model 1903 sniper rifles in World Wars I and II? How do you know if a Warner & Swasey Telescopic Sight and its mounts and base on that Model 1903 is real or fake? What characteristics identify a Model 1903 Sniper Rifle, particularly U.S.M.C. Model 1903A1 (Sniper) Rifle and its Unertl Telescopic Sight, from all of the fakes that are on the market? This now book, the first ever to define the exact points of identification for each Model 1903/1903A1/1903A4 Sniper Rifle tells all.

The Model 1911 and 1911A1 Military and Commercial Pistols (2nd edition, revised and expanded), by Joe Poyer ($35.95). The first new book on the Model 1911/1911A1 in over fifteen years. Provides a complete part-by-part by serial number range for both military and commercial models as well as several foreign models. Serial number charts are extensive and cover each variation individually. Additional charts compare military and serial numbers by year of manufacture and provide an annotated list of military serial numbers. All markings—factory inspection, military acceptance, and factory address and patent markings—are discussed and illustrated.

The .58- and .50-Caliber Rifles and Carbines of the Springfield Armory, 1865–1872, by Richard A. Hosmer ($19.95). This book describes the .58-

and .50-caliber rifles and carbines that were developed at the Springfield Armory between 1865 and 1872 and which led ultimately to the selection of the famed Allin "trapdoor."

Serbian and Yugoslav Mauser Rifles, by Branko Bogdanovic ($19.95). Thousands of Yugoslav Mauser rifles have been imported into North America in the last two decades and Mr. Bogdanovic's book will help the collector and shooter determine which model he or she has, and its antecedents. Every Mauser that found its way into military service in Serbia/Yugoslavia is listed and described.

Swiss Magazine Loading Rifles, 1869 to 1958, (2nd edition, revised) by Joe Poyer ($22.95). A complete part-by-part description for the Vetterli, Schmidt-Rubin, and K-31 rifles in all their variations by serial number range, plus a history of their development and use, their cleaning, maintenance, and how to shoot them safely and accurately.

The American Krag Rifle and Carbine, (2nd edition, revised) by Joe Poyer, edited by Craig Riesch ($22.95). A part-by-part description of the first magazine repeating arm adopted for general service in American military history.

The Model 1903 Springfield Rifle and Its Variations (3rd edition, revised and expanded), by Joe Poyer ($24.95). Includes every model of the Model 1903 from the ramrod bayonet to the Model 1903A4 Sniper rifle. Every part is described by serial number range, markings and finish.

The .45-70 Springfield (5th edition, revised and expanded), by Joe Poyer and Craig Riesch ($22.95), covers the entire range of .45-caliber "trapdoor" Springfield arms, including bayonets, tools and accoutrements.

U.S. Winchester Trench and Riot Guns and Other U.S. Combat Shotguns (2nd edition, revised), by Joe Poyer ($16.95). Describes the elusive and little-known "Trench Shotgun" and all other combat shotguns used by U.S. military forces.

U.S. M1 Carbines, Wartime Production (7th edition, revised and expanded), by Craig Riesch ($22.95), describes the four models of M1 Carbines from all ten manufacturers. Complete with codes for every part by serial number range.

The M1 Garand, 1936 to 1957 (6th edition, revised and expanded), by Joe Poyer and Craig Riesch ($22.95). This book covers such important identification factors as manufacturer's markings, proof marks, final acceptance cartouches stampings and heat treatment lot numbers plus detailed breakdowns of every part in minute detail.

Winchester Lever Action Repeating Firearms, by Arthur Pirkle
Volume 1, The Models of 1866, 1873 & 1876 ($22.95)
Volume 2, The Models of 1886 and 1892 ($22.95)
Volume 3, The Models of 1894 and 1895 ($22.95)
These famous lever action repeaters are completely analyzed part-by-part by serial number range in this first new series on these fine weapons in twenty years.

The SKS Carbine (4th revised and expanded edition), by Steve Kehaya and Joe Poyer ($19.95). *The SKS Carbine* "is profusely illustrated, articulately researched and covers all aspects of its development as well as . . . other combat guns used by the USSR and other Communist bloc nations." Glen Voorhees, Jr., *Gun Week*.

British Enfield Rifles, by Charles R. Stratton (each volume, $19.95)
Volume 1, SMLE (No. 1) Mk I and Mk III
Volume 2, Lee-Enfield No. 4 and No. 5 Rifles
Volume 4, Pattern 1914 and U.S. Model of 1917 Rifles

The British Army's famed rifles are analyzed in detail on a part-by-part basis, complete with all inspector's and military markings. Each volume above now in 2nd edition, revised.

The Mosin-Nagant Rifle (6th edition), by Terence W. Lapin ($22.95). A comprehensive volume covering all aspects and models from the Imperial Russian rifles to the Finnish, American, Polish, Chinese, Romanian and North Korean variations. Includes part-by-part descriptions of all makers plus all variants such as carbines and sniper rifles.

The Swedish Mauser Rifles (3nd edition) by Steve Kehaya and Joe Poyer ($22.95). A complete history of the development and use of the Swedish Mauser rifles is provided as well as a part-by-part description of each component. All 24 models are described and a complete description of the sniper rifles and their telescopic sights is included. All markings, codes, regimental and other military markings are charted and explained. A thorough and concise explanation of the Swedish Mauser rifle, both civilian and military.

A Shooter's and Collector's Guide Series

The AK-47 and AK-74 Kalashnikov Rifles and Their Variations (3rd edition, revised and expanded) by Joe Poyer ($22.95). The AK-47 and its replacement, the AK-74, are examined on a part-by-part basis to show the differences between various types of receivers, other parts, and the AK and AKM models. Also contains a detailed survey of all models of the Kalashnikov rifle from the AK-47 to the AK-108.

The M16/AR15 Rifle (4th edition, revised and expanded), by Joe Poyer ($24.95). This 155-page, profusely illustrated, large-format book examines the development, history, and current and future use of the M16/AR15. It describes in detail all civilian AR15 rifles and takes the reader step-by-step through the process of accurizing the AR15 into an extremely accurate target rifle.

The M14-Type Rifle (3rd edition, revised and expanded), by Joe Poyer ($19.95). A study of the U.S. Army's last and short-lived .30-caliber battle rifle. Also includes the National Match M14 rifle, the M21 and M25 sniper rifles, civilian semiautomatic match rifles, receivers, parts and accessories and the Chinese M14s. A guide to custom-building a service-type rifle or a match-grade, precision rifle.

The SAFN-49 Battle Rifle, by Joe Poyer ($14.95). This detailed study of the SAFN-49 provides a part-by-part examination of the four calibers in which the rifle was made, a description of the SAFN-49 Sniper Rifle and its telescopic sights, plus maintenance, assembly/disassembly, accurizing, restoration and shooting. A new exploded view and section view are included.

Collector's Guide to Military Uniforms

Campaign Clothing: Field Uniforms of the Indian War Army
Volume 1, 1866–1871 ($12.95)
Volume 2, 1872–1886 ($14.95)

Lee A. Rutledge has produced a unique perspective on the uniforms of the Army of the United States during the late Indian War period following the

Civil War. He discusses what the soldier really wore when on campaign. No white hats and yellow bandanas here.

A Guide Book to U.S. Army Dress Helmets, 1872–1904, by Mark Kasal and Don Moore ($16.95).
From 1872 to 1904, the men and officers of the U.S. Army wore a fancy, plumed or spiked helmet on all dress occasions. As ubiquitous as they were in the late 19th century, they are extremely scarce today. Kasal and Moore have written a step-by-step, part-by-part analysis of both the Models 1872 and 1881 dress helmets and their history and use. Profusely illustrated with black-and-white and color photographs of actual helmets.
